TESTIMONY

Whoever saves one life . . . saves the world entire.

TESTIMONY

The LEGACY of SCHINDLER'S LIST and THE USC SHOAH FOUNDATION

USC Shoah Foundation

Introduction by STEVEN SPIELBERG Preface by STEPHEN D. SMITH

A 20TH ANNIVERSARY COMMEMORATION

newmarket **press**
for it books
AN IMPRINT OF HARPERCOLLINS PUBLISHERS

This book was made possible with the generous support of
Ruth & Steven Katz and Deborah & Wayne Zuckerman
in honor of Abraham & Millie Zuckerman and as a tribute to the legacy of Oskar Schindler.

To the survivors, the witnesses,

and all who gave testimony

so that future generations might

know a world free of prejudice,

intolerance, and bigotry—and

the suffering they cause

CONTENTS

TESTIMONIES FROM THE VISUAL HISTORY ARCHIVE

FACE TO FACE WITH TESTIMONY

by Steven Spielberg

I am not an authority on the Holocaust.

The only authorities are the survivors themselves.

I am, however, a steadfast ally of the people who I encountered while making *Schindler's List*, and an advocate for the faces and voices of these survivors. Their firsthand accounts of the atrocities of World War II remind us that history is always relevant—not only because we can learn from these crimes against humanity, but because recalling and retelling can show us that one voice can change the world and the way we see the world. One voice can move us to act. This call to action is at the very core of *Schindler's List* and the work of the USC Shoah Foundation, and it says: *One person can change the world, and that person is you.*

As a filmmaker, I have always adhered to the old adage "seeing is believing," and this was never more true than with the making of *Schindler's List* and the creation of the foundation. It was in 1982 that my mentor, Sid Sheinberg, then president of Universal Pictures, shared with me the *New York Times* book review of Thomas Keneally's *Schindler's List*. Sid optioned the film rights to the story of Oskar Schindler, an opportunist who joins the Nazi party for business advantages and ends up saving the lives of more than one thousand Jews during the Holocaust.

LEFT: *Steven Spielberg with a dozen of the nearly 52,000 survivors and witnesses interviewed by the Shoah Foundation, c. 1995.*

"One voice can move us to act. This call to action is at the very core of *Schindler's List* and the work of the USC Shoah Foundation, and it says: *One person can change the world, and that person is you.*"

I knew survivors. In fact, some of them were my earliest teachers. My grandmother had taught English to Hungarian survivors when I was little, and they taught me how to read numbers by showing me the numbers that had been tattooed on their arms during their time in the concentration camps. It didn't take long for me to realize that I had a deep affinity for what Sid had found and, furthermore, a profound respect and curiosity for the plight of the survivors—what they experienced during the war and how they managed to live the rest of their lives with death and genocide entrenched in their subconscious. It all seemed unimaginable—but then again, to imagine a world where their stories were not documented seemed unconscionable.

While I was moved by the book, it was almost ten years after reading it that I found myself ready to make *Schindler's List*. I'd like to think that with age comes an increased empathy for others, and I think that is true with some of us, but empathy is relative to our own tragedies and personal struggles. And so is our understanding of mortality. It's not that after making *E.T.* and *Indiana Jones*, I suddenly decided to settle down and make more serious, more adult pictures. We don't just grow up overnight. But we do often have children, as I did, and through that experience I gained a deeper love for life and a belief in the need to contribute meaningfully to others' lives. Sure, I also had a fear of getting older, as we all do—but it was during those ten years after *E.T.*—in my professional life with *The Color Purple*, *Empire of the Sun*, and *Always*, and my personal foray into fatherhood—that I got a good grip on the idea of mortality. We will not be around forever to tell our stories, to teach our children, to make the contributions I so desperately wanted to make. *Schindler's List* would have to be more than a creative endeavor. Making a film about the Shoah would prove to be a great honor but also an enormous social responsibility.

We invited many survivors to visit us at each of our locations during filming, and I particularly remember one who visited us in Krakow, a woman named Niusia.

She asked me for a tape recorder. Then she asked me to write her story down. And then, like many others, she said, "Please, tell my story after you tell Oskar Schindler's." It was then that I understood: they were not looking for me to make a movie about their lives—they were looking for a voice. All of them inspired me to see the untapped educational value in testimony. With their voices, eyewitnesses could and should change the world. And I wanted to help them do this before they were gone, and with them, our ability to learn from them. I knew that we could not just give Niusia and the other survivors a tape recorder. We needed to see them as well as hear them—to interview them about their lives during the Holocaust, but also about life before and after the war. The important thing was to give them a platform to be seen, to be heard, and to be teachers.

That platform, Survivors of the Shoah Visual History Foundation, was established in 1994 to videotape interviews with survivors and other witnesses to the

ABOVE: Spielberg talks with Stephen D. Smith (left), executive director of the USC Shoah Foundation, and Holocaust survivor and educator Renée Firestone.

> **We made a promise to interviewees, a promise I feel we have honored—that their testimony would be saved and shared for the benefit and progress of humankind.**

Holocaust and World War II. Over the four years that followed, nearly 52,000 testimonies were recorded in 56 countries and 32 languages. It was and continues to be the largest collection of its kind in the world. We made a promise to interviewees, a promise I feel we have honored—that their testimony would be saved and shared for the benefit and progress of mankind. The fulfillment of this promise—which today continues to be made to Rwandans, Armenians, Cambodians, and other survivors and witnesses to genocide who give testimony—is pursued at the USC Shoah Foundation, whose Visual History Archive is a growing global resource for research, education, and ultimately, action!

The most important legacy of *Schindler's List* is the work of the Shoah Foundation. My hope with the film was to reach people with a compelling and deeply human story that would inspire them to think twice about their own humanity. My hope for the foundation was to expand upon that inner reflection, to make sure that once we bore witness to these deeply personal stories, we would figure out how to take that knowledge and make worthwhile contributions to the world.

With this book, we will share with you a behind-the-scenes look at the making of *Schindler's List*. We will recall the story of Oskar Schindler and his righteous deeds, and we will bring you face to face with testimony. We hope you will be drawn to the power of testimony, that you will be inspired to explore the work of the USC Shoah Foundation's Visual History Archive, and that, in doing so, you will gain conviction and a sense of responsibility to foster the creation of a more tolerant world.

Steven Spielberg

OPPOSITE: Spielberg with students at the IWitness Video Challenge launch, February 2013.

FULFILLING THE PROMISE

by Stephen D. Smith

One of the many outcomes of the *Schindler's List* film is the USC Shoah Foundation's collection of life histories, which today contains more than twelve running years of testimony given by survivors and witnesses of the Holocaust. This rich archive details the lives of tens of thousands and the painful period of history they lived through, but it is so much more than a historical record. The Visual History Archive is a rich tapestry of hopes and dreams, of loss and courage, of fear and sorrow and survival. It gives insights into the worst abuses of human endeavor, but also shows the strength and tenacity of the human spirit. Every testimony represents a whole life, and each of those lives in turn represents communities and generations of families that were lost and will never be recovered. The giving of each testimony was an act of memorialization, and so the archive at its most basic level is a living, enduring memorial.

The archive also represents the very fact of survival, because the vast majority of its contributors did survive the determined attempt of the Nazis to murder them. Their gesture of remembrance and retelling is in itself the last great act of defiance to the Nazi regime, whose intent was that its victims would never tell their stories. The last act of genocide is always denial and silence. For the witnesses to have the final word, inscribed in history and memory, is to overcome the attempt to silence truth. Most of the victims did *not* survive to give their final

RIGHT: A student watches testimony at Freie Universität Berlin in Germany.

word, but we know that during the Holocaust victims found many ways to "tell the world": through letters, diaries, secret archives, and conversations with fellow inmates of the camps—many of which are recalled in the testimonies. Thus this archive fulfills the wishes of those who did not survive as well as those who did.

Through the act of telling their own stories, through their many reflections on life and loss, in providing historical details, and in the analysis that can come only through experience, the witnesses of the Holocaust have also become teachers of future generations. How that teaching happens is critical to its effectiveness. Between the years following *Schindler's List,* when the testimonies were being collected, and the present, a whole new visual culture has emerged in which it is expected that audiovisual content will be delivered to the digital classroom via the Internet.

In pursuit of that educational goal, Steven Spielberg, a trustee of the University of Southern California in Los Angeles, in 2006 donated the archive to the university, and the USC Shoah Foundation: The Institute of Visual History and Education came into being. At USC Shoah Foundation the full archive is digitally preserved,

ABOVE: Stephen Smith at the IWitness Video Challenge launch, February 2013.

and the institute delivers a broad range of academic research and educational initiatives, in fulfillment of the promise made to the witnesses who gave testimony.

Using the same infrastructure and its experience of collecting testimonies from the Holocaust, the archive is now collecting testimony from the Rwandan Tutsi, Armenian, and Cambodian genocides; and the Nanjing massacre—and the work will go on. Human suffering cannot be compared, but its common causes and consequences must be understood. Through the Visual History Archive, students, teachers, and researchers are learning more about the genesis of genocide, and contributing to the mission of reducing its future incidence.

Today USC Shoah Foundation is one of the world's leading audiovisual digital libraries where technology is used to the benefit of humanity. It is an indelible voice of conscience in our world. But it requires detailed listening and is no panacea. Just because the witnesses have spoken does not mean that we will learn from what they have shared with us. That is why USC has committed itself to being a hub of educational activity, with scores of universities and thousands of schools connected to the archive, drawing on its rich resources as a part of their ongoing educational work.

At the heart of the USC Shoah Foundation's mission is the hope that viewers of the testimony collection will gain *insight*, develop *conviction*, and *participate* fully in civil society. Learning more from the witnesses of genocide is the first step toward putting words into actions.

From the moment when Steven Spielberg decided that he wanted to hear the stories of fifty-two thousand witnesses to this moment, when students and teachers and researchers can listen and learn at the click of a mouse, the Visual History Archive at the USC Shoah Foundation has come a long way. But twenty years is just the first milestone in a millennial purpose. If we give them space to be heard, these voices will speak and teach the world for many generations to come.

> " The last act of genocide is always denial and silence. For the witnesses to have the final word, inscribed in history and memory, is to overcome the attempt to silence truth. "

Part 1
SCHINDLER'S LIST
THE MAKING OF THE FILM

PROLOGUE

The story of the filming of *Schindler's List* begins in Krakow, Poland, on a bitterly cold day in 1993. "We had just started principal photography when Niusia Horowitz came to the set with Franciszek Palowski, a Polish journalist who served as an interpreter for survivors visiting the set," remembers unit publicist Anne Marie Stein. "Niusia heard about the film because she worked in the salon at the Forum Hotel where many of the crew were staying. She came to see what was happening, elegantly dressed in her best makeup and fur. She didn't speak English but, with the help of a translator, Niusia told Steven that she was a Schindler Jew—which of course amazed all of us. I remember Steven asked her why she was still in Poland, why she had never left. The question seemed to surprise her. She told us this was her home, it always had been. Why would she leave?"

Niusia Horowitz, as it turned out, was the first of many Holocaust survivors who found their way to the set during filming. Hearing that Steven Spielberg was filming a movie about the Holocaust in Krakow and in other Polish locations—moreover, the true story of Oskar Schindler, the industrialist who rescued eleven hundred Jews—inspired survivors to come forward and make a connection with the director. "When I was making the film in Poland," Spielberg later told a reporter, "at least a dozen Holocaust survivors journeyed there, using the film as a cushion to find closure with their nightmare. They showed up, and often through tears, began telling us their stories.

OPPOSITE: Steven Spielberg, on location in Poland, meets Niusia Horowitz, the first Schindlerjuden who came to the set. Standing next to Niusia is Franciszek Palowski, who served as her translator.

"I kept saying to them, 'Thank you for telling me, but I wish you could say this to a camera because this is important testimony.' I asked them if they'd be willing to do this, and they all said yes."

Today, in a world where there are seemingly no secrets, we may think it strange that no one had recorded these life stories, but in the early 1990s things were very different for people who'd experienced the trauma of war. "The survivors of the Holocaust and many of the World War II soldiers didn't have anybody to help them overcome the trauma of their experiences," Spielberg says. "In 1946, there weren't any books about post-traumatic stress, and they didn't have a national forum for dealing with their trauma. So they buried these events deep into their subconscious and tried to forget what happened. The result was that they became traumatically unhappy in their lives."

Many of these survivors had never told their stories to anyone before they showed up on the set to meet Spielberg. "People came up to him and just started telling him what they'd experienced," said Stein. "I think they just trusted that here was someone who could relate (and possibly use) their stories to tell the world what had really happened."

It seems safe to say that these survivors had found the perfect audience in Steven Spielberg. Producer Branko Lustig was among the first to recognize the impor-

ABOVE: On the set in Poland during filming: Mietek Pemper, a Schindlerjuden *portrayed in the film, Ralph Fiennes, and Branko Lustig.*
OPPOSITE ABOVE: Producers Gerald Molen and Branko Lustig on location in Krakow.

tance of what was happening between the director and these survivors. "When I was on the set of *Schindler's List* with Steven Spielberg, and other survivors were speaking to him, I could see how determined he was to ensure that their life histories were taken for the future, and before it was too late," says Lustig.

Spielberg understood the importance of the testimonies, both for the survivors to heal themselves and for future generations to learn what had happened. "Teaching is at the heart of Jewish culture," explains Spielberg, "as is the strength to take the most ineffable horror that could possibly happen to a human being and turn it into something constructive from which we derive positive lessons for the future. . . . I had four great teachers. They taught me that fabulous teachers who had relevant and compelling concepts to teach could impress their students indelibly. That's what we want to do with our survivor testimony collection. It's the only way to reach people.

"No one can do anything to fix the past—that's already happened. But a picture like this can impact on us, delivering a mandate about what must never happen again."

It has been twenty years since *Schindler's List* unleashed its powerful message of redemption and the first Holocaust survivors began recording their testimonies for posterity. Perhaps no other film has had a greater impact on audiences around the world or created such an indelible legacy. ■

SCHINDLER'S ARK

"Every big movie has a big history of how it came to be made," says producer Branko Lustig. "Good scripts are like fine prosciutto, they need time to age."

Perhaps no other film in the history of moviemaking made a more intriguing journey than *Schindler's List* as it went from historical event to historical novel to screenplay to screen and, finally, served as a catalyst for recording oral history.

The story of this extraordinary film begins in a Beverly Hills leather goods store owned by a Holocaust survivor named Leopold Page. Page, who was known as Poldek Pfefferberg in his native Poland, had come to California after the war. Pfefferberg was determined to bring his Holocaust story to Hollywood. It was said that he asked everyone who entered his shop if they wanted to hear a fascinating story about a man named Oskar Schindler.

One customer who felt the force of Pfefferberg's passion was the Australian novelist Thomas Keneally, who had come into the shop to repair a broken briefcase. Waiting for approval of Keneally's Australian credit card, Pfefferberg inquired as to his customer's profession. Upon learning that Keneally was a writer, Pfefferberg said that he had an amazing story he was sure Keneally would want to hear.

Over a four-hour lunch, Pfefferberg revealed everything that had happened to him during the war and everything he knew about Oskar Schindler, a German industrialist who single-handedly saved eleven hundred Jews from death by Hitler's hand—himself among them.

OPPOSITE: Poldek Pfefferberg expressing his obvious gratitude to Steven Spielberg during principal photography.

66 The minute you decide you are without any exit in the darkest situation, then you are doomed to perish. You have to have a hope that you will survive and you will overcome. 99 — Poldek Pfefferberg

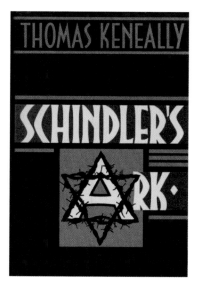

Keneally was fascinated by the story and promised Pfefferberg that he would write a book, but only if they could get documentation to verify the story. This would require interviews with other *Schindlerjuden* ("Schindler Jews"). After World War II, the *Schindlerjuden* had scattered to many different parts of the world, so money would need to be raised to finance the research and travel. Pfefferberg assured Keneally that he could raise the funds and make the necessary contacts for the interviews.

True to his word, Pfefferberg raised the necessary funds and began writing letters of inquiry to find the Schindler Jews. When he had secured enough names, Pfefferberg and Keneally set out to travel the world—from Poland to South America to Israel—to conduct interviews and research any available documents. Together, these two men pieced together the story of Oskar Schindler.

After six months, Thomas Keneally returned to Australia and wrote the novel, using a style he called "facticious," meaning that the book was a novel based on a true story. Acknowledging Pfefferberg's contribution, Keneally dedicated the book to both Oskar Schindler and Pfefferberg, "who by zeal and persistence caused this book to be written."

The book was published in 1982 in England and Australia with the title *Schindler's Ark*, in the United States later that year as *Schindler's List*, and then throughout the world. It became an international best seller and garnered both critical acclaim and many awards, including the prestigious Booker Prize. The *New York Times* hailed the book as "an extraordinary tale" and "a notable achievement." The *Los Angeles Times Book Review* called it "a masterful account of the growth of the human soul."

Sidney Sheinberg at Universal Pictures acquired the rights to the book and brought the project to Steven Spielberg. "Sid found the book and gave it to me," explains Spielberg. "I liked what I read. The thing I liked most about Keneally's book was that it took more of a documentary approach than anything else Hollywood had turned out about the Holocaust. I really admired and respected that and thought it was a good approach for a movie."

What attracted Spielberg to the book was its emphasis on the experiences of individual people, which help anchor the reader emotionally within the overwhelming events of the Holocaust. *Schindler's List* faithfully recounted episodes from the lives of its characters—real-life stories that would seem unbelievable if they were part of a work of fiction: Poldek Pfefferberg really did escape a roundup by convincing the SS commandant Goeth that he had been detailed to collect strewn suitcases; and, just as the book records, Oskar Schindler did play for the life of Goeth's maid Helen Hirsch in a single game of blackjack.

"I had a hunger to make *Schindler's List* a few months after the opening of *E.T. the Extra-Terrestrial*. I wanted to document it for the public record," Spielberg says. But timing and script obstacles precluded the film from being made for almost ten years. As he has said in many interviews, Spielberg was not yet ready in the early 1980s to tackle a subject so vast as the Holocaust. "I had a fear of doing *Schindler's List* that made me delay it year after year," he admits.

OPPOSITE: *The first edition cover of Thomas Keneally's* Schindler's Ark. ABOVE: *Steven Spielberg and Sidney Sheinberg, then president and COO of Universal Pictures, who originally acquired the film rights to* Schindler's Ark *for Spielberg to direct.*

Meanwhile, since Spielberg was slow to commit to the project, Universal offered the script to Martin Scorsese, who was keen to take it on but had problems with an early script Universal had developed. To rework the material, Scorsese hired script-writer Steven Zaillian and, together, they went through several drafts of the story.

"While Marty was developing *Schindler's List*, Steven was scheduled to direct a remake of *Cape Fear* for Universal," explains producer Branko Lustig. "Then, Steven decided that he wanted to direct *Schindler's List* instead, but Marty wouldn't give it up. In the end, they made a trade: Steven got *Schindler's List* and Marty got to make *Cape Fear*."

Looking back, it seems that the decade-long delay was fortuitous. "It took me ten years to develop a kind of maturation in order to say, *now* I'm ready to make *Schindler's List*," Spielberg said in many interviews granted after the movie was released. "I wasn't ready to make it in '82 because I wasn't mature enough. I wasn't emotionally resolved with my life. I hadn't had children. I really hadn't seen God until my first child was born. A lot of things happened that were big deals in my personal life that I didn't give interviews about, but they changed me as a person and as a filmmaker."

Of course, back in the early 1980s and even into the 1990s, *Schindler's List* was unlike anything the wildly successful director had ever before attempted. Spielberg, the most commercially successful director of his generation, had just finished shooting *Jurassic Park*, an instant blockbuster and about as far from *Schindler's List* as any story could get. Spielberg's reputation had been built on such megahits as *Jaws*, *Close Encounters of the Third Kind*, *Raiders of the Lost Ark*, and *E.T.*, among the best and most imaginative films in the history of Hollywood, so tackling a subject as serious and profound as the Holocaust was a daunting challenge.

> "Schindler gave me life and I tried to give him immortality." —Poldek Pfefferberg

"I have a pretty good imagination," Spielberg told *Newsweek* magazine, in an obviously colossal understatement. "I've made a fortune off my imagination. My imagination is dwarfed by the events of 1940 to 1945. Just dwarfed. And so I couldn't imagine the Holocaust until I went to Krakow, and to Auschwitz-Birkenau for the first time."

The enormity of this endeavor would have been overwhelming for any director, and it is easy to understand why it took Spielberg so many years to finally com-

mit to making the film. Those who would eventually come to work on *Schindler's List* realize that the ten-year pre-production period was exactly what this project required.

"Because he had been planning the film for ten years, he had an immense passion to get the film made," maintains producer Gerald Molen. Actress Embeth Davidtz, who plays the abused maid Helen Hirsch, suggests that the long gestation period also benefited the actors: "Since *Schindler's List* has been evolving in Steven so many years, he understands each of the characters so well." Liam Neeson speculates, "Steven *is* Oskar Schindler, he is also Itzhak Stern, Amon Goeth, and all the Jewish survivors."

Once Spielberg was ready to make the film, the first task at hand would be to develop a workable shooting script.

Enter Steve Zaillian. ▧

ABOVE: Steven Spielberg talking to novelist Thomas Keneally and his daughter Jane, who visited the shoot in Poland.

POLDEK PFEFFERBERG

When Steven Spielberg won the Academy Award for Best Director in 1993, he began his acceptance speech by thanking Poldek Pfefferberg. "Let me just start by saying that this [movie] never could have happened, this never could have gotten started without a survivor named Poldek Pfefferberg who Oskar Schindler saved from Auschwitz, from Belsen," said Spielberg. "He's the man who talked Thomas Keneally into writing the book. I owe him such a debt. All of us owe him such a debt. He has carried the story of Oskar Schindler to all of us. A man of complete obscurity who makes us wish and hope for Oskar Schindlers in all of our lives."

Born in 1913 to a Jewish family in Krakow, Poldek Pfefferberg became a high school teacher and then joined the Polish army, fighting against the Germans. After Poland's defeat and annexation to Germany, Poldek returned to Krakow. He met Oskar Schindler when the industrialist hired Poldek's mother to be his interior decorator. Soon Poldek, a born smuggler, was supplying Schindler with black market goods. Thanks to Oskar Schindler, Poldek and his wife, Mila, survived the war. His family was not so fortunate; 100 of his relatives were murdered in the camps, including his parents and sister.

In the early 1950s, the Pfefferbergs moved to Los Angeles, where Poldek was known, for a time, as Leopold Page. He opened a leather goods store and spent years fulfilling a self-imposed obligation to tell the world about Oskar Schindler. "I always talk about the war," Poldek said when he recorded his testimony for the Shoah Foundation on November 6, 1994. "I consider that the reason why Mila and I survived is for a purpose; otherwise there is no other way to make sense of why we survived."

One day he met Australian novelist Thomas Keneally, who, after hearing Poldek's story, agreed to write a book about Oskar Schindler. The book recounts part of Poldek's story, and he subsequently became a character in the movie. Played by Jonathan Sagalle, Pfefferberg is the Jewish smuggler who gets caught in the street during the liquidation of the ghetto and stands up to Amon Goeth with a snappy salute,

telling him that he was ordered to remove the abandoned suitcases from the street. Goeth laughs and walks away.

This true story was one of many times Pfefferberg defied the Nazis. In his Shoah Foundation testimony, interviewer Branko Lustig asks if Pfefferberg ever worried about the consequences of such dangerous acts. Pfefferberg smiles and replies, "If I'd been caught I wouldn't be talking to you." He shrugs. "I wasn't thinking about the danger. I was thinking I was so smart I can avoid anything."

"You were sure you would survive the ghetto?" asks an incredulous Branko.

Pfefferberg nods emphatically. "I was sure I would survive the ghetto, no question about it. I was sure I would survive the war, too."

Lustig seems bewildered by this statement and asks again how Pfefferberg could have been so confident. "The minute you decide you are with-

out any exit in the darkest situation, then you are doomed to perish," he responds, as if the answer was obvious. "You have to have a hope that you will survive and you will overcome. This is most important: your mental attitude. Your strength is in yourself to survive. In the darkest moment of your life you must think positively that you will overcome," he adds.

Not only did he overcome, Pfefferberg prospered in California, and his spirit of determination and positive mental attitude remained a hallmark of his personality. "The thing I remember most about Poldek," says producer Gerald Molen, "was his tenacity, his enormous appetite for life and for being a part of it all."

And Oskar Schindler was never far from Pfefferberg's thoughts. In the late 1950s, Pfefferberg learned that Schindler, living in South America, was broke and practically homeless. Then fifty-four years old, Schindler "didn't have a quarter to buy a pack of cigarettes," so Pfefferberg got a film studio to pay him $50,000 for his life story (so said Pfefferberg in his testimony, but details cannot be confirmed). Poldek sent Schindler a plane ticket and met him in Paris to present him with the check. "The check made him respectable again," says Pfefferberg, "because money was very important to him."

Though it took almost forty years, Poldek Pfefferberg lived to see Schindler become a household name. "A human being—a single person can change the world. That's what I've been trying to do since 1945 when I promised Schindler I would tell everybody his story," Pfefferberg told *Newsweek* in December 1993.

Poldek Pfefferberg died at age eighty-seven on March 9, 2001, in Beverly Hills, never having abandoned the memory of the man who saved him.

He established the Oskar Schindler Humanities Foundation, which recognizes acts by individuals and organizations, regardless of race or nationality. "Only when the foundation is a reality will I say I have fulfilled my obligation," he wrote before he died. "Because when I am no longer here, when the Schindler Jews are not here, the foundation will still go on."

"Schindler gave me life," Pfefferberg once said, "and I tried to give him immortality." ∎

OPPOSITE: Poldek and Mila Pfefferberg on the set with Steven Spielberg. Poldek Pfefferberg spent decades trying to get a movie made about Oskar Schindler. ABOVE: Pfefferberg, 50, and Schindler, 54, in Paris, November 1, 1962.

THE FILM STORY

Within weeks of the German invasion of Poland that launched World War II in 1939, the signs of Nazi occupation were unmistakable in Krakow. Tanks and soldiers paraded continually through the picturesque medieval city. A stream of directives and edicts made Jewish life increasingly precarious. Armbands displaying the Star of David became compulsory. Walls went up around the Podgorze district, creating a closed Jewish quarter of only sixteen square blocks, and all Jews were commanded to move there. Thousands of families trundled their belongings through the streets as speakers on trucks blared the latest edict, #44/91: "Failure to register with housing authorities is a violation and will result in summary executions."

Into this milieu the Sudeten German Oskar Schindler (Liam Neeson) arrived, hoping to set himself up in business as an entrepreneurial industrialist. Schindler knew how to make an SS bureaucrat happy and was rewarded with control of a Jewish-owned enamelware factory he named Deutsche Emailwarenfabrik. His lavish parties, shameless bribes, and coterie of girlfriends helped him secure lucrative contracts to produce mess kits and field kitchenware for the German army.

When Schindler's wife, Emilie (Caroline Goodall), visited him in Krakow, she was taken aback by his apparent success. She wondered aloud if it was all a charade. But Oskar let her in on a little secret: something had always been missing from his other business plans. Expecting him to say "Luck," she was startled when he smiled and instead proclaimed, "War."

Schindler staffed Emalia, as his factory became known, with unpaid Jewish workers. He placed one, Itzhak Stern (Ben Kingsley), in the position of accountant, and with his help amassed huge profits. Schindler's factory became a haven for Jewish workers. He used his connections to blunt every Nazi action that threatened "his" Jews, especially those that came from Amon Goeth (Ralph Fiennes), the savage SS commandant of the Plaszow forced labor camp.

In order to shelter his workers from Goeth's unpredictable and brutal assaults, Schindler came up with the idea of establishing his own subcamp at Emalia. He built and operated the camp at his own expense. No guards were allowed inside the camp to abuse the workers, and food and living conditions were infinitely better than at Plaszow.

Schindler dealt cleverly on the black market, procuring goods with the help of another Jew, Poldek Pfefferberg (Jonathan Sagalle). He was even able to traffic in such luxuries as liquor, chocolate, fruit, coffee, and silk stockings. This penchant landed him in good favor with the Nazis, who could have, with a mere shrug, consigned him to a death camp.

In 1944, when the Nazis ordered Plaszow and its subcamps closed as part of their "Final Solution," targeting all Jews to be sent to the Auschwitz, Gross-Rosen, or Treblinka extermination camps, Schindler redoubled his resourcefulness. Speed was vital: any delays could send his workers to their deaths.

Schindler capitalized on his skillfully cultivated Nazi connections, bargaining with Goeth to let him move his factory to Brünnlitz (Brnenec), a town on the Polish-Czechoslovakian border. He would be allowed to draw up a list of "essential" Jewish workers whom he could take with him as his workforce—not only workers from Emalia but any workers from Plaszow or its other subcamps, as long as he could justify each as having special talents he could use. Schindler paid Goeth for each human being on the list, draining his fortune in the process. When word spread among the Jewish community that there was a list, everyone prayed to be on it. With the help of Itzhak Stern, Schindler drafted a list of eleven hundred names. "The list is an absolute good. The list is life," Stern says in the film. "All around its margins lies the gulf."

The men on Schindler's list, numbering about eight hundred, were separated from the women and taken by freight train on an arduous journey to Brünnlitz, where Schindler had moved his operations to a munitions plant. He greeted them upon their arrival.

But something went horribly wrong with the women's train en route to Schindler's new factory, delivering them instead to Auschwitz-Birkenau (one of three camps in the Auschwitz complex). The terrified women were subjected to the unthinkable inhuman conditions of the extermination camp—virtually no food, paralyzing cold, little clothing, threats of death everywhere.

Once he learned where they were, Schindler worked feverishly behind the scenes to secure their release. Miraculously he succeeded. All three hundred Schindler women and children were called out by name and marched to waiting cattle cars that would deliver them to Brünnlitz. It marks the only known case in which specific individuals were ever released from Birkenau by name.

Once his workers were safely ensconced in Brünnlitz, Schindler saw to it that during the seven months his munitions plant was operational, the factory produced nothing that could be of use to the German army.

On May 7, 1945, the *Schindlerjuden* learned the news of Germany's surrender. Oskar knew that the Russians were about to enter Brünnlitz and that he had to avoid them and reach the Americans. It was painful for his workers to say goodbye. Before he and Emilie departed, they presented him with a gift—a ring they had made from the gold extracted from one of the worker's teeth. They had inscribed on it a Talmudic verse: "Whoever saves one life, saves the world entire."

—Adapted from the movie's original
production notes by Anne Marie Stein

"Other Priorities"

INT. JUDENRAT OFFICES—VACANT OFFICE

Schindler follows Stern into the small room, sits, takes a flask from his coat pocket, and pours a shot of cognac in the cap.

> **SCHINDLER**
> There's a company you did the books for on Lipowa Street, made what, pots and pans?

Stern stares at the cognac Schindler's offering him. He doesn't know who this man is, or what he wants. He could be a member of the Gestapo for all Stern knows.

> **STERN**
> By law, I have to tell you, sir, I'm a Jew.

Schindler looks puzzled; then shrugs, dismissing it.

> **SCHINDLER**
> Well, I'm a German, so there we are. Good company, you think?

He keeps holding out the drink. Stern declines it by not reaching for it.

> **STERN**
> Modestly successful.

Schindler nods, drinks, takes out a streamlined cigarette case and holds it out in offering. Stern declines again and Schindler tamps a cigarette and sets it between his lips.

> **SCHINDLER**
> I don't know anything about enamelware, do you?

> **STERN**
> I was just the accountant.

> **SCHINDLER**
> Simple engineering, though, wouldn't you think? Change the machines around, whatever you do, you could make other things, couldn't you?

He fires the cigarette with the flame of a lighter and lowers his voice in case anyone is listening in.

> **SCHINDLER**
> Field kits, mess kits . . . army contracts. Once the war ends, forget it, but for now it's great, you could make a fortune, don't you think?

He spits out a speck of tobacco and waits for a reaction. It doesn't come; Stern is waiting for the other shoe to drop. Schindler misinterprets his silence for a lack of understanding. He smiles broadly, good-naturedly, perhaps imagining the fortune he could amass. Stern dampens contempt with a matter-of-fact tone.

> **STERN**
> I think most people right now have other priorities.

Schindler tries to imagine what they could possibly be.

> **SCHINDLER**
> Like what?

ENTER ZAILLIAN

Once he had committed to making *Schindler's List*, Spielberg had to grapple with the complexities of bringing this often-overwhelming historical drama to the screen. As with all movies, the process began with the script.

Steve Zaillian had been working on the screenplay since 1988 and had gone through several drafts with Martin Scorsese. Prior to taking on the Keneally novel, Zaillian had written the screenplays to *The Falcon and the Snowman*, *Awakenings*, and *Searching for Bobby Fischer*. "The way I approach anything is in broad strokes first," Zaillian explained in an interview on *Nightline* in 1993, shortly after winning the Academy Award for Best Adapted Screenplay.

"What is the story about? In the case of *Schindler's List*, it was always a balancing act. You have the story of Oskar Schindler, but we also had a larger story, which was the story of the Holocaust and the experience of the Polish Jews. I felt very strongly that by telling Schindler's story we would tell the story of the Holocaust. I felt that was enough. Steven felt that he wanted an even larger picture, he wanted to follow certain stories of the workers."

Indeed, it was important to Spielberg that particular characters were showcased as individuals and not just part of the mob. "You get to know the Pfefferbergs, Dresners, Rosners, and Helen Hirsch not as frightened faces but strong people who were selected by God, destiny, and Oskar Schindler to survive," says the director.

Trying to balance those two elements of the story was the hardest and most time-consuming part of the writing process for Zaillian and Spielberg. They also had to grapple with different ways of telling the basic story.

Opposite: Screenwriter Steve Zaillian on the set with Steven Spielberg during filming at the Auschwitz death camp in Poland.

Zaillian's approach was much different from the way Spielberg usually worked on his films. "I tend to look for films that tell strong stories and have a beginning, a middle, and an end," says Spielberg. "I'm very much into a linear technique in my filmmaking. I tried for a very long time to impose a linear narrative into *Schindler's List* but I discovered it was not possible. This story is more like real life, where you can't predict what's going to happen tomorrow and you really can't analyze what happened yesterday. You go through your life, events unfold, and they don't always follow a perfect scenario. Once I was able to accept that for this film, I could accept Steve Zaillian's point of view. The screenplay he developed for us was pretty much a [clarification] of ever-unfolding events from the novel. He took these events and put them in chronological order and aside from that, there's not much narrative in this movie."

> ❝I have been searching for the meaning of Schindler for over a decade. And I am no closer today, having made the movie, to discovering it than I was when I first read the book.❞ —Steven Spielberg

In fact, it was the unfolding of seemingly random events that most interested Zaillian. He wanted to tell the story through a series of incidents that were not necessarily explained at every turn. "I don't think you need to have a character come out and make speeches. In fact, if you do, it just doesn't seem real," says the writer. "I think that sometimes people think of screenwriters as dialogue writers and they're not. A playwright obviously tells their story with dialogue and a screenwriter should, I think, primarily tell a story with pictures."

A great part of the challenge was how to depict the character of Oskar Schindler himself. A complex man, full of contradictions, he was first and foremost an entrepreneur who came to Krakow at the start of the war to build a fortune. Then, somewhere along the way, he developed a conscience that led him to perform the altruistic deeds that saved the lives of eleven hundred people, at the expense of the fortune he had worked so hard to obtain—and at the risk of his own life.

Most storytellers would want to answer the most obvious question: why did he do it? And surely most "Hollywood" movies would find a specific moment to explain Schindler's change of heart. But, in reality, a full answer to this complex question is elusive. "You add up all the elements—the expediencies and the decency—and you don't get the sum of what happened," author Thomas Keneally says. "Ultimately, he has no motive except to create a haven."

Liam Neeson, who so brilliantly brought Oskar Schindler to life on the screen, says, "Schindler's motives were perhaps a blend of selflessness and opportunism."

In an interview in *Time* in December 1993, months after wrapping the film, Neeson said, "I still don't know what made him save all those lives. He was a man everybody liked. And he liked to be liked; he was a wonderful kisser of ass. Perhaps he was inspired to do some great piece of work. I like to think—and maybe it comes across in the film—that he needed to be needed."

Some survivors are uncomfortable with any attempt to canonize Schindler. "We owe our lives to him," says *Schindlerjuden* Danka Dresner Schindel. "But I wouldn't glorify a German because of what he did to us. There is no proportion."

In the end, no one can explain Oskar Schindler's motives with any degree of authority. "If you talk to the survivors, the people who knew Schindler, they will all give you different reasons why he did what he did, and none of those reasons really fully explains it," says Zaillian.

Spielberg agrees. "No one is able to say why he did what he did. I've met witnesses who weren't able to tell me, with any clarity in terms of agreement, why he did it. Oskar Schindler was a shining star in an otherwise very stormy sky. He was a Great Gatsby kind of character. He was German, Catholic, and a war profiteer. He was in the Oskar Schindler business for most of his career, but something happened along the road that changed him. Somehow he took a turn when everyone else was continuing to toe the line. A lot of this was kismet, you know. Schindler was meant to happen. I think he decided to save his workers not because of any one precise moment, but because he got to know who they were as human beings.

"What motivated this character to do this? That's important. But I agree with most of the Jews who have told me themselves that what was really important was that he did it, not why he did it. I have been searching for the meaning of Schindler for more than a decade now, the way the characters in *Citizen Kane* searched for the meaning of Rosebud. And I am no closer today, having made the movie, to discovering it than I was when I first read the book."

In the end the filmmakers decided neither to try to give reasons for Schindler's motives nor to invent a defining moment that would easily explain his change of heart. They chose to let the story run its course and allow audiences to draw their own conclusions about why Schindler did what he did.

"I don't think there is just one answer," explains Spielberg. "The film poses more questions than it answers."

> "A screenwriter should, I think, primarily tell a story with pictures."
> — Steve Zaillian

"Luck"

INT. RESTAURANT—LATER—NIGHT

> **EMILIE**
> It's not a charade, all this?

> **SCHINDLER**
> A charade? How could it be a charade?

She doesn't know, but she does know him. And all these signs of apparent success just don't fit his profile. Schindler lets her in on a discovery—

> **SCHINDLER**
> Wait a minute. Take a guess how many people are on my payroll. My father at the height of his success had fifty. I've got 350; 350 workers on the factory floor with one purpose.

> **EMILIE**
> To make pots and pans?

> **SCHINDLER**
> To make money, for me. (pause) Does anyone ask about me?

> **EMILIE**
> Back home? Everybody. All the time.

> **SCHINDLER**
> They won't soon forget the name Schindler here. I can tell you that. Oskar Schindler, they'll say, everybody remembers him. He did something extraordinary. He did something no one else did. He came here with nothing, a suitcase, and built a bankrupt company into a major manufactory and left with a steamer trunk, two steamer trunks, full of money. All the riches of the world.

> **EMILIE**
> It's comforting to see that nothing's changed.

> **SCHINDLER**
> You're wrong, Emilie. There's no way I could have known this before, but there was always something missing. In every business I tried, I see now it wasn't me that was failing. Something was missing. Even if I'd known what it was, there's nothing I could have done about it, because you can't create this thing—and it makes all the difference in the world between success and failure.

He waits for her to guess what it is. His look says, It's so simple, how can you not know?

> **EMILIE**
> Luck?

> **SCHINDLER**
> War.

"Be a witness to my murder."

EXT. STABLES—DAWN

Ingrid climbs onto one of the horses, Schindler onto the other. As the animals gallop away with their riders toward a wood, the stable boys wave. . . .

EXT. HILLTOP CLEARING—DAWN

The galloping horses break through to a clearing high on a hill. The riders pull in the reins and the hoofs rip at the earth. Schindler smiles at the view, the beauty of it with the sun just coming up. From here, all of Cracow can be seen in striking relief, like a model of a town. He can see the Vistula, the river that separates the ghetto from Kazimierz; Wawel Castle, beyond it, the center of town.

Schindler begins to notice refinements: the walls that define the ghetto; Peace Square, the assembly of men and boys. He notices a line of trucks rolling east across the Kosciuscko Bridge, another across the bridge at Podgorze, a third along Zablocie Street, all angling in on the ghetto like spokes to a hub. . . . The wheels of the last truck clear the portals at Lwoska Street and the SS troops jump down. . . .

From here the action below seems staged, unreal, the rifle bursts no louder than caps. A man falls to the ground well before the sound of the shot that killed him arrives.

Dismounting, Schindler moves closer to the edge of the hill, curious. His attention is drawn to a small distant figure, all in red, at the rear of one of the many columns. . . .

EXT. HILLTOP—DAWN

Schindler watches as the girl in red slowly wanders away unnoticed by the SS. Against the grays of the buildings and street she's a bright moving target.

EXT. STREET—DAWN

A truck thundering down the street obscures her for a moment. Then she's moving past a pile of bodies, old people executed in the street, and Pfefferberg prying off a manhole cover. An elderly man, being dragged to a wall for execution, sobs for a world to hear:

> **OLD MAN**
> Be a witness to my murder! Be a witness to my murder! Be a witness to my murder!!

BEYOND THIS DAY

BY THIS TIME, of course, Schindler
had returned his horse to the stable.
. . . He was already in his office at
DEF, shut away for a time, finding
the news too heavy to share with
the day shift. Much later, in terms
uncharacteristic of jovial Herr
Schindler, Cracow's favorite party
guest, Zablocie's big spender, in terms,
that is, which showed—beyond the
playboy façade—an implacable judge,
Oskar would lay special weight on
this day. "Beyond this day," he would
claim, "no thinking person could fail
to see what would happen. I was now
resolved to do everything in my power
to defeat the system."

—from Thomas Keneally's *Schindler's List*

FILMING IN POLAND

Principal photography began on *Schindler's List* in Krakow on March 1, 1993, with a predominantly Polish crew complemented by workers from England, Croatia, Austria, Germany, Canada, Israel, and the United States, including many Polish-Americans. The multitude of languages on set was only one of many complications and challenges. At the time, *Schindler's List* was one of the most ambitious productions ever to be filmed in Poland. "We had about 148 basic sets and thirty-four to thirty-five locations in and around Krakow," explains producer Gerald Molen. "We shot this movie in seventy-five days." Incredibly, but not atypically for a Steven Spielberg movie, filming was completed four days ahead of schedule.

"When we got to Poland, communism had only been dead about two or three years," explains Molen. "This gave great impetus to [production designer Allan] Starski to make it as realistic as possible and to Steven to make his beautiful pictures with great accuracy. The challenge for Allan was in the places that had changed. He had to make them as accurate as possible, without spending a lot of money, of course."

Allan Starski managed to create an atmosphere in which everyone could do their best work, and his contribution to the film did not go unnoticed by the critics. "Among the many outstanding elements that contribute to *Schindler's List* . . . [is] the production design by Allan Starski, which finds just the right balance between realism and drama," wrote Janet Maslin in the *New York Times* on December 15, 1993. Starski's work was also hailed by his peers— he won the Academy Award for Art Direction and Set Decoration for *Schindler's List*.

OPPOSITE: *The scenes of the Jewish quarter in Krakow were shot in the actual location, though the filmmakers had to re-create the gate that separated the ghetto from the rest of the city during the war.*

KRAKOW

The advantages of shooting in Poland were obvious. Many of the original locations mentioned in the book were still standing, as Krakow was one of the few Polish cities to escape devastation during World War II. In fact, in 1978, Krakow was listed by UNESCO as one of the great historic cities of the world. "We had a tremendous set in Krakow itself," explains Molen. "It's a wonderful piece of history. We used the city in so many different ways: the streets, the buildings, and the ambiance. There was a lot of history in the city and we utilized whatever we could in making this movie work."

Authentic locations added to the realism of the filming and were priceless to the filmmakers and actors. Scenes were shot both inside and out of the actual apartment where Schindler lived during his time in Krakow. Also utilized were Schindler's original offices at the factory. Both the apartment building and the factory remained almost exactly as they had been fifty years before. An exterior shot of Schindler's enamelwork factory could have been taken in the early 1940s. The

ABOVE: Oskar Schindler's actual apartment, still intact from the 1940s, was used in the film.

DEUTSCHE EMAILWARENFABRIK

The photo at right was taken by Raimund Titsch (see page 27). It shows the staff of beautiful *Schindlerjuden* secretaries who worked at Oskar Schindler's factory. The re-creation of the scene in the film (below), shot in the original Deutsche Emailwarenfabrik (DEF) building.

filmmakers also shot in the interior of the still-standing SS headquarters and the interior and exterior of the prison.

Many renowned locations in and around the historic city of Krakow were shown in the film, including the fourteenth-century Saint Mary's Basilica, Krakow's most important church; Rynek Glowny, one of the largest and most distinctive market squares in Europe; the Krakow Glowny train station; many streets and buildings in Stare Miasto (old town); and the quaint town of Niepolomice, which doubled for Brünnlitz. ▪

Above: Liam Neeson in the original office Oskar Schindler occupied at Emalia, the enamelware factory he ran in the 1940s. Above right: Steven Spielberg and production designer Allan Starski, on the first day of filming in Krakow, a shot of Jews shoveling snow. Opposite: Shooting on location in Saint Mary's Basilica, one of Krakow's most beautiful architectural wonders. Built in the fourteenth century, the church was used for the scene in which Oskar Schindler first makes contact with black marketers.

The scene in which Amon Goeth spearheads the evacuation of the Jewish ghetto was shot on the streets of Krakow, which had not changed much in the fifty years since the events depicted in the film.

PLASZOW LABOR CAMP

The one set that had to be constructed from scratch was the forced labor camp at Plaszow. The location is central to the story of the *Schindlerjuden*, who suffered greatly under Amon Goeth's demonic rule at Plaszow.

At the time of filming, the original camp did still exist, but behind it loomed a fifty-foot monument in one direction and a modern skyline in the other, severely limiting camera angles for the cinematographers. The filmmakers needed to be able to shoot from all over the camp, including many exterior shots, so they decided they had to create their own camp. By any measure, this was an enormous undertaking.

"I've worked on many movies about the war, both Polish and European productions, but the Plaszow labor camp was the biggest set I ever built," says the Polish-born production designer Allan Starski.

To make Plaszow as authentic as possible, the crew used the original archival blueprints from the 1940s to construct the camp. Everything was built in the style of the original camp, with materials that would have been available at that time. Overall, the company built thirty-four barracks and seven watchtowers. They also re-created the road into the camp that was paved with Jewish tombstones, since the

ABOVE LEFT: Building Plaszow. ABOVE RIGHT: The thirty-four barracks built for the replica of the Plaszow camp. ABOVE: Original map of Plaszow. OPPOSITE: Production designer Allan Starski re-created such chilling details as the pathway to the Plaszow camp that the Nazis created out of tombstones taken from the Jewish cemeteries that had been destroyed to build the camp.

42

original camp had been built on the site of two Jewish cemeteries. In addition, the company built a replica of the villa that Amon Goeth occupied during his command of the camp. Like the original, the villa was perched above the labor camp, giving Goeth free access to oversee the workers and shoot them at will. The villa built for the film was less than a mile from Goeth's original villa.

"I had a team of twenty-eight, plus we hired local people to help us," says Starski. "Not only is this the biggest camp I ever built, but also it was built like a real camp. We built Plaszow to be as realistic as possible. We put in stables and a garage, Goeth's villa, the main gate, and everything else. Spielberg could shoot from any angle, from any corner, and all you see is the camp. It's built with so much accuracy that it was like coming into the real thing." ■

OPPOSITE AND ABOVE: *Views of the replica Plaszow camp, which allowed the camera to shoot from any angle without any obstruction in the far background.* ABOVE RIGHT: *Allan Starski, Steven Spielberg, production assistant Steve Bauerfeind, actor Osman Ragheb, and Branko Lustig.*

AMON GOETH'S VILLA

Below: Amon Goeth's actual villa was still standing and in fairly good condition when the filmmakers arrived at Plaszow. Above: A replica of the villa was built about a mile from its original location so that it would be close to the newly constructed camp set.

Below left: The finished villa, in its imposing hilltop location, as it was seen from the perspective of the workers at the camp. Opposite: In some of the most horrifying scenes in the movie, Ralph Fiennes, as Amon Goeth, stands on his balcony and randomly shoots workers in the camp. Survivors report that Goeth killed with impunity and that he seemed to enjoy it.

> **"** There wasn't a day on this movie where I didn't think that where I was standing, being a Jew, fifty years ago, was an automatic death sentence. **"**
>
> —Steven Spielberg

AUSCHWITZ-BIRKENAU

Nowhere on the shoot was the authenticity of the surroundings more emotionally charged than when the production moved to the Auschwitz-Birkenau death camp. Located in the industrial town of Oswiecim, the desolate camp stands today as a memorial to the millions murdered there by the Nazis. There, on that sacred ground, the filmmakers planned to shoot a symbolic scene of prisoners disembarking the trains and entering the camp.

It was an understandably upsetting place to work, and Spielberg had anticipated the difficulty of shooting at this camp. From his first visit to Auschwitz, he recalled, "I was all ready to cry in front of strangers, but I didn't shed a tear. I was just boiling inside. Freezing day, and I was so hot. I felt so helpless; that there was nothing I could do about it. And yet I thought, well, there is something I can do about it. I can make *Schindler's List*. I mean, it's not going to bring anybody back alive, but it maybe will remind people that another Holocaust is a sad possibility."

The filmmakers were not granted permission to shoot inside Auschwitz, but only directly outside the infamous gate to the camp. To overcome the problem, they built their set outside the camp gate as if it were on the inside. As Spielberg explained, "We were just outside the gatehouse, which is exactly as it looks from inside Birkenau. And we simply showed the other side of the gate and walls, looking back in. That worked fine."

Still, the entire cast and crew were deeply affected by being in such close proximity to the Nazis' most iconic death camp. "The ground is saturated in blood," actor Jonathan Sagalle told *Newsweek* magazine in May 1993. "It's like walking on tombstones."

ABOVE: *Constructing Auschwitz's outside gate.* OPPOSITE: *Shooting the arrival of the women at Auschwitz.*

It was hard not to feel the significance of working on such hallowed ground. "Every moment at Auschwitz was intimidating," admits Spielberg. "It was snowing like crazy and really cold, which made us feel like we were caught in a time warp. It was terribly frightening. There wasn't a day on this movie where I didn't think that where I was standing, being a Jew, fifty years ago, was an automatic death sentence. That feeling never left me, it was like a smell I couldn't get off my clothes. Working on the most notorious killing ground in recorded history was a feeling we all shared and, as a result, we clung to each other."

The emotions evoked at Auschwitz-Birkenau created a working atmosphere unlike anything that Spielberg and the other cast and crew members had ever experienced on a set. Perhaps no one was more affected than producer Branko Lustig, who had been prisoner #A3317 in this very camp as a young boy. Returning to the place of so much horror and devastation brought back searing memories. "When I entered Birkenau and came to this gate and saw this big, enormous emptiness, it was again winter," he said. "And I remembered this moment: I felt this thing; I felt that I am hungry again, and I felt the stench, the smoke, without seeing it. . . . I was crying. I couldn't get through." ∎

DRESSING THE SETS

Once the locations are selected and the sets are built, they have to be decorated. Great production design is in the details and *Schindler's List* was no exception. Allan Starski and his team scoured Poland for period pieces, or created realistic facsimiles. From stacks of suitcases and diamonds confiscated by the Nazis to the typewriter used by Ben Kingsley, every item had to be exactly right. Even the pile of bodies Goeth is ordered to burn had to look like the terrible real thing. These kinds of details often go unnoticed by the audience precisely because they are so perfectly attuned to the time and place being re-created on film.

"Today is history."

EXT. PARK, CRACOW—DAWN

Untersturmfuhrer Goeth, soon to be Commandant Goeth, stands before the assembled troops with a flask of cognac in his hand. He looks out over them proudly; they're good boys, these, the best. He addresses them—

> **GOETH**
>
> Today will be remembered. Years from now, the young will ask with wonder about this day. Today is history and you're a part of it.

EXT. PEACE SQUARE, GHETTO—DAWN

A fourteen-year-old kid hurries across to the square pulling on his O.D. armband. Several others of the Jewish Ghetto Police, Goldberg among them, are already assembled there. The clerks, the list makers, scissor open their folding tables, set out their ink pads and stamps.

> **GOETH (V.O.)**
>
> Six hundred years ago when, elsewhere, they were footing the blame for the

Black Death, Kazimierz the Great, so called, told the Jews they could come to Cracow. They came, they trundled their belongings into this city. They settled, they took hold, they prospered. Their children prospered. In business, science, education, the arts. They came here with nothing and . . . flourished. For six centuries, there has been a Jewish Cracow. Six centuries.

EXT. WOODS—DAWN

The horses panting hard. Their hoofs hammering at the ground, climbing a hill. Riding boots kicking at their flanks.

EXT. PARK, CRACOW—DAWN

The boots of Amon Goeth slowly pacing. He stops. Tight on his face, smiling pleasantly.

> **GOETH (V.O.)**
>
> By this evening, those six centuries are a rumor. They never happened. Today is history.

53

54

CINEMATOGRAPHY

One of the first and most defining decisions in the creation of *Schindler's List* was to shoot the movie in black and white. For Spielberg, it seemed obvious that this was the only way to go given the gravity of the subject matter, and also to help give the movie a documentary feel. "Virtually everything I've seen on the Holocaust is in black and white," explains Spielberg, "so my vision is what I've seen in documentaries and in books."

The use of black and white is a choice that focuses the subject matter for the audience. "Black and white is a tonal palate and it gives the audience fewer choices," explains the director. "In color, the audience has a lot of things to look at. In black and white, you have to look at the characters. You look into an actor's eyes and you're not seduced because he has blue eyes. You are seduced because there is a performance there. I felt that for a movie about the Shoah [the Hebrew term for the Holocaust], black and white was like a truth serum."

For his director of photography, Spielberg chose the Polish-born Janusz Kaminski. "I met Steven for the first time during the winter of 1991," recalls Kaminski. "He said he was going to shoot the film in the spring of 1993. He had just learned that I was Polish, and he wanted me to know that had nothing to do with him choosing me for the film. I started researching the period. I read the book about Schindler and I met several people with first-hand accounts. Of course, I continued working. I shot *The Adventures of Huckleberry Finn*. Afterward I flew to Poland with the

OPPOSITE: *Janusz Kaminski and Steven Spielberg on the set.*

production designer and producers for *Schindler's List*. I came back to the States to do another picture, then we flew to Poland in June of 1992 to scout locations with Steven."

THE LIGHTS

Next to the director himself, the director of photography is one of the most crucial jobs on a movie set. While the work involves a great deal of technical ability, a huge element of artistry is also required. In an interview on *Nightline* in 1993, after winning the Academy Award for Cinematography, Kaminski described his work quite succinctly. "What the director of photography does is to transfer the written word into visuals and hopes to create story through lighting and camera movement," he said. "The motion picture camera is not just an observer, it can play a very important part in contributing to the drama of the movie."

Demonstrably, Kaminski used all of the tools at his disposal to heighten the emotional impact of the story. "My biggest and most important desire was to allow

ABOVE: *In the opening nightclub scenes, Kaminski used a special eye light on Liam Neeson. The effect was to make the audience feel safe in Oskar Schindler's presence while showing that he was like a hunter sizing up his prey.*

the audience to feel the terror and the horror of that period," he explains. "Having the chance to photograph this movie in black and white was very unusual, of course, as there are very few modern-day movies being made in black and white. However, our perception of history and of the Second World War comes from black-and-white stills and documentary newsreel footage that during that time was black and white. So I think deciding to photograph *Schindler's List* in black and white was the right choice, was the only choice in my opinion."

The critics agreed. As David Denby wrote in *New York Magazine*, in December 1993, "The black-and-white images gleam with the glamorous and sinister promise that went out of movies when film stock turned to color."

In the course of researching images from the time period, Kaminski discovered the black and white photographs of Russian-born Roman Vishniac, whose work would come to greatly influence the look of the movie. "The guiding source for visual interpretation of this movie was a book of still photography done by Roman Vishniac, who photographed Jewish settlements in Eastern Europe between

ABOVE: Kaminski's talent is obvious in his use of light and shadow to create emotion in this tender scene between Oskar Schindler (Liam Neeson) and Helen Hirsch (Embeth Davidtz), a maid at Plaszow who was routinely abused by Amon Goeth.

1926 and 1939," says Kaminski, referring to the book *To Give Them Light: The Legacy of Roman Vishniac*. "I saw the pictures and said this is how the film should look. It felt realistic. He didn't have any lights, he didn't have a particular style. They were just beautiful representations of daily life in Jewish villages and cities. It felt contemporary. Very often he would photograph people near the window, silhouetted against a window or a doorway. Everything was lit with natural light and it was very contrast-y. One side of their face was always brighter; one side was darker. That was the biggest inspiration."

> 66 My biggest and most important desire was to allow the audience to feel the terror and horror of that period. 99
> —Janusz Kaminski

Vishniac's influence can be seen from the very start of the movie, when we are first introduced to Oskar Schindler. Kaminski uses light and shadows to reveal character and underscore what the character is thinking. "The movie is about the change that happens within Oskar. He was very glamorous, so I was trying to

ABOVE: Kaminski used shadows throughout the movie to underscore the sense of danger and fear of the unknown.

ROMAN VISHNIAC

Photographer Roman Vishniac was the main source of inspiration for cinematographer Janusz Kaminski, who drew upon Vishniac's naturalistic style and his use of shadows while filming *Schindler's List*.

Born in 1897 to wealthy Russian Jewish parents, Roman Vishniac grew up in Moscow, where he developed an interest in photography at a young age. In 1920, he immigrated to Berlin. Armed with a Leica and a Rolleiflex, Vishniac went on assignment to document Jewish life in small towns and urban centers of Eastern Europe, including Warsaw, Krakow, and Lodz. Between 1935 and 1938, he photographed evidence of Jewish poverty to aid in fundraising campaigns that provided relief. In so doing, he documented the people who would perish during Hitler's reign of terror.

Published in several books, Vishniac's images constitute the most extensive photographic record of Jewish life in Central and Eastern Europe before the Holocaust, and they stand alongside the best social documentary photography of his era.

Vishniac arrived in New York in 1941 and settled on the Upper West Side. He became a pioneer in photomicroscopy, but in 1947 he returned to Europe to document Jewish displaced persons camps and other evidence of the war's toll. Vishniac died in 1990 at the age of 92.

In 2010, the massive archive of Vishniac's work (more than 30,000 objects including some 9,300 negatives and 5,000 prints) became an intended gift to the International Center for Photography in New York City from his daughter, Mara Vishniac Kohn.

reflect his character through lighting," says Kaminski. "The scene in the nightclub represents the classic Hollywood glamorous lighting. You would like the audience to start sympathizing with Oskar, to feel very safe in his presence. I created this 'eye light' so when the camera is in close up you can see just his eyes and the rest of the face falls in shadow. I think that had a very dramatic effect because he was, in a sense, an animal looking for prey and we know that he is studying these German high officials who would eventually help him. He was trying to figure out how he could buy them."

The lighting helped define the character of Oskar Schindler and heighten the performance of the actor playing him. "Mr. Neeson, captured so glamorously by Janusz Kaminski's richly versatile black-and-white cinematography, presents Oskar as an amalgam of canny opportunism and supreme, well-warranted confidence," wrote Janet Maslin in the *New York Times* on December 15, 1993. "Mr. Spielberg does not have to underscore the contrast between Oskar's life of privilege and the hardships of his Jewish employees."

> " We wanted people to see this film years from now and not realize when it was made." —Janusz Kaminski

After the scenes at the nightclub, the mood of the film takes a decidedly different turn. Now we are in the offices of the Jewish administrative council, or *Judenrat,* where people are frantically looking for help. "Right after that scene we go away completely from that kind of lighting and that kind of feel," explains Kaminski. "Then we get the night action sequences, which are extremely dark and very sketchy—where you don't really know what's in the shadows with flares into the lens."

This instinctive use of light is not always obvious to the audience, but it is the very subtlety of lighting that is the hallmark of great cinematography. The quiet and unobtrusive brilliance of Kaminski's work involved an enormous amount of planning and forethought. "Sometimes I dream about lighting setups, and other times I don't know how I will light something until I turn the first light on," Kaminski said in an interview for *Film and Video* magazine in 1994. "In *Schindler's List,* we dealt with very large locations that had to be pre-rigged, so I tried to figure out what I was going to do in advance. It took two weeks of laying cables and putting the lights in place. I had three truckloads of lights and every single one of them was needed."

THE CAMERA

To create a feeling of authenticity, Spielberg decided to strip away all of the artifices, the tricks of the trade he'd perfected in his previous movies. His goal was to "bear witness" to the Holocaust in the most direct and realistic manner possible. "I didn't want a style that was similar to anything I had done before," says the director. "First of all, I threw half my toolbox away. I canceled the crane. I tore out the dolly track. I didn't really plan a style. I didn't say I'm going to use a lot of handheld cameras, I simply tried to pull the events closer to the audience by reducing the artifice." In the end, some 40 percent of the film was shot using handheld cameras, adding to the documentary feel.

The contributions of camera work to heighten the emotional impact of the story are exemplified in the scene in which Itzhak Stern (played by Ben Kingsley) comes out of his apartment building and is stopped by SS soldiers. They demand to see his papers, which he frantically struggles to find in his pockets. Panic mounts when he can't find the documents. In this scene, the camera is more than an observer of the action, it becomes part of the sequence. The shots are quick and confusing, reflecting how immediately, how fast, life could change or be taken away. The camera quickly pans left and right, just as a person would do when sur-

ABOVE: Janusz Kaminski and Steven Spielberg on the set; Liam Neeson in foreground.

rounded by danger. Here the camera feels very frantic and terrifying, emphasizing the panic the character is feeling.

"It's not just in the action sequences," adds Kaminski, "very often we see the camera looking through other objects, looking through people, windows, obstructions, just like a documentary filmmaker would do during the war." In many scenes, the camera was used to project a furtive feeling of hiding in the shadows.

As Spielberg puts it, "I tried to be close to a journalist in recording this re-creation, more than being a filmmaker trying to heighten the suspense or action or the pathos. The black and white and handheld camera gives the film sort of a cinema verité, documentary feel. It embodied the truth we were trying to explore and communicate what happened. It made it seem more real, somehow." Kaminski adds, "We wanted people to see this film years from now and not realize when it was made."

That the filmmakers succeeded is beyond question. The cinematography was, in fact, so brilliant that film reviewers nearly swooned in appreciation. In December 1993, David Denby wrote in *New York Magazine,* "The camera keeps moving in Steven Spielberg's *Schindler's List,* and moving fast, around corners and up stairways, racing across open squares filled with naked and terrified people. Spielberg wants to get it all in, the entire catastrophe of the Polish Jews, and you can feel the obsessional fury in his work, the anguish, the grief passing over into revolt. . . . Spielberg has given the material the rushed, spasmodic, almost inadvertent look of newsreel footage. Appalling things happen, just *happen,* without warning or emotion—a few pistol shots to the head, from point-blank range, and the bodies fall over, two, three, four people. . . . Under the Nazi occupation of Poland, people are dying everywhere, and the resistance of at least one German, Catholic Oskar Schindler, seems like a miracle. *Schindler's List* is an emblem of annihilation and of hope at the same time. The film is an astonishing achievement."

Opposite and above: The camera as witness. In these shots, the camera looks through windows as if it were hidden somewhere and not part of a staged scene. These techniques were used to create a more realistic and documentary feel, as if the characters are unaware that they are being filmed and we are surreptitiously eavesdropping on their conversation.

66 I tried to be close to a journalist in recording this re-creation, more than being a filmmaker trying to heighten the suspense or action or the pathos. The black and white and handheld camera gives the film sort of a cinema verité, documentary feel. It embodied the truth we were trying to explore and communicate what happened. It made it seem more real, somehow. 99

—Steven Spielberg

Work this fully realized can happen only when the filmmakers are in perfect synch and, clearly, the working relationship between Spielberg and Kaminski was both en-ergizing and creatively fulfilling for both artists. "Janusz Ka-minski was my favorite ally on the set," says Spielberg. "The sparks just flew between us and he was a great stimulus in our collaboration."

The experience was just as rewarding for the cinematog-rapher. "I had the greatest working relationship with Steven Spielberg on this movie," says Kaminski. "It was very open and he encouraged me to take visual chances. He was not afraid of being too dark. He allowed me to contribute and to tell the story from my heart and that's what it's all about. I think he did the same thing from his perspective. He allowed himself to take chances. He also worked from his heart. We all have ideas and the point is to allow us to choose the right ideas. I think we chose the right ideas in *Schindler's List*." ■

DRESSING THE ACTORS

From cinematographer Janusz Kaminski and production designer Allan Starski to costume designer Anna Sheppard and makeup artist Christina Smith, every department in the production of *Schindler's List* was affected by the creative decision to shoot the movie in black and white. "In black and white, the major difference is that you have to create separation through lighting," explains Kaminski. "With the absence of color, I had to throw light on the faces while shooting so they became the brightest object in the scene. I had to ask Allan Starski to stay away from colors that would be similar to either skin tones or colors earmarked for set walls."

Even though they were shooting in black and white—indeed, as a result of this decision—there were specific restrictions in terms of choosing colors for both the set design and the costumes. White, for example, was unacceptable because it stood out too prominently. Green was also off limits: "We found certain colors, like green, didn't look really good in black and white, so we made a green-free movie," says Spielberg. "The palette to the eye during the production didn't look very good, but on film it was perfect."

These restrictions led costume designer Anna Sheppard to quip, "Doing a film in black and white was something like doing two films at once. You wanted everything to look right in color, then transfer to black and white." To compensate for the

LEFT AND FOLLOWING PAGE: Some examples of Oskar Schindler's impeccable wardrobe. Throughout the movie he is dressed in finely tailored suits with beautiful accessories. He is far better attired than any other character—just one of many aspects that set him apart.

color restrictions, Sheppard incorporated a lot of textures, such as tweeds and lace.

The Polish-born Sheppard (her maiden name was Biedrzycka) felt that her birthplace helped her re-create the way people dressed in Poland in the 1940s. "The advantage I had was that I am Polish and because this film portrays part of my country, I can feel this period of history more than someone who never lived here," she claims. "This is my homeland and shooting here was part of my heritage."

While most of the costumes in the movie are either military uniforms or the tattered rags of the prisoners, the lead character, Oskar Schindler, is always elegantly dressed, sometimes in a tuxedo, though most often in expertly tailored suits. The real Oskar Schindler was a huge, bear-like man of great height and girth. While Liam Neeson is on the slender side, he is so tall that vintage clothes from the 1940s would not fit him.

"Because Liam is so tall, all of his costumes had to be designed and made, even the shoes," says the designer. "[Schindler was] very glamorous, so all his clothes were impeccable: silk shirts, beautiful ties with matching tie clips. I really had to think about all the details to make his costumes stand out in the film." In addition, because Spielberg wanted Neeson to look large and imposing, the shoulders in all his suits were extravagantly padded.

Dressing the small army of extras was an entirely different story. "We had to make eighteen thousand costumes for seven thousand extras," says Sheppard.

OPPOSITE: In researching photos from the period, costume designer Anna Sheppard noticed that the women were sometimes beautifully dressed when they were being hauled off by the SS, indicating that they had no idea what was in store for them—as shown in this production still.

" We had to make 18,000 costumes for 7,000 extras. "

—Anna Sheppard, costume designer

Her department tried to get as much original clothing and accessories as possible. "We advertised in local media—TV and newspapers—for people to sell their period clothes, jewelry, shoes, and accessories," she says. "I was astonished by seeing how many beautiful things survived the war."

Unfortunately, a great deal of the beautiful clothing had to be virtually destroyed for visual effect. "Of course, the costumes had to deteriorate and change shape during the course of the shoot," explains Sheppard. "We had to make them look distressed, dirty, and worn out, which was the most difficult part of the costuming. We went from beautiful antique silk dresses right down to almost rags; it really showed the characters losing their dignity and the inhuman conditions in which they suffered."

Israeli actress Adi Nitzan, who portrays prisoner Mila Pfefferberg in the film, gave Sheppard high praise for her work at enhancing the film's authenticity through costume design. "I remember my first day on the set, going to lunch and seeing six Nazis in uniform, eating, talking German," she says. "I couldn't accept them, sitting there and eating. They looked so beautiful and elegantly dressed. I looked down at my torn and tattered dress and wanted to cry."

Sheppard's research on the period revealed an interesting dichotomy in terms of the clothing people wore during these dreadful years. "When you look at original photos from the time, you are surprised seeing the way people were dressed going to the cattle cars," says the designer. "They didn't know what was waiting for them. There was this wonderful photo of a woman wearing elegant clothes with a fox stole around her neck. If I'd invented it myself I think it would've looked wrong. I'd look at the original photos and think, how can she wear that elegant hat when she's going to the gas chamber? But they did and it made it all so human. Seeing those photos really helped me create this atmosphere."

How to dress the prisoners was another question that had to be addressed. The dress of the concentration camp prisoner that first comes to mind is the striped uniform. However, careful historical research helped overturn preconceived notions that have sometimes been incorporated in media interpretations of the Holocaust. "Looking at documents and photographs of the period, our research showed that Jewish prisoners didn't wear striped outfits until the end of the war," says Spielberg. "Until then they wore street clothes, which wasn't the image we had."

Still, Anna Sheppard noted that the most difficult aspect of her job was not the camp uniforms or outfitting thousands of extras. "My biggest challenge was keeping up with Spielberg," she said. "He shoots with such speed and efficiency that everything must be perfect."

Opposite: The women prisoners wore period clothes, many of which came from the 1940s. As the film progresses, their clothes deteriorate accordingly. Above: It was only toward the end of the war that prisoners wore the striped uniforms we usually associate with the camps. Following pages: There were many scenes for which Sheppard had to provide costumes for hundreds, sometimes thousands, of extras, including children.

HAIR AND MAKEUP

From the construction of the barracks at Plaszow to the wigs worn by the prisoners of the camp, the fundamental directive in the making of *Schindler's List* was authenticity. While attention to detail is crucial to the success of any movie, this particular project brought with it the added pressure of being true to historical fact and accurately portraying such a horrifying time in the lives of the survivors while honoring the memory of those who were murdered.

Steven Spielberg was involved in every aspect of what went up on the screen, including the actors' hair and makeup. "I worked with Anna Sheppard and [makeup artist] Christina Smith, looking at photos and history books of the period for hairstyles and costumes so we could be as authentic to the period as possible," he says. The filmmakers were looking to re-create in exact detail "what people looked like, what kind of makeup they wore on their faces."

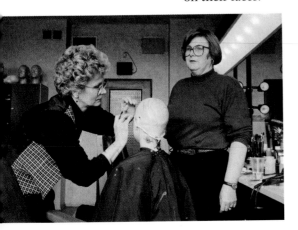

Hairstyles and makeup were relatively easy to duplicate from archival images. Perhaps the greatest challenge, though, to the hair and makeup department were the scenes in which the Schindler women were sent to Auschwitz and had their heads shorn. Bald skullcaps would be fine for long shots, but that was not what Spielberg wanted. To fully portray the terror these women felt when they were herded into the showers, the camera needed to show the emotion on their faces. "Steven wanted to be able to shoot extreme close-ups with the actresses in their bald caps, and present designs did not permit such shots," explains hair designer Judy Cory.

All available bald caps looked inherently fake in close-ups; they did not fit properly or seamlessly, and they did not extend down the nape of the neck. It always looked as though the actresses were wearing wigs, and that was not acceptable to the filmmakers. To solve the problem, Smith and Cory invented a different kind of wig.

"We designed and produced an entirely new kind of cap, with a new construction method that fit them not only to the head, but down the neck as well," says Cory. This involved a cap that fit over the head and down the neck without any discernable lines of latex. The results of their efforts were frighteningly realistic on screen, adding yet another dimension to an already fearsome scene. ■

LEFT AND ABOVE: Christina Smith, makeup supervisor, and Judith Cory, hair supervisor, had to create a new kind of skullcap for the close-up shots of the women whose hair is shorn at Auschwitz.

"Oskar, you're giving them hope!"

EXT. DEPOT—PLASZOW—LATER—DAY

Waves of heat rise from the roofs of the long string of cattle cars. Inside, those who "failed" the medical exams bake as they wait for the last cars to be filled. Schindler's Mercedes pulls up. He climbs out and stares transfixed. He notices Goeth then, standing with the other industrialists, Bosch and Madritsch, and strolls over to them.

> **GOETH**
> I tried to call you. I'm running a little late, this is taking longer than I thought. Have a drink.

There's a makeshift bar on a mahogany table, stocked with liquor and a pitcher of iced tea. Goeth glances away to the train. The idling engine only partially covers the desperate pleas for water coming from inside the slatted cars.

> **GOETH**
> They're complaining now? They don't know what complaining is.

> **SCHINDLER**
> What do you say we get your fire brigade out here and hose down the cars?

Goeth stares at him blankly. Then, with a what-will-you-think-of-next? look, laughs uproariously and calls over to Hujar—

> **GOETH**
> Bring the fire trucks!

What? Hujar heard him, he just doesn't get it. Finally he turns to another guy and tells him to do it. Streams of water cascade onto the scalding rooftops. The fire trucks are there, the hoses firing the cold water at the cars and on the people inside who are roaring their gratitude.

> **GOETH**
> This is really cruel, Oskar, you're giving them hope. You shouldn't do that. That's cruel.

> **SCHINDLER**
> I've got some 200-meter hoses back at Emalia, we can reach the cars down at the end.

Goeth finds this especially sidesplitting. . . . The DEF hoses are coupled to Plaszow's. As the water drenches the cars further back, the people inside loudly voice their thanks, and the guards and officers outside grin at the spectacle.

> **GUARD**
> What does he think he's saving them from?

81

POSSESSED

AS OSKAR MOVES along the string of cars, accompanied by the laughter of the SS, bringing a mercy which is in large part futile, it can be seen that he's not so much reckless anymore but possessed. Even Amon can tell that his friend has shifted into a new gear. . . . Amon was horrified by the way Oskar insisted on treating those dead as if they were poor relations traveling third class but bound for a genuine destination.

— from Thomas Keneally's *Schindler's List*

THE CAST

Early on, Steven Spielberg made a decision not to cast a well-known actor as Oskar Schindler, even though famous movie stars were vying for the part. "I was looking for . . . as close to the actual man as I could find," he told *Premiere* magazine in 1994. "I like the fact that although [Liam is] not an unknown actor, he's not a star either, and he won't bring much baggage to the character." (In 1992, Liam Neeson was not nearly the superstar he later became.) Like Neeson, Ralph Fiennes was also relatively unknown in the early 1990s—especially in America—when Spielberg cast him as Amon Goeth. Ben Kingsley was the only legitimate, Oscar-winning movie star cast by Spielberg—he was, as the director has said, the first and only actor Spielberg considered for the part of Itzhak Stern. All the supporting roles were filled by unknown actors, and the extras were cast in Poland for authenticity. Many of the extras were survivors of the Holocaust or the children of survivors, which helped fuel the aura of realism that was a hallmark of the film.

      The actors just did their best work. They didn't even work— they just *existed* in these characters. . . . We all kind of lived the experience even more than made a movie. —Steven Spielberg

LIAM NEESON / OSKAR SCHINDLER

Steven Spielberg:

I wasn't really concerned that [Neeson] look like Schindler. Liam had the charm and the bearing of Schindler. And he had the presence of Schindler. He had the charisma, just existing there without doing very much. And he also had the humanity that would always be there. It could be latent, but it would always come out when he summoned it. And so I felt that he was the best choice I could make for Schindler.

In terms of age and height, Liam wasn't as big as Schindler—Schindler was a big, portly man with huge shoulders. I had to actually pad Liam's costumes a lot to get his shoulders to even be two inches broader than they actually are. But I felt that he could carry it as sort of a figurehead of great deeds. I tested him on film, and his test was wonderful. And then [his performance in the stage play] *Anna Christie* just simply confirmed to me that of all the other actors I'd been talking to for a year and a half to three years, he was the one that I wanted the most.

Liam Neeson:

What I liked about this character was that he was a flesh-and-blood human being. He was full of contradictions, the way real human beings are. He wasn't a Francis of Assisi–type saint. He starts out as a businessman, purely for himself, to earn as much money as he can. He was a black marketer, earned millions, even by today's standards. By his shady dealings he earned this money and then spent every last cent to save these Jewish lives. It was a wonderful arc within the script to see him going through these changes.

Kenneth Turan, *Los Angeles Times*:

The brio of Neeson's performance knits *Schindler's List* together, and no greater compliment can be paid to it than to say its strength and assurance makes this unbelievable story believable and real.

Owen Gleiberman, *Entertainment Weekly*:

Neeson, with his overpowering physique, makes Schindler a man of hypnotic charisma, but we never quite feel we're inside him emotionally. His remoteness often plays as a dramatic "flaw," yet it's a flaw integral to the film's success. Watching *Schindler's List*, the audience becomes, in effect, the invisible protagonist, experiencing the insanity of Nazi Germany directly, with a minimum of melodramatic buffer.

REAL POWER

There is this beautiful piece of dialogue by Zaillian between Schindler and Goeth about the essence of power. It's about how it's much more powerful to forgive rather than take revenge for some injustice. Goeth tries it but doesn't have the power to withhold or to forgive. But it is a wonderful scene. When I first read the script I thought, "This is the one. If you can nail this scene, then everything else will come from it." —*Liam Neeson*

SCHINDLER
You have the power, Amon. But is that why they fear us?

GOETH
We have the fucking power to kill, that's why they fear us.

SCHINDLER
They fear us because we have the power to kill—arbitrarily. A man commits a crime, he should know better. We have him killed and we feel pretty good about it. Or, we kill him ourselves and we feel even better. That's not power, though,

that's justice. That's different than power. Power is when we have every justification to kill . . . and we don't.

GOETH
You think that's power.

SCHINDLER
That's what the emperors had. A man stole something, he's brought in before the emperor, he throws himself down on the floor, he begs for mercy, he knows he's going to die . . . and the emperor pardons him. This worthless man. He lets him go.

BROTHERS IN BUSINESS

OSKAR HAD the characteristic salesman's gift of treating men he abhorred as if they were spiritual brothers, and it would deceive the Herr Commandant so completely that Amon would always believe Oskar a friend. But from the evidence of Stern and others it is obvious that, from the time of their earlier contacts, Oskar abominated Goeth as a man who went to the work of murder as calmly as a clerk goes to his office. Oskar could speak to Amon the administrator, Amon the speculator, but knew at the same time that nine-tenths of the Commandant's being lay beyond the normal rational processes of humans.

—from Thomas Keneally's *Schindler's List*

BEN KINGSLEY / ITZHAK STERN

Steven Spielberg:

Stern really represents the collective Jewish consciousness. He nags at Schindler and acts like Oskar's mother most of the time. I didn't want to take a chance on casting an unknown to play Stern. I wanted someone who I had respect for as an actor. I probably had Ben Kingsley in mind from the moment I decided to make this movie. It was not like I struggled with a whole list of casting choices. Ben was the only man on my list for Stern.

Ben Kingsley knows so much more about acting than I ever will. I found it a relief to have an actor of that caliber on my movie set to help me make our story. When I have an actor like that, I am going to exploit his talent any way I possibly can in collaboration. Ben would continually say, "'Keep me on a level that's realistic. Please stop me from acting. I don't ever want to get caught acting.'" Ben is brilliant in this movie and as close to the guy as I imagined Thomas Keneally portrayed him in the novel.

Ben Kingsley:

Both the screenplay and the book isolate all those hoards of traumatized and distressed faces we've seen on the documentary footage of those terrible years. They draw a magic circle around each face, pulling it out of the crowd. This is what the screenplay achieves and why it is such an adventure for all the protagonists in the film. Everyone has a great moment where the camera zooms into this old black and white still and pulls a face out.

The systematic killing of six million people is something the mind is unable to grasp and to transmit that tragedy, you have to focus on the individual. Shakespeare did it. Whenever he had vast armies moving across the stage, there was always one remarkable scene between the first, second, and third soldiers. Spielberg and Zaillian used this device as well.

This period of history must be retold to every generation. I'm afraid if we don't, whatever year this film appeared, it would be relevant somewhere in the world. We have a long, long way to go before stories like this become ancient history.

RALPH FIENNES / AMON GOETH

Steven Spielberg:
Amon Goeth was one of the most satanically brutal—I hate calling him a person but don't want to melodramatize it by saying "thing" or "beast." As a man, he was closer to his two dogs than to anyone wearing the Star of David. He was just a bloodthirsty man and, on his menu, he would daily kill Jews.

Ralph Fiennes:
Someone told me that Goeth was a good-looking man and could smile like an angel. He didn't necessarily look like an evil monster but everyone was terrified

of him. So what do evil monsters look like? Goeth was terrifying not because of how he looked but because of his behavior, his unpredictability. You had no indication of what he was going to do. He had two dogs he trained to attack and kill, especially children. In the morning he would go on his balcony overlooking the camp and, with a rifle, pick off people. Poldek Pfefferberg says he was the devil.

Everyone concentrates on the evil sadist in Goeth, but there was also this other side to him. He thought of himself as a smart black-market operator. He was feathering his own nest with all the wealth he was accumulating by stealing from the Jews. I think his main interest was amassing a lot of wealth and making his life as comfortable as possible. Schindler was a part of that.

David Denby, *New York* magazine:
Fiennes, an English TV and theater actor, has a dyspeptic, malevolent gaze and a soft body that seems to be pouring out its wastes. He is a great, terrifying actor. . . . Goeth actually becomes an interesting and suffering man. He shoots Jews from his balcony, for sport: but as the war goes on and the atrocities mount, he looks miserable in his own body and he disintegrates. The role is a study of what happens to a man operating entirely without limits.

ABOVE: Amon Goeth at his villa at Plaszow in 1943, photographed by Raimund Titsch (see page 27). RIGHT: Ralph Fiennes recreates the scenes of Goeth shooting prisoners with a terrifying nonchalance. Photo also shows the Plaszow set.

SENTIMENTAL

GOETH'S FACE was open and pleasant, rather longer than Schindler's. His hands, though large and muscular, were long-fingered. He was sentimental about his children, the children from his second marriage whom, because of his foreign service, he had not seen often in the past three years. As a substitute, he was sometimes attentive to the children of brother officers. He could be a sentimental lover too, but though he resembled Oskar in terms of general sexual voraciousness, his tastes were less conventional, running sometimes to brother SS men, frequently to the beating of women."

—from Thomas Keneally's *Schindler's List*

CAROLINE GOODALL / EMILIE SCHINDLER

Thomas Keneally, *Schindler's List*:

There seemed to be at least a tolerance between Oskar and Emilie, a thorough mutual respect. At first sight she might have looked like a marital cipher, an abused wife who did not know how to get out. Some of the men wondered at first what she would think when she found the sort of factory Oskar kept, the sort of camp. They did not know yet that Emilie would make her own discrete contribution, that it would be based not on conjugal obedience but on her own ideas.

Steven Spielberg:

There's a whole other story, by the way, worthy of a film. Emilie Schindler made amazing contributions, especially in the medical area. I'd actually shot more scenes that involved Emilie. But once again, it didn't play into the themes, you know, and didn't play into the central theme of Oskar Schindler. But she made great contributions and he was unfaithful to her, of course, all his life. Even after the Holocaust. Basically abandoned her. But she came back to be with him. She was a very righteous Christian Catholic woman.

ABOVE: *Allen Starski, Steven Spielberg, and Caroline Goodall on set.*

EMBETH DAVIDTZ / HELEN HIRSCH

Steven Spielberg:

Helen Hirsch had to survive the war in the house of Amon Goeth. She was a real survivor, who had maybe the worst time of anyone. She is played by Embeth Davidtz, a wonderful South African actress who is pretty much an actress for all seasons and countries. She can do any accent. She can do an American accent and fool you into thinking she was born in Oklahoma. She does a perfect Polish accent. She did a remarkable job in this movie.

Embeth Davidtz:

Helen Hirsch lived with Goeth. The other women in the camp envied her but basically, she was a caged animal living with a very crazy, volatile man. She was there to serve him as his maid but she suffered the most awful abuse from him. She must have been very gifted and something special to have made it out of there alive. Knowing she was such an extraordinary human being really helped me in preparing for the part.

Schindler's presence in Helen's life was like having a guardian angel. His story is the incredible triumph of the faith of one man.

Ralph Fiennes:

Goeth perceived himself as being very fond of Helen Hirsch. When he was in prison at the end of the war, he wrote to her asking if she could send him a few things. To him, she was like a faithful house servant. There is a scene in the movie where he tries to articulate his feelings for her but he is not clear about them and I think that makes great psychological sense.

JONATHAN SAGALLE / POLDEK PFEFFERBERG

Jonathan Sagalle:

Poldek Pfefferberg . . . was the go-between for Schindler with the black market. He supplied most of what Schindler needed to bribe the Germans—expensive herring, liquor, clothing, and other things they could only get on the black market.

Poldek is a survivor and everything he does is to insure his survival. There's a scene where he's caught in the street by Goeth and he makes this decision to say he was ordered to pick up the bundles in the street and he salutes him. Goeth doesn't believe this kind of Jew exists—someone who would stand up to him. The problem with Poldek is that he was sort of a stray cat. He had a lot of secrets and even his wife didn't know where he got all the liquor, the furs, the sardines, and other stuff. He would just disappear from the ghetto.

I didn't want to meet Poldek in person because it was better for me if he remained this kind of vague character for me to play. So I avoided him until about the sixth week of shooting when he came to the set. I was pleasantly surprised to discover that he was a nice man and very funny. He was eighty years old but still strong, muscular, and tough. You could see he had all this physical strength to go through the tunnels and stand up against the terror and horror of his situation.

I myself come from a family of Holocaust survivors. I don't know if Schindler was a hero, but he was certainly a survivor. He had to make a living and he tried to make the best of his situation. He used the Jews for forced slave labor but I think he very slowly fell in love with the people who worked for him and that deep down he was probably a good man.

ABOVE: *Jonathan Sagalle meets Poldek Pfefferberg, the character he plays in the movie, on the set in Krakow.*

ADI NITZAN / MILA PFEFFERBERG

Adi Nitzan:

Mila Pfefferberg . . . was married to Poldek and Schindler saved her, too. Her story is not very dominant in the movie or the book. She was an orphan who married Poldek when she was young.

It felt very strange to meet her and Poldek. I didn't know what to expect. But then she came up to me and said, "'I don't believe they took such a beautiful actress to play me. I don't look so nice.'" She made me feel very comfortable, she was so friendly and casual.

FACES OF THE EXTRAS

Steven Spielberg:

Branko Lustig rewarded the movie with great authenticity. For example, he found me some of the best faces among the extras.

Branko Lustig:

Steven and I were both concerned that we would not find Jewish-looking extras in Krakow. The city was once one of the biggest Jewish communities in middle Europe. There were about three hundred thousand Jews here. But today (in 1992) you have only like three or four hundred because they were all either killed or went to America or Israel. About six months before shooting, we came to Krakow and put an ad in the papers and on television and radio. We asked for people to play Jews in the movie. We didn't know how many people would want to come but, on that Sunday, we had about ten thousand people show up. It was raining but people stood there all day while we took pictures.

I took the photos to Steven in Los Angeles and we ended up with our extras from here. We had about three hundred with us all the time and some days we had as many as two thousand for the Plaszow camp scenes.

David Denby, *New York* magazine:

Spielberg was right to stay away from familiar stars, right to use so many unknown actors, many of them the Israeli children of survivors. The faces are authentically Eastern European. We get to know many of those faces: we see the people working, taking care of their families, hiding, pricking their fingers with pins and smearing the blood into their ashen cheeks so as to appear healthy (and not be sent to Auschwitz). They are a community, a people.

"The list is life."

INT. STERN'S OFFICE—PLASZOW—NIGHT

To the faint tapping of the typewriter keys across the room, Schindler runs his finger down several pages of names, counting to himself. Eventually, quietly—

> **SCHINDLER**
> That's it.

Stern heard him and stops typing, glances over.

> **SCHINDLER**
> You can finish that page.

Stern resumes where he left off, but then hesitates. Glances over again. There's something he doesn't understand.

> **STERN**
> What did Goeth say about this? You just told him how many people you needed, and he . . . ?

He trails off. It doesn't sound right. And Schindler doesn't answer. He's avoided telling Stern the details of the deal struck with Goeth, and balks at telling him now.

> **STERN**
> You're not buying them. (*no answer*)
> You're buying them? You're paying him for each of these names?

> **SCHINDLER**
> If you were still working for me, I'd expect you to talk me out of it. It's costing me a fortune.

Stern had no idea. And has no idea now what to say. He's astonished by what this man is doing. Schindler shrugs like it's no big deal, but Stern knows it is. Silence. Then—

> **SCHINDLER**
> Finish the page and leave one space at the bottom.

Stern turns back, does as he's told. Schindler drinks. Nothing but the sound of the typewriter keys. And then nothing at all. The page is done. Stern turns and looks Schindler in the eyes.

> **STERN**
> This list is an absolute good. The list is life. All around its margins lies the gulf.

TALMUDIC LEGEND

THERE IS the Talmudic legend of the *Hasidei Ummot Ha-olam*, the Righteous of the Nations, of whom there are said to be—at any point in the world's history—thirty-six. Stern did not believe literally in the mystic number, but the legend was psychologically true for him, and he believed it a decent and wise course to try to make of Schindler a living and breathing sanctuary.

— from Thomas Keneally's *Schindler's List*

THE CREW ON SET

Opposite: Production associates Bonnie Curtis and Karen Kushell, executive producer Kathleen Kennedy, Steven Spielberg, and director of photography Janusz Kaminski on the set in Krakow. Above: Spielberg with executive producer Kathleen Kennedy. Right: Producer Branko Lustig with an actor playing a German soldier.

ABOVE: *Spielberg, co-producer Lew Rywin, Branko Lustig, and two actors playing German officials on the set in Krakow.* LEFT: *Producer Gerald Molen and film consultant Rabbi Marvin Hier, dean and founder of the Simon Wiesenthal Center, the Museum of Tolerance, and Moriah Films. In 2007, Newsweek named him the most influential rabbi in America.* OPPOSITE: *Spielberg's good friend George Lucas visited the set; here, with Spielberg and his wife, Kate Capshaw.*

WAKING UP AND
GOING TO HELL

Schindler's List was shot in Poland over a three-month period that was plagued by cold and inclement weather. In all of the behind-the-scenes photographs, the crew is wrapped in down jackets, scarves, hats, and gloves. Not only was it bitterly cold, which complicates many different aspects of filming, but it also either rained or snowed almost every day, and the filmmakers had to work around the weather conditions. In the end, though, the weather was not nearly as problematic for the actors and the crew as the emotional toll of the material.

In nearly every interview Steven Spielberg gave after Schindler's List was released, he talked about the emotional strain of shooting this movie, admitting that it was the first time he cried on set. "I never cry on sets making films," said the director. "I've often protected myself with the movie camera. The camera has always been my golden shield against things really reaching me. I put that thing in front of my face; it stops the bullet.

"I can't tell you the shots I did on Schindler's List or why I put the camera in a certain place. I re-created these events, and then I experienced them as any witness or victim would have. It wasn't like a movie.

"So every single day was like waking up and going to hell, really. There was sadness on the set every day. I had actors breaking down from the stress of the re-

OPPOSITE: The weather in Poland was always an issue as it either rained or snowed every day throughout the three-month shoot.

112

creation. I had crew members that would walk away from the camera in tears and not come back for ten minutes. I was as strong as I could be . . . but I cried more making this movie than I cried during any three- or four-month period in my whole life."

Yet, despite everything, Spielberg managed to bring the film in on time, and crew members reported that his energy never flagged, that he was constantly in motion. One day, in fact, Spielberg managed to complete an amazing fifty-one setups, which would have been something of a miracle even on a much less emotional shoot.

Producer Gerald Molen reported that Spielberg operated in an aura of "austere calm" and that to everyone there he seemed to be "a man at peace with himself." Perhaps it was because, as Richard Schickel suggested in *Time* magazine, "At some point, impeccable professionalism simply merged with obsession."

While many scenes were painful to film, several of the filmmakers pointed out two particularly difficult sequences. The first was the scene in which the prisoners at Plaszow were forced to strip naked and run in circles around the doctors. The

more healthy-looking ones would be allowed to stay in the labor camp, while the others would be shipped off to the gas chambers at Auschwitz.

To make the scene work, the actors (most of them extras, not professional actors) would be required to strip naked in front of hundreds of others. This was not an easy thing to ask of them, and the filmmakers worried about their reactions to this direction.

"We talked to everybody beforehand. For one thing, they had to know why they were taking off their clothes," says Spielberg. "The clothes came off so easily once the Polish people who were in those scenes understood what we were trying

OPPOSITE: According to Spielberg, the sequence where the prisoners are stripped naked and forced to run in circles around the camp in front of the doctors was one of the most emotionally draining scenes to shoot. ABOVE: During the scene in which the children at the camp are taken away from their mothers, listening to the women's screams was very hard for many of the crew members. They knew that many of the actors and extras in these scenes were from Holocaust families.

to do and that it was a health action at the hands of the German physicians. Nobody came over and said, 'I'm Catholic, I can't do this.'"

Spielberg seemed quite surprised that the extras were so willing to participate in this scene. "The clothes came off, the people did it without question," he repeated. "*Without question*. And they were humiliated, and we caught the humiliation on film. We only did this a couple of times. It wasn't that way all day long, but they were, you know, undressed for a number of hours, and it was hard on everybody. It was hard on me to be there, I couldn't look at it, I had to turn my eyes away, I couldn't watch. It was easier to see it in black and white than it was in color, actually. I couldn't watch but I shot it. It's kind of hard to get across to you what that means. But it was one of the worst days on the movie, I think for everybody involved."

The scene took three days to shoot, and after the first day, Spielberg said he was "trying to find a way not to come back to work." Of course he somehow found the wherewithal to finish shooting the scene, although everyone had a difficult time with the sequence. "None of us looked," admits the director. "I said to the guy pulling the focus on a very difficult shot, 'Do you think you got that one?' And he said, 'I don't know. I wasn't looking.' And when the man on the focus doesn't look, you know, it's interesting."

The other especially hellish scene was the one in which the women in the camp see their children being herded up and put on trucks to be taken away, presumably to Auschwitz. The women prisoners break ranks to run after the trucks, screaming for their children. Anne Marie Stein, the unit publicist on set that day, said that these scenes were so realistic that she had to walk away.

> "The ghosts were on the set every day in their millions." —Ben Kingsley

It was hard, if not impossible, for the filmmakers to avoid the feeling that they were actually living through this terrible time in history. This was surely the result of working in an atmosphere that was so realistic. Unfortunately, in terms of working conditions, there was little to alleviate the tension inherent in the material, which everyone approached with a certain reverence and respect.

On most movie sets, the actors and the crew will create their own amusement between takes, and practical jokes are common to break up the tedium, but the experience on this movie was quite different. "I went there thinking you could separate work from life," said actress Embeth Davidtz. "It's the first time that didn't happen."

Opposite: The director, deep in thought, during filming.

Richard Schickel wrote, "The goofing around that usually makes the boredom and hardships of difficult movie locations bearable was not available to this company. 'The ghosts were on the set every day in their millions,' says Ben Kingsley. As Spielberg recalls, 'There was no break in the tension. Nobody felt there was any room for levity,' and people were always 'breaking down or cracking up.' This he had anticipated, he says, 'but I didn't expect so much sadness every day.'"

They couldn't escape, even in their spare time. When they weren't filming, there was one particular event that, for Spielberg, proved as emotional as anything he experienced during the shoot. "The most moving thing that happened for me was on Passover," says the director. "We had Passover at the hotel, and all the young German actors who were playing Nazis came in with yarmulkes and Haggadahs and sat with the Israeli actors and took part in the Passover service. I wept like a baby." ▪

"Three minutes of silence"

INT. BRUNNLITZ FACTORY—POWER ROOM—DAY

All eleven hundred workers and all the guards are gathered for the first time on the factory floor.

> **SCHINDLER**
> The unconditional surrender of Germany has just been announced. At midnight tonight the war is over. Tomorrow, you'll begin the process of looking for survivors of your families. In many cases you won't find them. After six long years of murder, victims are being mourned throughout the world. We've survived. Some of you have come up to me and thanked me. Thank yourselves. Thank your fearless Stern, and others among you, who, worrying about you, have faced death every moment. Thank you,

He's looking at the guards, thanking them, which thoroughly confuses the workers.

> **SCHINDLER**
> You've shown extraordinary discipline. You've behaved humanely here. You should be proud of yourselves. I know you've received orders from our Commandant—which he's received from his superiors—to dispose of the population of this camp.

Apprehension waves across the factory. To the guards:

> **SCHINDLER**
> Now would be the time to do it. They're all here. This is your opportunity. Or . . .

you could leave. And return to your families as men instead of murderers.

Long, long silence. Finally, one of the guards slowly lowers his rifle, breaks ranks, and walks away. Then another. And another. And another.

> **SCHINDLER**
> I'm a member of the Nazi party. I'm a munitions manufacturer. I'm a profiteer of slave labor. I'm a criminal. At midnight, you'll be free and I'll be hunted. (*pause*) I'll remain with you until five minutes after midnight. After which time, and I hope you'll forgive me, I have to flee. In memory of the countless victims among your people, I ask us to observe three minutes of silence.

THE FACTORY SPEECH

While *Schindler's List* is a fictionalized account of a true story and all the dialogue was, of course, imagined by the screenwriter, the final speech on the factory floor was taken from notes transcribed and saved that day by one of the *Schindlerjuden* secretaries. Thus, this is one of the most authentic scenes in the movie.

In researching his novel, Thomas Keneally interviewed as many *Schindlerjuden* as he and Poldek Pfefferberg could find. Many of the former prisoners told Keneally that, by the end of the war, Schindler was recklessly out of control and that his speech on the factory floor did not comfort them. "He was traveling around with pockets full of diamonds doing [black market] deals. He was deliberately running along an edge of risk because it suited his temperament," Keneally told *Entertainment Weekly* on December 13, 1993. "That factory floor speech [bidding the guards and inmates farewell] didn't make [the workers] misty, it made the hair stand up on the back of their heads. [Schindler's] getaway car was stashed full of diamonds in the seats and the hubcaps, although if you show that, you've got to show that later they were all confiscated or stolen."

Given the tenor of this speech, Keneally wondered how the ending of the movie would sit with the former prisoners. Had they glorified Oskar Schindler too much? "I met one of the prisoners at the New York screening," adds Keneally. "He'd been in Oskar's camp a long time and he knew the ambiguities of Oskar, the contradictions. When I asked him if he thought Oskar wasn't idealized too much at the end of the movie, he said, 'No. What Oskar did was so remarkable, you can't overdo the idealistic side.'"

To shoot the climactic scene in which Oskar Schindler announces Germany's surrender to his factory workers, Steven Spielberg decided to use eleven hundred extras when he could have shot the scene with far fewer people. "It is widely known that Schindler had eleven hundred people on his list," explains the director. "I could easily have shot the final scene with two hundred extras and asked the audience to believe there were eleven hundred in the shot. But I really wanted an exact count. I wanted you to see how many people he was attempting to save. I thought that would make us realize what a hero he really was in their lives and for the generations that followed."

ALL ALONE WITH THE PICTURE

"You can do anything in the editing room," says Steven Spielberg. "Film is so malleable. I could have made six films out of what we shot for *Schindler's List*."

Once filming on *Schindler's List* wrapped and the cast and crew disbanded, work began on editing the footage. Many people think that at the end of shooting, the film is more or less completed. This could not be further from the reality of filmmaking. "When a film is shot, it's not a movie yet, it's all in various pieces that have to be put together," says film editor Michael Kahn, who won an Academy Award for his work on the film. "There's close-ups and masters, and the editor goes in and he puts the film together; he decides the pace, the angles, the symmetry, and the rhythm."

Kahn had been a film editor for Spielberg for almost two decades before they worked on *Schindler's List*. "Steven and I started together on *Close Encounters of the Third Kind*, and we had worked together for about eighteen years when we made *Schindler's List*," explains Kahn. "We made so many movies that after a couple of years there's a shorthand between us. I understand when he says something, what he means and how he feels, and I try to implement that on film."

In explaining the way he works with Spielberg, Kahn says, "You can't put a scene together unless there's a point of view, so Steven and I discuss that and then I go and put the scene together. I bring it back, we run it and make changes, then we run it again and make more changes. We hone the scene down to where we feel it should be."

OPPOSITE: *Actor Piotr Polk plays Leo Rosner, one of the* Schindlerjuden, *who along with his brother, Henry, survived the war by playing music for the Nazis.*

This is painstaking, precision work, as every frame of the film is carefully considered. The editing room is a place where the film is brought to life, and it is the most contemplative time in the filmmaking process. It is, of course, quite a different working environment than filming on set. "I like the intimacy of the editing room," says Spielberg. "It's just me and Michael Kahn and our assistants sitting in a very small room with all the movie in the can. A movie is completely collaborative and social and noisy and there's a thousand questions asked of me every day. You never get a moment's rest. In the editing room, no one asks you questions. You're alone with the picture and it's much more the experience that an artist has painting his canvas."

Kahn points to two sequences in the movie that were substantially enhanced in the editing process. The first was the scene in which Schindler's women workers were mistakenly sent to Auschwitz. "The men are at Brünnlitz, they've just arrived," says Kahn. "These women felt they were going to freedom with Schindler, with the men. But then one woman senses that something is wrong. I started to go through

a couple of cuts. Initially, when I did these scenes, we didn't have close-ups. So what Steven did with these close-ups is that he internalized what these women were feeling through their eyes and through the motion of the light coming through the slats in the car. I think it works; you can feel the terror. What happened? They were supposed to be going to Brünnlitz and here they are at Auschwitz. They know what it means, it means that they could be liquidated."

The second sequence that Kahn cites is the one involving three kisses. "Steven shot three scenes: a wedding scene, a nightclub scene, and the scene where Amon Goethe talks to Helen Hirsch in the basement," explains Kahn. "The scenes were supposed to be intercut, so we edited each scene separately and then tried to figure out how to intercut them. This took quite a while and was difficult to do." In the end, these three scenes, all very different but connected spiritually, are seamlessly edited together and add to the contrasting emotions of these characters. Here, as in the rest of the film, the editing is so expertly done that it is almost invisible—the hallmark of great editing. ▪

Opposite: Script supervisor Nada Pinter, film editor Michael Kahn, and director Steven Spielberg on the set at the Plaszow camp location. Above: These three separate and seemingly disparate scenes— Oskar Schindler being seduced at a nightclub, the wedding scene in the prison camp, and Amon Goeth terrorizing Helen Hirsch in the basement of his villa—were seamlessly woven together during the editing process to make one sweeping and powerful sequence. Kahn's editing of these three scenes exemplifies how the editing process can convey emotion and enhance the story.

"Whoever saves one life . . ."

EXT. COURTYARD—BRUNNLITZ CAMP—NIGHT

Schindler and Emilie emerge from his quarters, each carrying a suitcase. In the dark, some distance away from the Mercedes, stand all eleven hundred workers.

> **LEVARTOV**
> We've written a letter trying to explain things. In case you're captured. Every worker has signed it.

Schindler sees a list of signatures beginning below the typewritten text and continuing for several pages. He pockets it, this new list of names.

> **SCHINDLER**
> Thank you.

Stern glances away to the assembled workers who are parting for Pfefferberg, Wulkan, and a couple of others coming through. They reach the group by the car and Wulkan hands Stern, who hands Schindler, the finished ring. Schindler sees that it's a gold band, like a wedding ring. He notices the inscription and glances up to Stern.

> **STERN**
> It's Hebrew. It says, "Whoever saves one life, saves the world."

Schindler slips the ring onto a finger, admires it a moment, glances to Stern and Wulkan and Pfefferberg nodding his thanks, then seems to withdraw.

> **SCHINDLER** (to himself)
> I could've got more out . . .

Stern isn't sure he heard right. Schindler steps away from him, from his wife, from the car, from the workers.

> **SCHINDLER** (to himself)
> I could've got more . . . if I'd just . . . I don't know, if I'd just . . . I could've got more . . .

> **STERN**
> Oskar, there are eleven hundred people who are alive because of you. Look at them.

> **SCHINDLER**
> If I'd made more money . . . I threw away so much money, you have no idea. If I'd just . . .

> **STERN**
> There will be generations because of what you did.

> **SCHINDLER**
> I didn't do enough.

> **STERN**
> You did so much.

THE *SCHINDLERJUDEN*

To find people who could work as extras on the film, producer Branko Lustig placed ads in local newspapers in various cities around Krakow. Thousands of people showed up to audition, but the ads had another benefit. "Interestingly, we found some Schindler Jews in Krakow," says Lustig, "and they came to the set to talk to Steven."

The arrival of the *Schindlerjuden* on set was a bonus for the filmmakers. They had amazing stories to tell the director (some of which found their way into the film), and their involvement helped the filmmakers be more authentic in telling these stories.

In 2013, Caroline Frost of the *Huffington Post* had the opportunity to meet Niusia Horowitz, the first of the *Schindlerjuden* to visit the set. As Frost reports, "An elderly lady of beauty and spirit, she remembers little of Oskar Schindler himself, whom she encountered as a child, and her life was complicated by the fact she told no one, not even her family, about her extraordinary background, until Spielberg came along.

"'He made it acceptable to bring these things out into the open,' she explains over dinner in one of Krakow's liveliest restaurants, where the cast and crew of *Schindler's List* often dined together. But it is clear, too, that Niusia is not consumed

Right: Niusia Horowitz and Magdalena Dandourian, the little girl who plays her in the film; she's the child that Schindler kisses at his birthday party in the factory.

by the past, talking about her makeup, her hair, her life in America. She lives in the present, which is the biggest victory anyone with her history can claim. There are an estimated 7,000 descendants of the names on Schindler's List living in the world today."

Spielberg was amazed to discover that many of these survivors had never before told their stories to anyone. He immediately understood the importance of these testimonies and was inspired to start thinking about how these stories might be preserved for future generations. In short, the unexpected appearance of these survivors would eventually become the inspiration for the Shoah Foundation. ■

ABOVE: Schindlerjuden *Henry Rosner and his wife, Manci, in Poland, with cast, crew and other survivors.*

ABOVE: *Israeli actress Adi Nitzan and Mila Pfefferberg, the woman she plays in the movie; Poldek Pfefferberg and the actor who plays him, Jonathan Sagalle; Liam Neeson; and Steven Spielberg.*

ABOVE: *Poldek Pfefferberg shares his photo album and his memories with Spielberg and other members of the cast and crew.* LEFT: *The actor Grzegorz Kwas and Mietek Pemper, the* Schindlerjuden *he plays in the film. As a stenographer to Amon Goeth, Pemper was one of the only Jews with access to the commandant's confidential files. After liberation, Pemper used his photographic memory to testify against Goeth. (See page 232 for an excerpt of the testimony Pemper gave to the USC Shoah Foundation's Visual History Archive.)* OPPOSITE: *Poldek Pfefferberg and Liam Neeson on the set in Poland. It was because of Pfefferberg's efforts to bring Oskar Schindler's story to the screen that Neeson got the opportunity to play this landmark role.*

SCHINDLER'S LEGACY

The dramatic epilogue of *Schindler's List* was shot in Israel, at the gravesite of Oskar Schindler. In this scene, a procession of the actual *Schindlerjuden* and some of their family members approaches his grave bearing small stones, a Jewish symbol of respect for the dead. These 128 survivors were flown to Israel from all parts of the world; also present was the frail, wheelchair-bound Emilie Schindler, Oskar's widow.

The sequence is shot in color, propelling the audience out of the 1940s and into the 1990s. We see the actual people whose stories have been immortalized in this film. And we see the children and grandchildren of these survivors, some seven thousand people who would not be alive today but for Oskar Schindler. They are his true legacy.

It is one of the most profoundly moving moments in a film that is defined by profound moments. By bringing us into the present, we are reminded of the adage that without acknowledging the past, we are doomed to repeat it. That message could not be more meaningful or important today.

Once this scene wrapped, the weary filmmakers flew home to Los Angeles. It had been three grueling months of work and everyone felt emotionally drained. Yet something happened on the flight home from Israel that energized the exhausted filmmakers.

On that flight, Spielberg began talking to producers Gerald Molen and Branko Lustig about his dream of shooting a twenty-minute documentary of each of the

Schindlerjuden, an idea that had come to him during production. As the flight continued, Spielberg became more and more animated. Production assistant Karen Kushell speculates that he may have experienced an epiphany similar to the one Oskar Schindler went through on the road to saving his eleven hundred Jewish workers.

Why limit the documentaries to only the *Schindlerjuden*? Spielberg then wondered out loud. Why not get the testimonies of as many Holocaust survivors as possible? Thus, the idea for the Shoah Foundation was conceived, and work on the project began almost immediately.

Anne Marie Stein, unit publicist for the film, recently came across a memo from the producers to Spielberg dated April 14, 1994—the earliest document to follow up on the initial discussion on the plane. Here the producers calculate the actual numbers involved in taking on a project of this scope and set a target of fifty thousand interviews. Interviewing 50,000 survivors in three years would involve recording 16,666 testimonies a year—that meant 1,388 a month, or 320 a week, or 64 a day! Numbers, as they say, don't lie, and even the best of intentions needs to be rooted in reality. The three-year deadline was expanded to five years. Everyone involved was eager to get started.

Less than two weeks later, on April 29, 1994, the first official testimony for the Shoah Foundation was recorded with Holocaust survivor Jacob Abram. Five years later, on January 31, 1999, Gerald Molen interviewed Auschwitz survivor Branko Lustig for the fifty-thousandth testimony. In all, more than fifty-two thousand testimonies are now archived at the Shoah Foundation at the University of Southern California in Los Angeles. ▪

OPPOSITE: Oskar Schindler and Schindlerjuden *Abraham Zuckerman on a visit to Jerusalem. TOP: The* Schindlerjuden *gather at Oskar's grave; Emilie Schindler is in wheelchair. ABOVE: The final shot in the film, re-created by the* Schindlerjuden *in Israel.*

BRANKO LUSTIG: TELLING THE WORLD

One of the most moving moments in the history of the Academy Awards was when producer Branko Lustig accepted the 1993 Oscar for Best Picture on behalf of himself and the film's two other producers, Gerald Molen and Steven Spielberg. After a thunderous standing ovation, Lustig said, "My number was A3317. I am a Holocaust survivor. It's a long way from Auschwitz to this stage. I want to thank everyone who helped me come so far.

"People died in front of me at the camps. Their last words were, 'Be a witness of my murder. Tell to the world how I died. Remember.' Together with Jerry [Molen] we helped Steven make this movie. I hope I fulfilled my obligation to the innocent victims of the Holocaust. In the name of the six million Jews killed in the Shoah and other Nazi victims, I want to thank everyone who acknowledged this movie. Thank you."

Even without knowing the details of Lustig's life, this was a memorable and stirring moment for everyone in the audience and anyone watching the broadcast. Indeed, the story of Lustig's journey from the concentration camps

to the stage of the Academy Awards is worthy of its own movie.

Branko Lustig was born in Croatia in 1932. His family was swept into the Holocaust, and most of them died in the camps, including his grandmother and his father. At twelve years old, weighing only sixty-six pounds, Branko was liberated from Bergen-Belsen after three long years. Eventually he was reunited with his mother. In 1955, he studied theater in Croatia and got a job as a translator on a film crew, in time working his way up on various movies from translator to assistant director. In the 1980s he worked on *Winds of War* and the sequel *War and Remembrance*, which brought him in 1988 to Los Angeles, where he decided to relocate.

His involvement with *Schindler's List* started long before Spielberg agreed to direct the film. "One day in 1981 or '82, I got a call when I was working in Yugoslavia," Lustig recalls. "I was sent a script for *Schindler's List* [an early version, not the Zaillian script] and asked to come up with a budget for shooting in Zagreb. There was still the Iron Curtain in those days, so you couldn't shoot in Auschwitz

OPPOSITE; Branko Lustig, Schindlerjuden *Poldek Pfefferberg, Janusz Kaminski, and Steven Spielberg on the set in Krakow.*

or anywhere in Germany. We looked at locations, made a budget, and nothing happened. The script got sold to Universal and I didn't hear back from them."

He directed a movie with Rutger Hauer and worked on Volker Schlöndorff's epic World War II tale *The Tin Drum* and the tragic Meryl Streep movie, *Sophie's Choice*. "Then I was convalescing from heart surgery when I got a call that Spielberg was going to make a Holocaust movie," he remembers. "I had introduced myself to Kathleen Kennedy and, through her, to Spielberg. They asked me to have lunch with Jerry Molen, who gave me a script. I realized I'd read the story before. Only this time, the script was much better. I had a meeting with Spielberg. It was supposed to be five minutes and it lasted a half hour. He was so excited when I told him my background. He said, 'You are my producer.'"

Spielberg remembers his first meeting with Lustig very clearly. "He said, 'Here are my credentials,' and rolled up his sleeve and there were the numbers from Auschwitz.' He said, 'I want

> **Branko said, 'Here are my credentials,' rolled up his sleeve and there were numbers from Auschwitz.** —Steven Spielberg

to produce this movie. I know these people. I know these individual stories, and I think I can be of great benefit to you.' And he absolutely was. One of the best decisions I made was to reward his persistence, because he turned around and rewarded the story with great authenticity."

After *Schindler's List*, Lustig produced many other films, including *The Peacemaker, Black Hawk Down, Hannibal,* and *Gladiator,* for which he won a second Academy Award in 2001.

In addition to his film work, Branko Lustig was instrumental in the establishment of the Shoah Foundation. "As the testimonies came in, I would spend hours and hours each day reviewing them," he recalls, "especially those in Croatian. I was totally absorbed, as I could see history coming alive before

my very eyes. As a filmmaker, I am interested in how we communicate the story of the Shoah. It is clear to me that the next generation will tell their own story in their own words with whatever means they have at their disposal. Our job is not to dissuade them from using their voice and the technology at their fingertips but rather to encourage them to do it with care, with dignity, and with humanity."

On a more personal mission, April 2011 marked the sixty-eighth anniversary of Lustig's liberation from the concentration camp. To commemorate the event, he returned to Auschwitz, where, in front of barrack 24A, he celebrated his Bar Mitzvah, a rite of passage denied him as a young man. (The event was captured in a short film, available on the *New York Times* website.)

In May 2013 he and his wife, Mirjana, moved back to Croatia. "I am leaving Hollywood and going back home," he said two days before his return. "I am eighty-one years old and I don't want to make movies anymore. I am

> **Today Steven said that without me he would not have made *Schindler*. I am not ashamed to say that I cried.** —Branko Lustig

going to Croatia to talk about the Holocaust. I have a feeling it is more important that a survivor of the Holocaust go to Europe than to stay here. In Europe, there is still anti-Semitism. We are only 60,000 of [those] left after the war, and we will all be gone soon. When I go to a meeting here, there are only old people. Young people don't come. I don't need to talk to old people about 'Never again!' The only reason I am going to Europe is to spend the rest of my days talking to young people. They will remember what I tell them, and that is more important than sitting in this big house in California."

By any measure it was a very long journey from Croatia to Auschwitz to Hollywood and back home again. Along the way, Lustig did what he set out to do when he was only a boy: he bore witness for those who couldn't and he helped tell their stories to the world.

Before he departed, Lustig had one last meeting with Steven Spielberg. "We had coffee together and we talked about old times and how we made the movie," he recalled, somewhat wistfully. "I reminded him how he played the clarinet in a klezmer band—that made him laugh. Today Steven said that without me he would not have made *Schindler*. I am not ashamed to say that I cried." He shrugs. "I did my best. *Schindler's List* was the best movie made about the Holocaust." ■

ABOVE: (from left to right) Steven Spielberg; Sid Sheinberg from Universal, Kathleen Kennedy (seated); Tom Pollack from Universal; Pollack's wife, the actress Lorraine Gary; Janusz Kaminski; Peggy Pollack; and Branko Lustig on the set in Poland.

THE FILM'S LEGACY

I f ever a film production could be described as a labor of love, it would be *Schindler's List*, the making of which was a profoundly moving experience for all involved. And the motivation for making it went far beyond the quest for fame and fortune that typifies most Hollywood films. In fact, as the film was being launched, the filmmakers had relatively low expectations as to how it might fare with audiences.

In 1993, when *Schindler's List* was released, Steven Spielberg was the top-grossing director of all time, but it almost seemed as if he'd done everything possible to ensure that this film *wouldn't* make money. Here was a very long movie (clocking in at 3 hours and 25 minutes), shot in black-and-white, starring relatively unknown actors, which depicted in excruciating detail the genocide of millions. Not exactly your average feel-good "date" movie.

In May 1993, *Newsweek* ran a story about the apparent prospects for the film: "Spielberg claims he has no illusions that the $23 million movie, which opens in December, will recoup its investment," wrote Andrew Nagorski. "Citing its length and his insistence on black and white to remain true to the spirit of documentaries and stills from the period, [Spielberg] laughs: 'I'm stacking the deck against this one.' Universal studio officials unsuccessfully tried to persuade him to shoot in color and then make a black-and-white print, allowing possible reconsideration—and, particularly, the opportunity to sell it later to TV in color. His decision to shoot in black-and-white negative was to ensure 'a point of no return.' Profits, he insists, are not anyone's motives on this project: 'Perhaps indecently, I am making this film for myself, for the survivors, for my family—and for people who should understand the meaning of the word 'Holocaust'.'"

So perhaps no one was more surprised than Spielberg by the film's astounding success—which could be measured by any Hollywood yardstick. The film earned critical acclaim and financial success, garnered twelve Academy Award nominations, and won seven Oscars, including Best Picture and Best Director. Its other awards and nominations from film institutions around the world—from the Amanda Awards in Norway to the Writer's Guild of America—constitute an almost unprecedented roster of accolades. The film has been re-released several times in various formats over the past two decades.

Of course, many films enjoy great acclaim and success, but perhaps no other film has left such an enduring legacy. Beyond its commercial accomplishments, *Schindler's List* generated a huge wave of emotional support and allowed many survivors to open their hearts for the first time. As testimonies began pouring into the Shoah Foundation, it soon became apparent that Spielberg had created a venue for people to begin a healing process previously unavailable to them. Letters of gratitude began landing on Spielberg's desk from around the world. One example was quoted in *Reader's Digest*, April 1996: "After videotaping their testimonies, Rita and Sam Starkman, both survivors of Auschwitz-Birkenau wrote to Spielberg. 'You opened hearts locked up for 50 years,' they said in their letter. 'We feel free again. We fulfilled promises we made when we were lying among the dead—that if we survived, we would tell what happened. Never again!'"

On numerous occasions, Steven Spielberg has acknowledged that *Schindler's List* and the Shoah Foundation are the greatest accomplishments of his career, despite the fact that he keeps on creating blockbuster, Oscar-winning films. In a 2013 interview for *Mania* magazine, on the eve of the 20th anniversary commemoration of the film and the foundation, he did so again.

Asked if he believed *Schindler's List* had the greatest impact of any of his films, he replied, "Yes, by every measure. I still think *Schindler* has made the most amount of material change in the world. When I went to Poland twenty years ago, I quickly realized that this wasn't just a natural reflex of my filmmaking instincts. This was going to be something that changed my life. I didn't presume to think that this was going to have an impact on the world entire, I just knew that I wasn't going to be the same when I came out of it.

"I thought the film was a stepping stone. Most movies are posited in terms of the various ancillary markets. It'll be in theaters, and it'll come out on DVD, and it'll come out on television, and that will be it. The shelf life of *Schindler's List* has renewed my belief that films can do good work in the world, but it's up to the people to allow those images to last, and to do something about it."

Spielberg is well aware that this work is far from over, and that it's the task of the Shoah Foundation to carry it on. "Over the last few decades, I'd always hoped that the film and the Shoah Foundation would know no bounds of age or generation or geography. . . . [I]n an age when we have unprecedented technological advancement, I was sure that our consciences would evolve along those same lines. But sometimes it seems as if there are still people immune to the notion of empathy or compassion. . . . and in many cases, technology has become a vehicle for voyeurism rather than a vehicle for change. This persistence of inaction is one of the reasons I think the Foundation is even more important today."

It has been twenty years since *Schindler's List* was first screened, and its power has not waned. Movies can influence culture, fashion, taste, and music; rarely do they shape millions of lives. It is only the simple truth that no film has had a greater impact on audiences around the world or created such an indelible legacy for generations past, present, and future. ▪

“Though it is not a happy ending, I think the ending is uplifting because it is about salvation and deliverance. The biggest message of the movie is that because of what Schindler did, generations live on.”

—Steven Spielberg

Part 2
LIVING TESTIMONIES
THE STORY OF THE SHOAH FOUNDATION

A RACE AGAINST TIME

In March 1994, when Steven Spielberg accepted the Academy Award for Best Picture for *Schindler's List,* he implored the world's teachers to make sure that future generations learned from the trove of wisdom resident in the last living survivors of the Holocaust. "There are 350,000 experts who just want to be useful for the remainder of their lives," he said. "Please listen to the words and the echoes and the ghosts—and please teach this in your schools."

Behind Spielberg's words lay a vision for the Survivors of the Shoah Visual History Foundation—a vision that grew from his momentous encounters with Holocaust survivors on the set of *Schindler's List,* when he realized that the story he was telling on the screen echoed the stories they were telling him. "They came to reconnect with their history," he later said. "They would say, 'Please tell my story when you're finished telling Oskar Schindler's.'"

To the world's preeminent visual storyteller, who had rediscovered his own Jewish identity in the emotionally wrenching process of making the film, it was a

Opposite: Surviving Schindlerjuden were invited to visit Oskar Schindler's grave with actors from Schindler's List *for the final scene of the film, Jerusalem, 1993. Above: Steven Spielberg, with fellow producers Gerald Molen (left) and Branko Lustig, accepts the Academy Award for Best Picture for* Schindler's List, *1994.*

call to action he could not decline. His fellow producers, with whom he first shared the idea of preserving survivor stories on videotape, saw what was happening. "It was very clear to us how committed Steven was to survivors and to recording their firsthand accounts," says Branko Lustig. "The experience of making this film was very powerful for all of us," affirms Gerald Molen, "so it was no surprise that Steven was driven to do something more."

> 66 Steven Spielberg opened the set of *Schindler's List* so that survivors could see what was happening. They told him their personal stories on the set. That's where the Shoah Foundation began. 99
>
> —Anne Marie Stein, publicist, *Schindler's List*

Having committed himself, Spielberg knew that he had to move quickly. In one interview about the Shoah Foundation—as the project soon came to be known—he bluntly articulated the urgency of its mission to record on video the testimony of Holocaust survivors—and the breadth of his ambitions for that mission: "We want to be ready for anyone who approaches us," he said. "We have no time to lose."

PRESERVING VISUAL HISTORY

In the spring of 1994, there were likely several hundred thousand survivors of the Shoah. It was nearly a half-century after the end of World War II, and most people who were middle-aged and older during the Holocaust were gone: the patriarchs and matriarchs of families, the community elders. (In its first two years, the foundation took testimony from five people over one hundred years old.) Those

who had been young adults during the war were now seniors; with every day that passed, more of them were lost. In another two decades—that is, by the twentieth anniversary of the foundation—most survivors would be those who were children or youths during the Holocaust, their memories no less important to preserve but necessarily different.

June Beallor and James Moll, founding executive directors of the new organization, remember the excruciating awareness of time not being on their side. "It's the last opportunity for many of these survivors to tell their stories," Beallor said in a 1995 article. Literally every week they would receive reports that a survivor had passed on after telling her story, or before she could be interviewed.

The coinciding of a new ethnic conflict in Europe with the foundation's birth served as a stark reminder—if one were needed—of Spielberg's overarching purpose for the Shoah Foundation: using the stories of survivors to teach future citizens, to shape hearts and minds in directions that make future genocides less likely. "The eternal theme is: why do we hate?" Spielberg said in an interview with the German magazine *Der Spiegel*. "Why does man have so deplorably little compassion for those who are different? Our children must learn that ours is a history of intolerance which has in no way been overcome."

It was a monumental vision, grounded in the unique catastrophe of European Jewry but reaching for the universal in human experience. "There are so many

THESE PAGES: Portraits of Holocaust survivors in the Visual History Archive, taken in the years surrounding World War II. Left to right: Anita Lasker-Wallfisch; Steve Mendelsson; Edith Ostern; Kitty Hart; Israel Dubner (left) and his brother Yulek Dubner, who perished in the Lodz ghetto; and Mark Nusbaum.

ways you can apply the Holocaust to other examples of social injustice," Spielberg went on. "The Holocaust has great relevance to the history of racial prejudice in this country, not to mention what's happening in Bosnia and Rwanda." The Rwandan genocide, also occurring just as the foundation was getting started, would become the impetus for a new round of testimony-taking.

The vision was also anchored by Spielberg's fundamental belief that testimonies of Holocaust survivors viewed on screen would make a greater impact than written accounts. Thus the project's mantra became: "See the faces, hear the voices." And because time was running short, the immediate goal was to start interviewing Holocaust survivors on videotape as soon as possible.

PEOPLE ON A MISSION

A handful of Spielberg's film production colleagues responded to the challenge he had issued. First was Karen Kushell, who worked in Spielberg's production office at Universal Studios and had spent the previous year on *Schindler's List* as a production associate. Kushell had done research on Holocaust resistance and was moved by her own experiences on the set of *Schindler's List*. "There was a palpable sense of purpose beyond moviemaking among the cast and crew on *Schindler's List*," says Kushell. "It was clear that Steven was making a very powerful film. When presented with the opportunity to expand the experience into a project that could have real-world impact, I was determined to ensure that Steven's idea would not fade away as an unrealized great intention." At the director's behest, she began researching options, reaching out to known experts in the field of Holocaust remembrance and education.

Acting on the keynote of preserving history, Kushell urged Spielberg to bring in a team to carry out his ambitious new project. "There were a handful of respected survivor testimony collection projects," notes Kushell. "I wanted to protect and build on that impor-

> **"This is a rescue mission and a race against the clock to get as many survivors on tape as possible in the amount of time they have left to remember and communicate their experience."** —Steven Spielberg

Opposite: June Beallor and James Moll in 1994. Above: *Steven Spielberg and Karen Kushell at the Shoah Foundation office in 1995.*

" Oskar Schindler saved my life. But it was Steven Spielberg who gave me a voice. "

— Celina Biniaz, speaking to students at the Barrack Hebrew Academy in Philadelphia in 2013. She explained that she had never spoken about her experiences in the Holocaust until after seeing *Schindler's List*.

tant, established work, yet with the freedom to move quickly and efficiently, and to work on a larger scale."

The people who could move such a project forward would need a particular skill set that included production logistics savvy, sensitivity to the subject matter, respect for academic methodology, and the raw energy to believe that such a massive undertaking could actually be accomplished. Spielberg and Kushell found those qualities close at hand in a young documentary filmmaking team, June Beallor and James Moll, who were already working in a modest production trailer behind Spielberg's Amblin Entertainment offices. Moll, a graduate of the USC School of Cinematic Arts, had worked on several documentaries; Beallor had begun her career in New York at ABC News Closeup, the network's long-form documentary unit, and at ABC Primetime Specials, before moving to Los Angeles. Neither had been involved with *Schindler's List,* but they had developed a relationship with Kushell and gained Spielberg's trust while collaborating on Amblin projects.

Moll and Beallor were enlisted to continue the research and to create proposals for how to proceed swiftly with interviewing Holocaust survivors. They hit the ground running.

From the start, the questions were endless. How should survivors be approached about being interviewed? What form should the interviews take, and how long should they be? Should they be edited, or made into short documentaries? What recording medium should be used, and how should the recordings be handled, stored, and preserved for posterity? How many interviews would it be possible to conduct? How large a staff would be needed, and with what skills? How much would all of this cost, and who would pay for it? Most important, how could the collection of testimonies best be used in the service of education?

In seeking answers, Spielberg and his new project team were guided by their faith in the power of eyewitness accounts, of the individual story—and of the visual medium for transmitting it. From that conviction a decision gradually emerged that the collected testimonies would always exist primarily in visual form. It was a practical matter as well: given the scope of the undertaking Spielberg imagined, transcribing all of the interviews would take far too long and cost far too much.

Moll and Beallor continued to engage in conversations with historians and scholars. They included Michael Berenbaum, then director of the U.S. Holocaust Memorial Museum's Holocaust Research Institute; Avner Shalev, chairman of the Directorate Yad Vashem; Yaacov Lozowick, then director of the Archives at Yad Vashem; Abraham Foxman, national director at the Anti-Defamation League; Geoffrey Hartman, cofounder, and Joanne Rudof, archivist, of the Fortunoff Video Archive at Yale University; David Altshuler, then director of the Museum of Jewish Heritage; and Rabbi Marvin Hier, founder and dean, and Rabbi Abraham Cooper, associate dean, at the Simon Wiesenthal Center.

From those discussions, it became apparent that the most valuable contribution Spielberg could make to the historical record would be a broad collection of unedited life histories, with the geographic and linguistic diversity to cover the entire spectrum of experience of surviving victims of the Holocaust. What they were learning about Holocaust eyewitness testimony also validated Spielberg's instinctive commitment to get as many interviews as possible. At that time, fewer than ten thousand videotaped interviews with survivors had been completed by previously existing institutions or projects.

OPPOSITE: *Celina Biniaz, who became one of the "Schindler Jews," on her first day of school, Krakow, 1937. Celina's surviving family immigrated to the United States in 1947.* ABOVE: *June Beallor watches testimony in her trailer office, c. 1995.*

As Spielberg, before a worldwide TV audience of millions watching the Academy Awards, promised to preserve the experiences of survivors of the Shoah, his project team felt the weight of that promise on their shoulders. Just a month later, with the support of Kushell, Lustig, and Molen, Beallor and Moll presented Spielberg with a proposal that outlined a basic framework for the project he envisioned. Their April 1994 memo outlined a six-month pilot program, during which time they would develop an interviewing methodology, and then test it by conducting some four hundred interviews. In January 1995, if all went well, they would ramp up to a three-year process of gathering a projected fifty thousand interviews.

By the end of April, the team had set up shop in the trailer Beallor and Moll occupied on the Universal Studios lot. A key group of Spielberg's close associates, including Bruce Ramer, Jerry Breslauer, and Mickey Rutman, helped guide them in setting up a 501(c)3 nonprofit foundation and became its founding board. Beallor and Moll had hired a small staff and worked full-time to move the project forward. In this first incarnation, the organization had Spielberg as founder and chairman, with Karen Kushell and Spielberg's fellow *Schindler's List* producers, Branko Lustig and Gerald Molen, each holding the title of executive producer. Consistent with the film production background of the entire team, Beallor and Moll were named

ABOVE: Visitors to the United States Holocaust Memorial Museum pass under this gate, a cast taken from the original entrance to the Auschwitz death camp, inscribed with the ironic phrase Arbeit Macht Frei (Work Makes One Free). *OPPOSITE: Survivor Paula Lebovics, who gave testimony to the Shoah Foundation, is among the child survivors of Auschwitz-Birkenau, shown here just after liberation.*

WHO IS IN THE VISUAL HISTORY ARCHIVE?

The Visual History Archive consists of interviews with individuals whose experiences fall under these primary experience groups (listed in order by the number of testimonies for each). This list covers only WWII-era survivors and witnesses; more recent additions to the archive are discussed on pages 297-306.

JEWISH SURVIVORS

About 48,000 testimonies

Individuals who were targeted for persecution under laws and/or policies against the Jews.

RESCUERS AND AID PROVIDERS

About 1,000 testimonies

Individuals who rescued those targeted for persecution and/or interviewees who were involved with the planning and implementation of aid programs during and after the war.

LIBERATORS AND LIBERATION WITNESSES

About 360 testimonies

Individuals who participated in the liberation of concentration camps and/or who entered concentration camps immediately after liberation because of assignments in or around camps.

SINTI AND ROMA SURVIVORS

About 360 testimonies

Individuals who were targeted for per-

ABOVE: *Linda Eifer (right) demonstrates how the testimonies are catalogued and indexed (see "Building an Intelligent Archive").*

secution under laws and/or policies against the Sinti and Roma peoples ("Gypsies").

POLITICAL PRISONERS

About 220 testimonies

Individuals who were targeted for persecution based on their political convictions and/or expression of those convictions.

JEHOVAH'S WITNESS SURVIVORS

About 80 testimonies

Individuals who were targeted for persecution based on their religious convictions and/or expression of those convictions as Jehovah's Witnesses.

WAR CRIMES TRIALS PARTICIPANTS

About 60 testimonies

Individuals who were involved in war crimes trials after the war.

SURVIVORS OF EUGENICS POLICIES

13 testimonies

Individuals who were targeted for persecution under eugenics laws and/or policies.

HOMOSEXUAL SURVIVORS

8 testimonies

Individuals who were targeted for persecution based on their homosexuality or suspected homosexuality.

senior producers. The project's leaders had embarked on an endeavor that would call on all of their formidable production skills and personal energies, but would also demand that they acquire an education in the documentation of history.

It was a historically significant time for Holocaust remembrance. *Schindler's List* had made a profound impact on audiences around the world, and the United States Holocaust Memorial Museum had just opened in the nation's capital. Consciousness of the Holocaust period had never been higher. So the time seemed absolutely right, even if the task itself seemed overwhelming.

ABOUT THE TESTIMONIES IN THIS BOOK

We are pleased to present in this book excerpts of testimonies from USC Shoah Foundation's Visual History Archive. These provide a small sampling of the nearly 52,000 firsthand accounts recorded by the foundation beginning in 1994. Most come from Holocaust survivors or witnesses and were given in English; a few are from the more recent testimony collections, or are translated from other languages including German, Hungarian, and Portuguese. Because reading a transcript is a different experience than watching videotaped testimony, the excerpts have been edited for clarity. Aside from editorial interpolations [in brackets], nothing has been added, and we have aimed to preserve the interviewee's voice and intent. To learn about accessing the video and data for the full unedited testimonies, visit sfi.usc.edu.

"We sidestepped the fact that it didn't seem possible," Moll said. "People kept telling us this project was too ambitious. It couldn't be done. But we remained focused."

"It all had to happen so quickly," Beallor recalls. "After we'd been working for about a week, Steven asked, 'How many interviews do you have?' He was understandably concerned about the time passing and the steadily declining number of Holocaust survivors." Spielberg had taken a year off filmmaking after *Schindler's List*, leaving time to focus most of his attention on the new endeavor.

The first interview for the Shoah Foundation was recorded on April 18, 1994, with Holocaust survivor Isabella Goldstein. Beallor and Moll's proposal had outlined the format for the interviews, based on conversations with Spielberg and with contacts at other oral history organizations. The interview structure came from the director's desire to tell a complete life story; survivors would be asked to talk about their background before the war began, describe their experiences during the war, and relate how their lives had unfolded in its aftermath. This three-part design carried all the way through the project, with important implications for how the testimonies would later be used.

Through the remainder of 1994, the tasks multiplied exponentially: getting the word out to survivors and the public, assembling teams of interviewers and videographers and coordinators around the world, raising funds, and making countless crucial decisions about how, what, when, where, and with what resources.

THE TESTIMONY OF **AUGUSTA GLAZ**

Date of birth . . . . January 3, 1924
Place of birth . . . . Antwerp, Belgium
Date of interview . . . . September 11, 1996
Location of interview. . . .Sao Paulo, Brazil
Language . . . . Portuguese
Experience . . . . .Jewish survivor,
active in resistance

AUGUSTA GLAZ *recalls being severely beaten by the Gestapo for her involvement with the resistance movement in Belgium. Augusta was then incarcerated at the Mechelen concentration camp outside Brussels, where she lived under harsh conditions in an underground bunker.*

I was held for only five days by the Gestapo. After the five days, they took me to an underground bunker in the Mechelen concentration camp in Belgium, where they had built under-ground cells specifically for female political prisoners. I was there for thirty days and thirty nights, without sleep, with a bright light I kept shining on me, because I was afraid that I might talk, should they find me asleep. I did not wish to talk, no way.

> **In order not to go out of our minds and stay awake, we would think of writers, of all the books we had read, of well-known authors. We would start from A to B and so on. And this is how we lived from day to day.**

Once while I was there, they came to interrogate me and they beat the side of my head, on my ears, so that there would be no evidence of the beating. You may lose your hearing, but there is no trace left of the beating. A friend of mine, a partisan, was in the camp, but I did not betray him. They could not get any information out of me so they brought me back to my cell.

There was no air to breathe because these underground cells had a wooden door with just a small hole in it. And on this door there was a sign, written in chalk, stating in German: *Jiddisch, Kommunist, Terrorist Augusta Finkelstein*—Jewish, Communist, and Terrorist Augusta Finkelstein [her maiden name]. This was on the door so that every soldier, every SS entering the hallway, should know who was there. There was a hallway where they built five underground cells. They would place a woman in each cell.

There was another woman there and we would yell out to one another. In order not to go out of our minds and stay awake, we would think of writers, of all the books we had read, of well-known authors. We would start from A to B and so on. And this is how we lived from day to day. ∎

LEFT, clockwise from top: Glaz and a fellow resistance fighter, Brussels, 1944; Glaz in Brussels, 1942; identity card issued to Glaz by the Belgian government in 1949 for her efforts as a political prisoner during the war.

"Working out the logistics was nonstop, from early mornings to late at night," says Moll. "But there are certain times in life where you know you're in the right place at the right time, doing the right thing."

A COMMUNITY OF SUPPORT

Beyond the logistical issues, the fundraising requirements were daunting. Moll and Beallor had been busily crunching numbers—a sobering exercise, Moll says. "When we first entered numbers for what it would take to hire video crews for every location we wanted to cover, there weren't enough spaces on the calculator."

Spielberg provided seed money for the project, "But it was very important from day one that the project be funded from a broad base of support," says Beallor. "This was a project for all humanity, and it was important that support came from many sources, not just from Steven." The director did, however, call upon his well-developed network of connections within and outside of the film industry to raise money for the foundation. "Once Steven approved the proposal, we met with him and his longtime mentors at Universal, Lew Wasserman and Sidney Sheinberg," Beallor recalls.

It was a pitch meeting of a very special kind. The two executives had run MCA/Universal for several decades; it was Sheinberg who gave Spielberg—still in college at the time—his first shot at directing television. It was also Sheinberg who brought Thomas Keneally's book about Oskar Schindler to Spielberg and who, while others at the studio were skeptical about making a Holocaust movie in black and white, championed the film project. Wasserman, whose marketing savvy was legendary, had made *Jaws* into the first blockbuster in the 1970s and later presided over an array of other Spielberg hits. "In that room, we received a commitment for $3 million, which was a fitting tribute to their relationship with Steven and to *Schindler's List*," says Moll.

The rest of the early funding came from "many sources, including individuals and foundations," according to a press release from Marvin Levy, longtime publicist for Spielberg and Amblin. "There was a great deal of pressure to keep the donations coming in,"

Beallor adds. "But we also received large commitments from big companies and individual contributions from all kinds of people. Every bit was needed and helped us get off the ground." There were significant in-kind gifts as well: for example, Maxell Corporation offered substantially discounted pricing on videotape, UPS donated $3 million worth of shipping for the worldwide operation, and Sony contributed $1 million toward the cost of hundreds of videotape decks to support the operation.

The base of support would continue to expand along with the Shoah Foundation's work. An important and satisfying moment of validation came in July 1996, when the U.S. Senate bestowed a $1 million Department of Education grant on the foundation.

A FUNDAMENTAL MORAL CHOICE

When I was drawing up this project, sensible people said to me 'It's impossible! Take five thousand survivors and you will have a good representative cross-section of the entire Holocaust." But . . . this story is universal and you cannot separate any one section. This crime was perpetrated against millions of individuals, and as in the film *Rashomon,* each one has their own subjective view of it. It is not possible to select five thousand people and exclude all others. . . . That is a fundamental moral choice. —*Steven Spielberg*

REACHING OUT

In preliminary statements about the Shoah Foundation's purpose, Steven Spielberg expressed his desire to videotape every living Holocaust survivor. Considering the realities of time and resources, however, that lofty goal was refocused to fifty thousand interviews.

The founders also recognized that not every survivor would be willing or able to come forward. Yet the impulse toward inclusion remained a defining trait of the organization. As Karen Kushell described it, "Steven almost went through the same epiphany . . . that Schindler does at the end of the movie, where he said, 'No, no, I want them all.' I don't want to just do the Schindler survivors. I want to get everybody's stories."

OPPOSITE: Sidney Sheinberg, Steven Spielberg, and Lew Wasserman c. 1994. ABOVE: June Beallor and Ari Zev, who joined the fondation in 1994 to direct the collection of testimonies, review plans on worldwide outreach to survivors, 1995.

WHO IS IN THE VISUAL HISTORY ARCHIVE?

The Visual History Archive consists of interviews with individuals whose experiences fall under these primary experience groups (listed in order by the number of testimonies for each). This list covers only WWII-era survivors and witnesses; more recent additions to the archive are discussed on pages 297-306.

JEWISH SURVIVORS

About 48,000 testimonies

Individuals who were targeted for persecution under laws and/or policies against the Jews.

RESCUERS AND AID PROVIDERS

About 1,000 testimonies

Individuals who rescued those targeted for persecution and/or interviewees who were involved with the planning and implementation of aid programs during and after the war.

LIBERATORS AND LIBERATION WITNESSES

About 360 testimonies

Individuals who participated in the liberation of concentration camps and/or who entered concentration camps immediately after liberation because of assignments in or around camps.

SINTI AND ROMA SURVIVORS

About 360 testimonies

Individuals who were targeted for persecution under laws and/or policies against the Sinti and Roma peoples ("Gypsies").

POLITICAL PRISONERS

About 220 testimonies

Individuals who were targeted for persecution based on their political convictions and/or expression of those convictions.

JEHOVAH'S WITNESS SURVIVORS

About 80 testimonies

Individuals who were targeted for persecution based on their religious convictions and/or expression of those convictions as Jehovah's Witnesses.

WAR CRIMES TRIALS PARTICIPANTS

About 60 testimonies

Individuals who were involved in war crimes trials after the war.

SURVIVORS OF EUGENICS POLICIES

13 testimonies

Individuals who were targeted for persecution under eugenics laws and/or policies.

HOMOSEXUAL SURVIVORS

8 testimonies

Individuals who were targeted for persecution based on their homosexuality or suspected homosexuality.

ABOVE: *Linda Eifer (right) demonstrates how the testimonies are catalogued and indexed (see "Building an Intelligent Archive").*

Who would those fifty thousand witnesses be? Here Spielberg held fast to his declaration that the foundation would interview "anyone who approaches us." The foundation included a wider range of experience than other oral history projects that were smaller in scope and narrower in focus. Its inclusive approach would seek interviewees from a range of backgrounds who experienced persecution under the Nazis from 1933 to 1945. Beyond Jewish survivors, whose testimonies ultimately would constitute about 95 percent of the Visual History Archive, interviewees included members of other groups that had been targets of Nazi persecution, or had been key witnesses to the Shoah. Ari Zev, the foundation's director of administration and longest-serving employee, explains, "We decided to broaden our reach to those who had been rescuers or liberators, and to members of other persecuted groups." Because the foundation welcomed such a wide range of eyewitness experiences from the start, the ways in which the archive is used today are that much more diverse (see opposite page).

Figuring out how to contact those fifty thousand potential interviewees was the first challenge. How to accomplish the actual interviews would become the foundation's core task over its first half-decade. A dedicated staff member to helm this operation was found in June 1994 with the arrival of Zev, a Jewish community professional and educator at schools and synagogues in the Los Angeles area. As head of research and training—the first of his many leadership positions at the foundation— Zev would oversee outreach to Holocaust survivors, witnesses, and interviewers in communities around the world, then spearhead training for interviewers. Eventually, more than 2,500 interviewers would be trained in thirty-three cities in twenty-four countries. Outreach to both survivors and interviewers began in Los Angeles, New York, and Toronto, and soon expanded to cities worldwide.

It was a global effort. Both during the Nazi period and in the wake of World War II, Jewish refugees and Holocaust survivors emigrated far and wide, taking up new lives around Europe and in Canada, China, South Africa, Australasia, Latin America, and the former Soviet Union—with large pluralities of Jewish survivors resettling

ABOVE: Early foundation staff: at left, Michael Engel (bearded) and Andy Nicastro, who managed the international production of interviews; at right, Ari Zev and Kim Simon.

in the United States and Israel. Survivors who had returned to their home towns in Europe were especially important to foundation leaders because they had been heard from so little since the war. "These survivors have rarely been interviewed," Zev has noted. "Their experience was vastly different from those who emigrated. But the distinctions did not end there. Survivors in Israel had a totally different experience than those in North America or South Africa. We wanted to make sure the testimonies reflected this diversity of postwar experiences."

Along with Zev, Kim Simon, who joined the team in November 1994, helped develop the foundation's international work. After college, Simon (then Hillman) lived in Prague for several years, where she did research in how Jewish survivors were living in central Europe, and she also worked in film production. On returning home in 1994, she says, laughing, "My mother called and said, 'I read that Steven Spielberg is starting this foundation—you'd be perfect for it!' in that way mothers do." Originally hired as an international production coordinator, Simon soon began to focus on small communities in Eastern Europe, where the interviewing effort faced unique cultural and logistical challenges; today she is the organization's managing director.

"As word got around, we heard from so many people outside the original geographic scope we'd established," Simon recalls. "They all were saying 'I want my

ABOVE: *Karen Fox (foreground) and other volunteers in the Shoah Foundation office, 1995.* OPPOSITE: *Los Angeles regional coordinator Michelle Kleinert with survivors Freddie Diament (left) and Sigi Hart in Birkenau, Poland, 1996.*

community and country to be included'—they were passionate about how 'their' community of survivors could be represented in the archive. It began to seem almost as if a kind of collective awareness was accumulating. Someone in New York would talk to someone in Budapest, and we'd hear about it the next day. And this was long before social media, even before e-mail became ubiquitous."

The foundation wanted to make sure, to the extent possible, that every living Holocaust survivor or eyewitness was aware of the invitation to record testimony on videotape. Well before the first interviews were conducted, a small item appeared in *People* magazine stating that Steven Spielberg was seeking Holocaust survivors to interview; a telephone number was published. Only Beallor and Moll were manning the office when the phone began ringing. And ringing. And ringing. "It was clear that survivors wanted to tell their stories, and they would make every effort to contact the Shoah Foundation," says Moll. While some of the eventual interviewees had been speaking for years about being Holocaust survivors, many found the confidence to do so for the first time in these videos. The public's embrace of *Schindler's List* created a climate in which some survivors found the strength to share their intensely personal stories and devastating memories. But for many, it always remained too difficult.

" We come forward because we are aware of our own mortality and how important it is to share what happened."

—Daisy Miller, survivor and director of community relations

By now, the lone production trailer near Spielberg's office had expanded to a small fleet of trailers to house the growing number of full-time staffers. Multiple phone lines were installed to receive toll-free calls from survivors all over the world, and the foundation needed people to answer those calls. Willing volunteers came forward, including some of the very first survivors who had contacted the foundation to be interviewed. Not surprisingly, this outpouring of on-site support from survivors had additional benefits.

"More often than not, it was difficult for a survivor to pick up the phone and call us. When they did, it was comforting to be able to speak to another survivor on the other end," says Daisy Miller, the foundation's director of community relations.

THE TESTIMONY OF **HENRY ROSMARIN**

Date of birth . . . . October 7, 1925
Place of birth . . . . Czeladz, Poland
Date of interview . . . . .December 11, 1998
Location of interview . . . . Van Nuys,
California, USA
Language . . . . English
Experience . . . . .Jewish survivor

HENRY ROSMARIN *remembers when he was called into the commandant's quarters at the Dyhernfurth concentration camp in Germany late one night and told to play a musical piece by Schubert on the harmonica. Henry credits his skill on the instrument with saving his life.*

One night, as I was contemplating the next day, ordeal, someone shakes me and says, "Henry, get up. Get up!" And I recognized this guy from the other forced labor camp . . . he became a runner or organizer for the commandant in this new camp. "The commandant wants to see you." I said, "Who, me? What did I do?" He said, "Don't worry, he's a harmonica buff. He plays the harmonica. He thinks he plays. He blows that thing but doesn't know a damn thing how to play, and I told him about you." And I say, "I don't have a harmonica." He says, "But he has a bunch of harmonicas. Come on, he wants to see you."

I had no watch. I had no idea what time it was. It must have been midnight. So I quickly put on my wet pants and my jacket, and shuffled along with my wooden shoes, and came to the commandant's quarters. Here it is nice and warm. He's sitting there drinking schnapps or whatever. He certainly wasn't skinny. His cheeks were red and puffy. He even had a stomach, too. You could see this guy was eating well . . . he was a German national and was a prisoner himself, a political prisoner, but he was in charge of the whole camp. The only one over him was the SS guy. And he says *"Spiel etwas!* Play something! Here!" and throws a harmonica at me.

And I caught it. I shouldn't have asked him, *"Was soll es sein?* What should it be? What do you wish?" And he says *"Spiel was von Schubert.* Play something from Schubert." I didn't play Schubert. The only Schubert I remembered was a serenade from when my uncle bought me my first harmonica and he got me a book of songs. There was a Schubert song, I remember it was called "Ständchen" ["Serenade"], and I learned a few opening bars from that . . . and I kind of liked that melody. But I hadn't practiced anything. And I hardly played it, even today.

I shouldn't have asked him what to play. I could have picked a polka, something easy. And he said, *"Spiel was von Schubert."* I wasn't going to say, "Let's play something else." You don't say no to him.

I took that harmonica . . . praying to God for a good performance here because, if I don't do right, who knows what he'll do with me? I shouldn't have asked him what to play. I could have picked a polka, something easy. And he said *"Spiel was von Schubert."* I wasn't going to say, "Let's play something else." You don't say no to him. So, I started to play the "Ständchen" von Schubert, "Serenade" by Schubert, and it goes like this [Henry hums the melody]. It's a beautiful melody.

When I finished, he started to look around . . . and I see something in his hand, something bigger than a harmonica . . . and he threw it at me. "Here!" I caught it like a football player. I used to be a goalie on my soccer team. I caught it and it was a loaf of bread! A whole loaf of bread! And the face, the poor face of my dad came to mind and I said, "Dad why aren't

you here? I have a whole loaf of bread I could share with you." I stood at attention and thanked him. And he said, "Get out of here!" But before, he said, "What does he do?" And [the runner] says that I worked on the so-and-so detail, mixing concrete. And he says, "Get him a job in the kitchen."

As this encounter was ending, the commandant directed the runner to find someone among the prisoners who played the guitar.

Two or three days later, I'm working in the kitchen. I have potatoes, carrots. I'm scrubbing. I'm eating. I have extra soup. In the evening [the runner] got hold of a guitar player and said, "You are going to the mess hall where the guards are eating, and will play something for the mess hall." We played polkas, waltzes. The guitar player was a gypsy, accompanying me. And after that, we would have to clean up the tables and that was the perk.

That was a wonderful perk because I was supposed to take the trays of uneaten food with leftovers to the dog pound for the German Shepherds to eat. But on the way out, I would have to pass a long corridor and an out-

side door and a fence . . . I would look over my shoulder, and if they weren't looking, I would bite into that steak or piece of chicken and I would eat. If [the commandant] would catch me eating the food that was meant for the dogs, he would kill me. The dogs were more important than this little Jewish guy.

In terms of miracles, every day was a miracle in camp. But in terms of real miracles, this was the one single incident that actually saved my life, playing that harmonica. Playing the harmonica one evening for the commandant and getting a better job. I had a better job and gained weight, so I actually survived that horrible camp because of that harmonica. My days were numbered, perhaps in single digits. I would not have lasted a week, perhaps. ■

Opposite, from top: Henry and his harmonica during his interview; with his brother Max in 1940, in the ghetto of Czeladz, Poland (Henry is about fourteen); and during his postwar professional career. Left: Henry took this photo of friends (including his future wife, Janet) in Czeladz, 1940. Right: Henry and Janet at their wedding in Austria, 1947, and in 1997.

Miller began as a part-time volunteer but soon became a full-time employee overseeing the entire volunteer department. A child during the Holocaust, she survived by hiding with her family in a crowded farmhouse in the hills of Italy. "Survivors can be uncomfortable about coming forward at first. Some of us haven't spoken about our experiences in forty years," she said in 1996. "But we come forward because we are aware of our own mortality and how important it is to share what happened."

Telephone volunteers were usually the first point of contact for survivors, offering a sympathetic ear, answering questions, providing reassurance, and eliciting basic information. This material was passed on to a regional coordinator, who set up the interviews, matching up survivors and interviewers with care.

At the hub of this increasingly intense activity was regional coordinator Michelle Kleinert, who left her job as a studio publicist when she heard Steven Spielberg speak about the Shoah Foundation at the Academy Awards. "After weeks of begging and bugging June Beallor and James Moll, I was finally granted an interview for the regional coordinator position," Kleinert recalls. "Los Angeles would be the prototype for how interviews around the world would be conducted. June and James asked me if I could schedule twenty interviews a week, including survivors, videographers, interviewers, and volunteers. 'Sure,' I said, having no clue what that entailed. The day I got the call from June saying I got the job is still one of the more memorable days of my life."

Above: Hillary Clinton views testimony with James Moll and Steven Spielberg during a 1998 visit to the foundation.

TECHNOLOGY FOR HUMANITY

Behind the efforts to locate survivors and start taking testimonies loomed the technological challenge of how the interviews would be recorded, preserved, and made accessible—in other words, how to fulfill Steven Spielberg's promise of a revolutionary visual history resource. "The idea was to quickly begin collecting the testimonies," says Moll, "while at the same time collaborating with major technology companies specializing in nonlinear digital storage systems that would someday enable us to preserve and access the interviews. This technology is so common now, it's hard to imagine that it was such a challenge in the early nineties. We were pushing the envelope for mass media storage that could be accessed through searchable databases."

A small cadre of young technical wizards was enlisted to make it happen, including Sam Gustman—another veteran from the charter year 1994 who is the foundation's chief technology officer. In addition to puzzling out the key components of the system—the handling of taped interviews and their transfer to digital media, and imagining the eventual user interface—Gustman doubled as the resident handyman, fixing electrical wiring when not busy with complex programming. Of his role in the new cyber-archive, Gustman said in 1995, "It just hits a lot of heartstrings for me. It does exactly what I'm best at, technology-wise, and . . . the Holocaust is a large part of every Jewish person's life. It has formed us."

Gustman, who has been behind every major technological innovation the organization pioneered, describes the Shoah Foundation's interview-gathering network. "The very first system we put in place, "explains Gustman, "was a way to essentially put people in the same room while in different parts of the world." Behind the human network of interviewers, videographers, and regional coordinators was a global computer network linking the Los Angeles base with the field, tracking the entire project, and enabling data exchange. "We were using dial-up connections, which at the time were state of the art," Gustman recalls, "with an array of computers to track what was happening in Boca Raton, Melbourne, or Kyiv. And sometimes teaching someone, somewhere how to use a computer."

CONNECTIONS

The dial-up connection, however ancient it might seem today, was an excellent tool that enabled us working in the field to connect, brainstorm, and keep updated. Global coordination and communication across a country and overseas were essential to advance our project. And it was a striking feeling to be in the same "virtual" room with people living so far away, who you might never have met—yet who shared the same vision and passion. — *Andrea Haas, regional staff member in Slovakia and Hungary*

SURVIVORS
of the SHOAH

Davia Berman
Ana Maria Bruner
Esther Bulka
Helen Chalef
Bela Cislowski
Blanka Wurzberge
Malvina Engel
Eugene Feld
Marie Glasser
Rachel Goldman–
Irwin (Yisroel Zvi)
Mitchell Gordon
Zelda Gordon
Rose Gottdiener
Joe Guttman
John Helman
Alice Hemar
Otto Herskovic
Dora Holland
Ella Jackson
Fred B. Jackson
Emil Menahem–M
Erica Jacoby
Klara Klein
Josef (Joe) Kreiten
Marlene Laufer Kr
Alexander Kuechel
Lilo Kuechel
Agnes Kun
Alex Lauterbach
Ann Lauterbach
Sidonia Lax
Sol Liber
Ella Mandel
Mickey Montage
Mary Natan
Sonia Pepper
George Pollack
Csia Carol Redlich

SEARCH CRITERIA

BIOGRAPHICAL INFORMATION

LIBRARY OF CON CLASSIFICATIO

NAME SEARCH

CU

SUMMARY

Helen lived in a traditional household with a younger brother, parents, and a grandmother, whom she loved very much. One day, after a midday meal, she took a nap with the grandmother in her big bed. The grandmother rubbed her head until she went to sleep. During that nap she had a peculiar dream, in which the grandmother, in a very persistent voice, kept repeating "You are not hungry, you are not thirsty, you are not tired, don't look around, just keep walking!" When Helen awoke the family discovered that the grandmother had died during that nap.

After 2 brief resettlements (the first one to

MAKING A PLACE IN VISUAL HISTORY

Unquestionably, the Shoah Foundation was breaking new ground and operating on a different scale than any prior oral history effort. But it was far from the first such effort, and its entry on the scene was met with mixed reactions by some established institutions and academic experts in the field. Some of the concerns stemmed from the project's film industry roots. Beyond this cultural divide, legitimate questions were raised about the foundation's interviewing methods, the quality of interviews that might result, and how the testimonies would be protected if Spielberg's professed goal to put the archive online were realized.

Among those with initial reservations was Geoffrey Hartman, project director of the Fortunoff Video Archive for Holocaust Testimonies at Yale University, where the production and archiving of video interviews with survivors began in the late 1970s. (At the time, the Fortunoff Video Archive held approximately 3,600 videotaped testimonies.) Hartman's concerns had mainly to do with how the interviews were going to be presented and who would have access to them. "These survivors are people who have gone through hell," Hartman said in a 1995 article. "Those to whom access should be given are educators and researchers and young people seriously interested in what happened."

The foundation acknowledged the concerns raised by Hartman and other critics, but ultimately chose to develop its own methodology to match the scale of the project. For example, the foundation departed from the standard practice of requiring that only specialists—historians or therapists—conduct oral history interviews. The argument had been that only academic experts possessed the training and

LEFT: *An early prototype of the interface designed to search the Visual History Archive.*
ABOVE: *Original Beta SP videotapes of interviews. This video format was chosen for its quality and wide availability internationally.*

knowledge to place personal testimony in context. Some also believed it necessary to correct a person who might give inaccurate information in testimony. "Our method was to allow people to talk about their lives in the way they wanted, with minimal intervention," says Beallor. "We always supported the survivor in speaking about the aspects of their lives that were most important to them."

Today Holocaust scholars from around the world—including some who were early critics—make use of the Visual History Archive in innumerable ways, and the foundation has a leadership role among institutions that study and memorialize the Holocaust. Far from acting in isolation, it steadily built bonds in Jewish and other religious communities as well as with governments, businesses, and foundations, nationally and internationally.

And its staff have microscopically examined the thorny question of access over the foundation's two decades of existence. Decisions are based on a complex interplay of factors and a vigorous ongoing debate. Once the collected testimonies were catalogued and indexed—a challenging new frontier for videotaped interviews—the foundation began to share them with designated repositories in the United States and abroad, where scholars and researchers could explore the entire Visual History Archive. Smaller samplings of the archive began to be made available, carefully, on the Internet in 2001.

While always ready to collaborate, adapt, and learn, the foundation's leaders never strayed from certain key principles they believed would best serve its mission and honor the witnesses. First, that the opportunity to give testimony would be open to any survivor, anywhere, who met their broad criteria. Second, that the interviews should be deeply personal, wide-ranging stories that treat the person's whole life experience, not just the central trauma of the Holocaust.

OPPOSITE: Richard Walton working at a transfer station where the videotapes of testimony were copied and digitized, 1998.

THE VISUAL HISTORY ARCHIVE AT A GLANCE

- The Visual History Archive (VHA) contains approximately 52,000 interviews—the equivalent of 105,000 hours, or 12 years, of continuous video.

- The complete VHA is available at 44 institutions in 57 countries.

- Approximately 1,200 interviews are available at the VHA Online (http://sfi.usc.edu/explore).

- Interviews were conducted in 36 languages in 57 countries.

- The Holocaust-related interviews were conducted from 1994 to 2000. Interviews in the Rwandan collection were recorded between 2008 and 2011.

- At just under 16 hours, the longest interview in the VHA is that of Moshe Bejski, one of the *Schindlerjuden* and a former supreme court judge in Israel.

- The shortest completed interview, conducted in Russian with Ukrainian survivor Roza Kulchitskaia, lasted 9 minutes, 49 seconds.

- In the Holocaust collection, the most common year of birth for interviewees is 1924.

- When the war began in 1939, roughly one-third of interviewees were adults, one-third teenagers, and one-third children.

Finally, they were committed not just to archiving as many of these stories as possible, but to using them in potent ways, helping to shape a world in which the impulse to persecute fellow humans cannot endure. That mission profoundly shaped how the foundation grew and developed: from the initial collection phase, through the painstaking work of digitally cataloguing and indexing the tapes for retrieval, and ultimately to the programs it would develop to bring survivors, their families, scholars, and especially young people into contact with the testimonies.

■

By the end of 1995, the Shoah Foundation had a presence in twenty-five cities around the world, had trained interviewers to take testimony in all these cities, and had completed 9,000 interviews with survivors and witnesses. The office trailers on the Universal Studios lot buzzed with a staff of more than one hundred; there were also staff and volunteers in distant time zones, interacting in many languages and filling the calendar with more and more interviews. Deliveries of interview tapes were rolling in, each to be meticulously labeled, stored, and prepared for the databank. That daunting goal of conducting and preserving fifty thousand eyewitness accounts of the Holocaust was starting to look achievable.

In fact, in its first five years, the Shoah Foundation would record more than fifty thousand interviews with Holocaust survivors and witnesses in fifty-six countries and in thirty-two languages. This capacious body of oral and visual history represents many things. It is an eloquent monument to the millions who did not survive, except in the memories of loved ones. It is a deeply inspiring, massively scaled exemplar of human fortitude and resilience. It is a vast database of material for scholars of the Holocaust and twentieth-century history, as well as for those who study human and social behavior in all its myriad forms. Finally, it is an innovative prototype for a twenty-first-century approach to education, using information technology to bring us face to face with people who—to quote Martin Šmok, an early European recruit who is the foundation's senior international program consultant, based in the Czech Republic—"look like your grandparents, whoever and wherever in the world you are."

Launching this project took a toll on those involved—not just the long days but the emotional impact of being in constant touch with survivors and their singular

> “ The foundation was born at a perfect historical confluence where new information technology was overlapping the later years of Holocaust survivors—technologies that would make it possible for us to carry out a global survey of this magnitude. ”
>
> —James Moll, founding director

but often terrible stories. Yet none would have chosen to be anywhere else. "The whole project had an energy I can't describe, and I've never experienced since," says Moll. "Things happened that I can't explain. Circumstances came together in ways we never expected. We often remarked that we must have had higher powers on our side." Beallor has similar memories of that first year, recalling the magnetic pull the foundation's work seemed to exert. "It was striking how many people came to us," she says. "Survivors, volunteers, key staff . . . all coming together at the right place and time."

Having set all this in motion, Steven Spielberg tracked the explosion of activity day to day from a television monitor in his nearby Amblin office. As he reported in a 1996 interview, "It shows the new interviews being copied every day. I regularly select an interview and listen to it." He admits that this could be painful, but the force of those encounters only fueled his drive to build the archive in the teeth of time. Spielberg correctly sensed that the narrative vision that had enabled him to make *Schindler's List* might also "allow fifty thousand people to trust me with their life stories." And he and his team were forging a technological and organizational vision that would "allow the memories to speak." ■

ABOVE: Sir Ben Kingsley, who played Itzhak Stern in Schindler's List, *is introduced to the archive by James Moll during a visit to the foundation in 1995.*

GATHERING THE TESTIMONIES

I n December 1998, the number of videotaped testimonies in the Shoah Foundation Visual History Archive reached the target number of fifty thousand, the goal set when the project was first conceived. Fittingly, interviewee number fifty thousand was none other than Branko Lustig, the Holocaust survivor who co-produced *Schindler's List*—together with Gerald Molen, who conducted the interview. At the ceremony marking this milestone, Lustig told an audience of staff, supporters, and fellow survivors:

"As we all know, fifty thousand is only a small fraction of the total number of Holocaust survivors. There were thousands of others who passed away before their stories could be told or simply because the memories were too terrible to talk about and instead chose to keep them buried inside, safe from the scrutiny of the outside world. But within these fifty thousand stories there exist . . . stories for the six million who

didn't survive, but who continue to dwell in each and every one of us who did. The work being done by the foundation continues to fulfill the visions and prayers of the six million who will never come back. We must never forget their words: 'Don't forget us. Tell the world how we died, and always remember us.'"

OPPOSITE: *Holocaust survivor George Citrom being interviewed, February 2010.*
ABOVE: *Gerald Molen interviews survivor Branko Lustig, January 1999.*

These statements distill the motives of survivors who shared their stories, and certain premises of the foundation's work. First, that fifty thousand testimonies, however few in comparison with the six million, would encompass such breadth of experience that virtually anyone who came in contact with them could feel a connection. Further, that the survivors who testified often spoke for those who did not survive: by naming them, by telling what they did, by passing on messages on their behalf. Finally, that all who came forward—from Isabella Goldstein in April 1994 to Lustig and beyond—were impelled by a sense of deep obligation to memorialize the six million so they would not be lost to history.

Collecting testimonies was the first major phase in the life of the Shoah Foundation. Its founders hoped and believed that many thousands would share the impulse that led a handful of survivors to seek out Steven Spielberg on the set of *Schindler's List*—that they would choose *not* to keep their stories buried.

The Visual History Archive's size and breadth resulted from early determinations about who would be interviewed—and the crucial decision was made to open the archive to a broad range of survivor experience. "Survival can take many forms," Ari Zev emphasizes. "Some people survived with false papers. Some children survived in hiding. It was important for us to document them all."

NARRATIVE MEMORIALS

The interviewees also gave the names of 1.2 million individuals to the Visual History Archive; these are the names of parents, grandparents, siblings, and extended family, many of whom did not survive the Holocaust. In their absence, their names have become memorials in their own right. —*Stephen D. Smith, executive director*

"Different communities have different understandings of what it means to be a survivor," says Karen Jungblut, the foundation's director of research and documentation. Jungblut took part in interviewer training while still a graduate student in Berlin, and in 1996 joined the Shoah Foundation as a cataloguer. "We were interested in anyone who had been a target of persecution in the years from 1933 to 1945 under the Nazi or Axis influence—mostly Jews, whether they were sent to camps, went into hiding, were deported to the Soviet side after the partition of Poland, or fled before the borders were closed."

WHY GIVE TESTIMONY?

During the interview, survivors and witnesses were often asked why they wanted to tell their stories. Given the great diversity of backgrounds represented in the archive—in nationality, language, culture, and life experience—the answers were remarkably consistent. A frequent reason given was that survivors were nearing

I CANNOT BE SILENT

My parents, two sisters, two brothers and I arrived in the U.S. from Poland eleven days before WW2. I was seventeen years old. I have learned in detail of the inhuman treatment and torture to the people of my town, Wolkowysk. Not of soul of my [remaining] family or friends survived. I have turned in my story to the Shoah Foundation.

—Lissa Streusund, in a letter to Steven Spielberg, December 1995

My lifetime mission is to keep alive the memory of the six million. . . . Most of my family members were among the victims, including my beloved father. They were all silenced forever by the Nazis. I was fortunate to be given a second chance. God saved me so I could return to remind the world of their unjust suffering and death. . . . Many [survivors] are not willing to talk about their experiences. . . . My mother was a survivor who kept her silence. I cannot be silent. . . . No matter how difficult it is to relate such shocking experiences, I feel that I have a strong obligation to do it for the sake of my family members and fellow prisoners who perished in the Holocaust. *—Magda Herzberger, survivor of the Auschwitz, Bremen, and Bergen-Belsen camps*

the end of their lives and feeling the same sense of urgency that drove the project founders. Most of them hoped that their testimony would be used to help educate the world, specifically to prevent future genocides. "Never again!" is the phrase used over and over. The same sentiment was implied in the foundation's original call to action: *"So generations never forget what so few lived to tell."*

Most who testified also wanted to honor family members, close friends, or fellow camp inmates. Simply by naming names—which might otherwise have vanished from the historical record—they achieved this goal, as every name in every testimony is catalogued and indexed for ready access by families, scholars, and other users of the archive.

Above: *Steven Spielberg and survivor Irina Maksimova (with Anna Lenchovska, the foundation's regional consultant in Ukraine, center) at the premiere of the documentary* Spell Your Name *in Kyiv, 2006.*

THE TESTIMONY OF **ESTHER JUNGREIS**

Date of birth . . . . April 7, 1936
Place of birth. . . . . Szeged, Hungary
Date of interview . . . . January 9, 1995
Location of interview. . North Woodmere,
New York, USA
Language . . . . English
Experience . . . . Jewish survivor

ESTHER JUNGREIS *remembers the blowing of the shofar as an act of spiritual resistance and faith in God. It took place during a clandestine celebration of Rosh Hashanah in Bergen-Belsen in 1944. Esther relates how the shofar was obtained in exchange for cigarettes.*

On Rosh Hashanah we wanted to blow the shofar. And we didn't have a shofar. So we collected three hundred cigarettes, which was an incredible feat. That was really the revenue in the concentration camp, cigarettes. And for three hundred cigarettes, we were able to get a shofar. How they did it, I do not know, but they did. And they blew the shofar.

For three hundred cigarettes, we were able to get a shofar. How they did it, I do not know.

Adjacent to our Hungarian camp was the Polish camp. Now the Polish camp did not have the same privileges as we did, unfortunately, for some reason. We were treated better than they were at that particular time. The boys [there] were working in their battalions. And when they heard us blow the shofar, they stopped, and they made the *brucha* [blessing]. And I'll never forget. They stopped where they were, and they made the *brucha* on the shofar, and the Nazis came and started to beat them mercilessly, but not

one of them moved till they finished making the *brucha*.

We didn't have a *mahzor*, the High Holy Day prayer book. So once again, they made a collection, and my father and all the rabbis got one *mahzor*.

But what do you do with one *mahzor*, one prayer book, when you have an entire camp? So the rabbis decided that each family should learn at least one prayer by heart. And once you learned that one prayer by heart, you are able to celebrate Rosh Hashanah with that one prayer. Now the question is: which prayer should it be? And the prayer they decided upon was *Shebohen et libam beyom hadin*, "He who examines the heart on the Day of Judgment." We said to God, come look at our hearts in Bergen-Belsen, and see if despite all our pain and our suffering, if we abandon you.

And the first Rosh Hashanah in Bergen-Belsen, we never gave it up. We were always connected. ■

ABOVE RIGHT: Esther in Israel, after the war. She had planned to make it her permanent home but fell ill and had to return to the United States, where her family had immigrated after the war. ABOVE: Esther and her brother, Jacob, in Szeged, Hungary, 1936.

Some, especially in the United States, said that they came forward because they trusted Steven Spielberg to do justice to their stories—in part because he was America's favorite storyteller on film, but above all because of *Schindler's List*. Knowing that he was the force behind the Shoah Foundation was immensely reassuring because of the impact the film had made, and the integrity and accuracy they understood it to have. Jacob Jungreis, a Hungarian Jew who survived the Bergen-Belsen death camp, said in his testimony, "I should also express my most deep-felt gratitude to *Schindler's List* . . . to Mr. Steven Spielberg. He did an unusual kindness to the dead, that they are not forgotten, with the film. . . . God should bless him for that."

> 66 The Shoah Foundation seems to have enabled [my father] to overcome the paradox between reluctance to burden the next generation with the horrors of war and the urge to tell his story. 99
>
> —Ralph Levie, executive secretary for the Joods Historisch Museum (Jewish Historical Museum) in Amsterdam

We will never know how many survivors may have considered giving testimony but decided against it. "Some people won't talk to us," Spielberg once acknowledged. "There are many survivors who want the story to die with them because it is too horrible for them to confront." Choosing not to speak publicly about one's Holocaust experience is a deeply personal and complex decision, especially for those in hostile environments, or for those whose family and friends still did not know that they were survivors of the Holocaust.

Some survivors who contacted the foundation were hesitant at first but gained confidence in the project after learning more about it. Frequently, talking to a fellow survivor was enough to allow the caller to dare imagine what it would feel like to have the weight of secrecy lifted. Henry Rosmarin (who passed away in 2001) gave his testimony and then volunteered to take calls from other survivors. "Most survivors feel comfortable talking with me," he said. "I simply told them, remember in the days when we said, 'If I live through this, I will tell the world.' This is one way of telling the world . . . not only today's world, but tomorrow's world."

ABOVE: Holocaust survivor Henry Rosmarin (see pages 164-165) during his interview in December 1998. He was interviewed by Emil Jacoby.

BRINGING SURVIVORS FORWARD

Although many survivors came to the foundation on their own, its leaders knew that they had to publicize their aims to achieve the robust response they sought. The staff organized a campaign that ranged from major TV appearances by Steven Spielberg to grassroots work in distant Jewish communities. It encompassed mailing information to survivor groups, networking with synagogues and Holocaust organizations, distributing printed notices, placing items in the Jewish and popular press. The campaign produced spectacular results—and turned up unexpected challenges.

The most indispensable tool was a one-page flyer, translated into twenty languages, that described the project's goals, stated the invitation clearly, and provided space for the person to fill in contact information and essential background. The appeal was direct: "By sharing these stories firsthand, survivors play a vital role in making sure that one of the most devastating events in human history is never forgotten." The prospective interviewee could mail the form directly to Los Angeles, call a toll-free number to respond verbally, or—most practical outside the United States—return it to the nearest regional office; flyers were customized with this information. Flyers poured in from all over the world. "Many survivors would write personal and

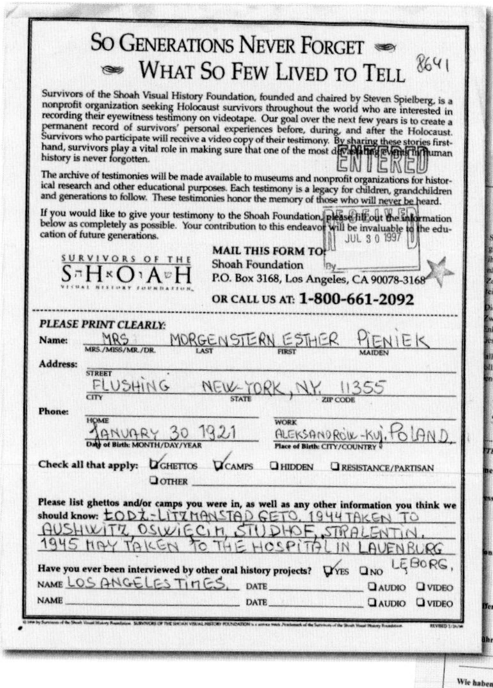

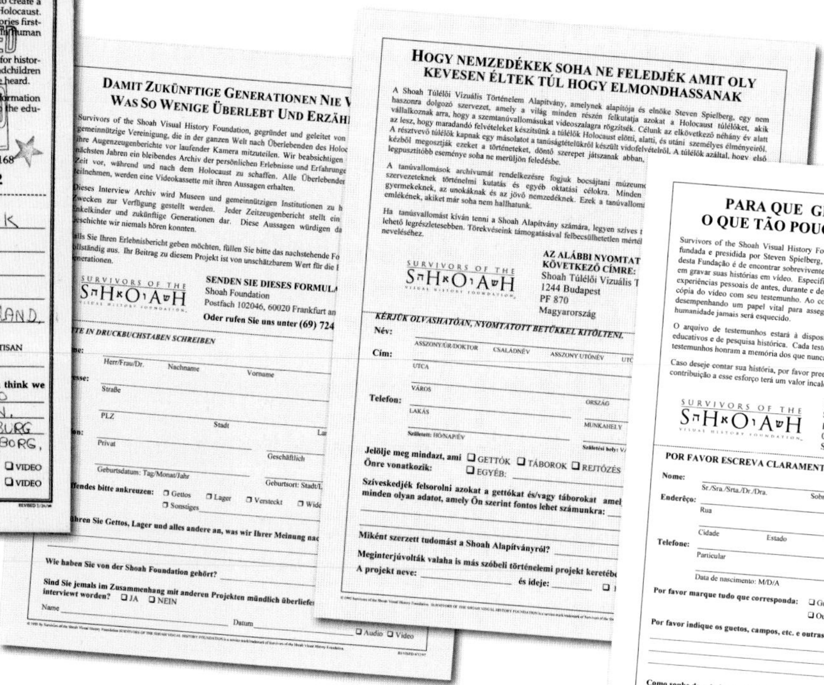

ABOVE: *The one-page flyer that invited witnesses to give testimony was translated into many languages, including (shown above) German, Hungarian, and Portuguese.*

poignant messages on their flyer, about their experiences or lost family members," recalls Ari Zev.

Outreach to survivors had to be adapted to each country and culture. In Europe, many of those who had been persecuted for being Jewish preferred to remain discreet about their Jewish identity, while others simply did not affiliate with their Jewishness at all—either out of fear of lingering (or renascent) anti-Semitism or just because no substantial Jewish community infrastructure remained. In such cases it was especially important to publicize the project via national and daily newspapers and other media outlets, as well as in Jewish community publications. Cultural nuances called for adjustments in method: in Venezuela, for example, survivors were more likely to respond to a phone call than a written invitation. In some rural areas, telephone contact was highly problematic; this was in the era before mobile phones or e-mail. Even obtaining postal mail addresses could be challenging. The regional coordinator often had to visit survivors in person and develop relationships in communities. Not surprisingly, these communal conversations generated long-lasting friendships and led to contacts with other Holocaust survivors.

In the end, Kim Simon notes, conversations circulating through an informal survivor network may have been the key. "This was especially important in Europe," she says. "Of course we were doing the classic kinds of outreach through the press, but word of mouth, and the credibility that gave us, was incredibly powerful." A highly effective tool in spreading the word—and building trust—was giving each interviewee a copy of his or her testimony (on VHS videotape, then the standard for home viewing). "That simple act had immense consequences," Simon says. As the interviewing proceeded, word continued to spread through the survivor communities, encouraging still more to come forward.

Each person who gave testimony

> ❝In Poland and other places in Eastern Europe, some survivors discovered their Jewish roots only recently. Some had used false identities since their early youth and were only beginning to process the history of anti-Semitism in their countries and their own newly discovered Jewish identities.❞
>
> —Ari Zev, director of administration

> ❝In order to present firsthand accounts of the Holocaust, I urge other survivors to break their silence even if it is difficult to do so. The story of the Holocaust should not die with us. It should be kept alive through our testimonies. I wish that more survivors would open up their hearts.❞
>
> —Magda Herzberger, survivor

THE TESTIMONY OF **MENACHEM RUBIN**

Date of birth . . . . June 22, 1922
Place of birth. . . . . Reghin, Romania
Date of interview . . . . June 5, 1997
Location of interview. . . . . Brooklyn,
New York, USA
Language. English
Experience. . . . . Jewish survivor

Grand Rabbi MENACHEM RUBIN *describes a typical Passover Seder at his home in Rhegin, Romania, before the war, detailing the strict Hasidic observances in the preparation of matzo baking for Passover. Some of these preparations, such as baking matzo on the eve of Passover, had to be done very quickly. During the war he was imprisoned in the Mauthausen camp in Austria. He says, "I didn't experience something that had to be so fast and so in a hurry until I came to Mauthausen, where I had to do certain things in the same type of hurry."*

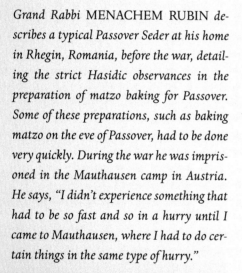

It is a joyous type of a story. First we had to go out in the field and cut wheat for the matzos. Then we had to sit down in the *beit hamidrash* [house of study] and go over each particle of the wheat and make sure it was not affected by water. After we went through with this, we had to grind it ourselves in a hand grinder because grinding with electricity or other means makes it hot in the middle and could become *chametz* [leavened].

They came in the middle of the Seder and everybody was placed. All the matzo, all the food in the house was made available. And they were listening to my father's Seder with such, such a high level of *kadisha* (holiness) that he will never forget that.

Then we had to do a lot of work. For instance, my father had a full room, all the walls full of *sefarim* [books]. We had to take all of it out—the children, the *bocherim* [students], the *gabbai* [religious functionary]—and everybody else put it out [in] the wind for the whole day to make sure that the wind goes through in case, during the year, a little piece of bread remained there, it should be cleaned out.

Then we had to do so many special precautionary works for *Pesach* [Passover]. And then came the time for the matzo baking and then came the second time of matzo baking of *erev* [eve of] *Pesach*, which was a special type of activity. There were always a number of *orchim*, guests, at the Seder. The women were not sitting immediately at the table and [if] there were too many, they were sitting in a different room, if not at the end of the table. ∎

ABOVE: Grand Rabbi Menachem Rubin during his interview. Left to right: Yitzhak Mais, George Klein, Rabbi Rubin, New York state senator Seymour Lachman, and Michael Berenbaum, former president and CEO of the Shoah Foundation.

also received a thank-you letter from Steven Spielberg (word got around about that, too). But the ultimate nudge to all of the regional outreach efforts was the international impact of *Schindler's List*, and Spielberg's commitment to publicly speaking about the foundation's work. When he appeared on Oprah Winfrey's show with survivors Sigi Hart and Renée Firestone in May 1996, more than six thousand calls flooded the foundation's phone lines. Hart, who also volunteered

on the phone at the office, wrote afterward, "The greatest gratitude I felt was when I came to the foundation on the day the showing aired, and I heard the [toll-free] lines ringing off the hook."

But the project's range exceeded even its founder's fame. The foundation made a special effort to reach out to ultra-Orthodox survivors in the New York area and Israel. As Ari Zev explained, "The Holocaust had such a tremendous impact on these communities, and survivors were not coming

ABOVE: *The phone bank in the foundation office on the night in 1997 that* Schindler's List *first aired on television.*

SCHINDLER'S LIST MAKES TELEVISION HISTORY

On February 23, 1997, NBC broadcast *Schindler's List* in its three-and-a-half-hour entirety, uncut and uninterrupted by commercials, as Steven Spielberg had requested. About 65 million viewers watched the film at home that night—more than double the number who watched it in the theater when it was released in 1993. Commercials for the broadcast's sole sponsor, Ford Motor Company, aired before and after the showing. At the film's end, Spielberg appeared to give a 90-second message about the Shoah Foundation.

The foundation's staff had prepared for the event as best it could. James Moll and June Beallor had set up a phone bank and were among those on hand at the Los Angeles headquarters that night. Jerry Cohen, one of the volunteers manning the phones, remembers, "Many volunteers, survivors, and staff were present, and the energy in the room was palpable. We knew there would be a lot of calls, but the tremendous response was overwhelming." The broadcast not only attracted much-needed support in the form of

donations to the foundation, but it also was instrumental in bringing more survivors forward to give testimony.

On the same February date in 2013, the USA network aired the film commercial free again, to coincide with the film's twentieth anniversary. On that occasion, NBCUniversal Cable Entertainment chairman Bonnie Hammer described *Schindler's List* as "the ultimate example of the profound difference an individual can make when he takes a stand against hate and intolerance."

forward." In 1998, the foundation held a special interviewer training session in Israel for the ultra-Orthodox (known as the Haredi) community. Recalls Kim Simon, "They didn't have any idea who Steven Spielberg was. Didn't know his films. And the partner we worked with told us, 'We don't need letters from Spielberg—we need a letter from the rabbi vouching for this project.'" After the foundation had done some two hundred interviews with members of the Haredi communities, says Simon, "They began asking, 'Who's this Steven Spielberg? We are so grateful to him for this. We want to thank him.' Their connection to him was solely his work with the foundation."

ON THE FRONTLINES

Reaching out to survivors was one side of a complicated equation: the other was forming field teams to record their testimonies. Interviewers, videographers, and regional coordinators were recruited internationally. The people who composed this

OPPOSITE: The Hall of Names at Yad Vashem. BELOW RIGHT: Dana Schwartz and Helen Chalef.

A SPECIAL BOND

As the Shoah Foundation celebrated its tenth anniversary in 2004, two women who had been child survivors of the Holocaust renewed a bond formed a decade earlier, when Dana Schwartz interviewed Helen Chalef for the Visual History Archive. While it was unusual for survivors to interview each other, there were sometimes good reasons to make an exception, as with these two pioneers in testimony. Recalling the interview, when Dana gently guided Helen through her harrowing story, Helen says, "The softness of Dana's voice, the way she encouraged me without probing, made it possible for me to continue."

Dana, who barely escaped with her mother from a Polish ghetto, conducted more than one hundred survivor interviews and recalls them in razor-sharp detail—for example, how the ten-year-old Helen lay down for a nap with her grandmother and dreamed she heard these words from her: "You are not hungry. You are not cold. You are not tired. Keep walking." When she awoke, Helen saw that her grandmother had died in her sleep. Years later, as a prisoner in a Nazi death march, Helen helped save herself by repeating these words over and over.

Helen is glad to have shared her story. "I hope it helps make people aware that segregating a group and negating their humanity is a very dangerous thing—not only to those they degrade but because they too become dehumanized," she says. And of the friend who helped her through the experience, even as her voice sometimes cracked and her hands shook: "To this day, I find myself calling Dana just to hear her voice and feel reassured," says Helen. "She makes me feel that all is going to be well."

185

flesh-and-blood network were a remarkable group, drawn from a wide array of backgrounds, communicating in scores of languages, but united by a fierce dedication to work they felt called to do.

The interviewers were thus the core of the effort, and were chosen with great care. A key early decision was that while interviewers should be bright, well educated, and highly committed, they need not have special credentials to be considered for the job.

"Reaching our goal of fifty thousand interviews meant that we needed to recruit and train a large number of interviewers," notes Zev, "and the diversity of backgrounds and experience among the interviewers made the archive richer." Many were indeed historians or other academics, but just as many were educators, journalists, lawyers, doctors, or therapists. There were Jews and non-Jews. Many were the children of survivors; a very few were even survivors themselves. "Some of the interviewers in Germany were the children of Holocaust perpetrators," says Zev, "people who had been connected in a negative way to that history all their lives and wanted to do something positive about it." In this way the interviewing project became yet another avenue toward healing.

The best interviewer candidates came to the endeavor with not only a strong base of knowledge about the Holocaust but also good listening skills and the appropriate sensitivity for interacting with survivors. Each brought his or her own perspective and experience to the process, and some also had specialized expertise in particular aspects of the Holocaust. If it was known that a prospective interviewee had an unusual experience to share—being in a certain camp or on a certain transport—the interviewer might be chosen for knowledge in that area and would do research.

The foundation also hired and trained about one thousand local videographers, who worked with volunteer camera assistants to

ABOVE: Left to right, Jeff Cooper, production coordinator; Michael Engel, director of production; Andy Nicastro, manager of production; and Bill Steinberg, production manager. OPPOSITE: Per Anger, a rescuer and aid provider in the Holocaust, during his interview in Stockholm, 1996, with videographer Thomas Wester.

THE TESTIMONY OF **HANNAH PICK**

Date of birth . . . . .November 12, 1928
Place of birth. . . . . .Berlin, Germany
Date of interview . . . . . . .August 19, 1996
Location of interview. . . . Jerusalem, Israel
Language . . . . Hebrew
Experience. . . . . .Jewish survivor

HANNAH PICK *describes her family's arrival and adjustment to a new life in Amsterdam. Hanah remembers the first time she met Anne Frank; they were neighbors and attended the same Jewish school. She also recalls the disappearance of the Frank family in 1942.*

In Holland I remember that we rented a very small apartment with three rooms. In one of the rooms, my father opened an office, together with a lawyer. [My father] was an economist. He wanted to help refugees whom he knew would come needing advice. And my mother, who was a teacher, became the secretary of that office. We also brought with us a girl, a refugee that was supposed to help my mother

ABOVE: *Hannah with her fiancé, Major Pinhas Pick, and her little sister, Rahel, after the war.*

with the home chores. It was a *mitzvah* [moral obligation] to bring someone else and get her out of Germany.

I remember signing up for kindergarten. I didn't know anyone besides Anne [Frank].

Either my mom or that girl [and I] went to the grocery store, where we spoke in German and where [we] met another woman that spoke German as well. With this woman was a little girl, who was six months younger than me, and that girl was Anne Frank. We lived right next to each other so we immediately connected.

I remember signing up for kindergarten. My mom brought me there. I didn't know the language, I didn't know anyone besides Anne, [whom I had met for only] five minutes in the grocery store. She was playing the bells, turned around, I ran to her hands, she ran to my hands, and that was it. My mom could go home.

I remember, in the beginning of '42, in June, when we finished the year in the Jewish school. Anne and I had to repeat a math test. Anne disappeared, so I had to do the math homework. When I came back a few days later, [the Franks] were not there. And this made me think, because Mr. Frank was always very optimistic. When he would visit us, everything was always fine; he said that the war will end soon, and the Americans will arrive. The pessimist was *my* father.

We didn't know that they went into hiding, we were told that he left for Switzerland—because his mother was in Switzerland. I came home and I couldn't understand. Then, on my way home, I met a friend, and he told me, "I am so glad to see you because I received an order and tomorrow morning I need to [report] to a work camp." The friend was only fifteen years old.

Later on, I heard that Margot [Anne's sister] got a similar order. Then Mr. Frank, who had already started to prepare the place [for hiding], decided that the time had come: it's all of us or none of us, and they went into hiding. ■

record the interviews. Videographers used their own camera equipment for the most part, and followed creative guidelines provided by the foundation to maintain consistency.

The foundation hired Michael Engel and Andy Nicastro to oversee the setting up of the regional coordinator network and the worldwide production of interviews. Says Engel, "I was working with a band of brothers and sisters to make sure we [had] capable videographers all over the globe. We couldn't simply hire anyone. . . . In most cases we were sending them into the homes of Holocaust survivors, so it was a unique situation indeed."

TRUE KNOWLEDGE

I thought I knew about the Holocaust. I knew what happened, and I knew how terrible it was. At first, I didn't know the difference between reading or watching a testimony and having it told to me. I had never met a survivor before. I had seen them on television and read about them in books, but I had never listened as a survivor, in his own words, told me his stories. It struck me hard, and then I understood what it means to survive. You don't get this realization when reading a textbook. It's one of those intangible feelings you get from speaking to someone who knows first-hand. To me, that is true knowledge. —*Adam Rokhsar, who volunteered as an assistant videographer while still in high school*

Nearly all of the interviewers and videographers worked as volunteers, receiving a small stipend for each interview. "So many skilled people from around the world wanted to lend their talents," says Moll. "But it's tough for people to make such a commitment of time and effort without at least some compensation." Videographers were given a modest allowance to compensate them for the cost of camera rental, and interviewers were reimbursed for expenses such as ground transportation.

Critical links among the many constituents in this human network were the regional coordinators, who became the foundation's representatives in more than thirty countries. "They were our eyes and ears on the ground, serving as bridges between cultures," as Michael Engel says. "Collectively these seventy dedicated people spoke to more than 50,000 survivors and witnesses in five years." The regional coordinators' core responsibility was

Right: Regional coordinators and staff at the Shoah Foundation, c. 1997.

contacting survivors and scheduling interviews, so they needed to know as much as possible in advance about both the interviewees and the interviewers—their expertise, language skills, and so on—to match them up. They kept information flowing in all directions before and after the interview, distributed tape supplies to videographers, and conveyed the precious tapes to headquarters. In turn, the Los Angeles office had to be expanded and equipped to handle the tapes once they started to arrive.

GUARDIAN OF STORIES

They had my number: the survivors, the interviewers, the videographers, and the volunteer camera assistants. They all called me after each interview with details, paperwork, tapes, stories of the interview day itself, and any recollections they had heard or told that were too weighty a burden to carry. [A regional coordinator was] a guardian of confidential anecdotes that had shaped the life of the original teller and would, in some small or huge way, shape the lives of all who heard them. — *Marla Dansky, regional coordinator, Philadelphia*

"A day in the life of a regional coordinator was an adventure," says Rebecca Saltman, a regional staffer in New York and Boston. "We had a list of names; we called, people cried, we were yelled at, or they simply hung up on us. On the other hand, people blessed us for doing this work, prayed for us, cooked us homemade goodies, and told all of us how grateful they were for the work of preserving and documenting these important times." Staff members were already busy building a database of potential interviewees from the calls and flyers coming in. More than once, a regional coordinator would pass on a name and information to be entered in the database, only to call back a few weeks later with news that the survivor had passed away before the interview could be conducted.

LEARNING TO INTERVIEW

With a roster of interviewers that ultimately topped 2,500, from many lands and many backgrounds, the foundation had to make sure that all were well trained in a consistent methodology for interviewing. "One of the primary goals was to prepare interviewers for the wide range of survivor experiences they might encounter, with emphasis on the survivor's comfort and well-being," explains Ari Zev. Interviewers were trained around the world in places where significant numbers of survivors lived, so they could be interviewed locally, in the language most comfortable for them—often in places where Holocaust events took place.

In July 1994 the first training session for interviewers was conducted in Los Angeles. Early training sessions took two days; later they grew to three or even four days. Ultimately those 2,500-plus interviewers attended intensive training sessions in twenty-four countries, led by multilingual teams with assistance from local historians and psychologists. Prospective candidates had to apply and be accepted;

after the training, they were evaluated and informed whether they had been chosen to join the team.

The training program was developed by the foundation's staff, building on the examples set by established organizations. They included the Yale Fortunoff Archive, led by Geoffrey Hartman and Joanne Rudof; the Department of Oral History at the U.S. Holocaust Memorial Museum, led by Joan Ringleheim; the San Francisco Bay Area Oral History Project, a pioneering effort run by Lani Silver; Iris Berlatsky at Yad Vashem in Jerusalem; and the Center for Holocaust Studies, Documentation & Research, founded by Yaffa Eliach, where trainer Bonnie Gurewitsch was archivist and oral historian.

Training sessions typically included lectures by foundation staff and guest speakers on Holocaust history, psychology, and interview methodology; practical exercises in techniques; screening and critical review of previously recorded testimonies; and practice in conducting interviews one on one—usually on the final day. Survivors from the region sometimes volunteered to be interviewed

THE TRAINERS

Remarkably just a handful of training leaders, traveling ceaselessly for several years, carried out the foundation's far-flung training program. Instrumental in developing and leading the training were Darlene Basch, a clinical social worker and daughter of Holocaust survivors, and Dr. Paula Draper, director of the Oral History Project at the Toronto Holocaust Memorial and Education Centre. Other trainers who served as regular presenters were Bonnie Gurewitsch, Lani Silver, Carol Stulberg, Dana Schwartz, and Renée Firestone. Among other experts taking part as trainers and presenters were Iris Berlatzky, director of oral history at Yad Vashem; Claudine Drame and Regine Weintrater, both interviewers for the Yale Fortunoff Archive's project in France; and historians Michael Berenbaum (then director of research at the U.S. Holocaust Memorial Museum and later to become the foundation's president), Yehuda Bauer, and Peter Hayes.

ABOVE: Darlene Basch, co-lead interviewer trainer (far right), and Ari Zev talk with an interviewer, c. 1996.

for the practice sessions, or spoke about their experiences. For trainings in Europe, lectures focused on local history, and interpreters provided simultaneous translations of the English-speaking trainers. There was always a trained professional on hand to help trainees deal appropriately with the sensitive issues inevitably raised by the process—and to prepare them for the emotional impact of working with survivors.

KINDRED SOULS

By 1994, I had been involved in several Holocaust survivor documentation projects in Canada. Traveling with the Shoah Foundation, I met kindred souls who, like me, had felt they were alone in racing to record the voices of survivors. In every country I made new friends who immediately felt like old friends. We reveled in sharing knowledge with the hundreds of interviewers we trained to join us in saving each unique story of the Holocaust.
— *Paula Draper, training leader*

"The trainings became very powerful experiences for the interviewers," says Diana Stein-Judovits, research and training manager, "partly because they were meeting so many like-minded people." In particular, interviewers who were children or family members of survivors shared a special bond, giving rise to deep and lasting friendships. "Both during and after the testimony-collecting phase, we held gatherings for interviewers all around the world," Zev adds. "These were opportunities to share updates about the project, educate and coach people on history and interviewing technique, and help everyone adjust to the emotional impact of what they had been exposed to."

Rolling out a training program internationally posed special challenges in planning and logistics as the team adapted to new languages and cultures. The human network proliferated, and local community leaders who had helped spread the word to survivors now became more deeply involved—often as liaisons with potential interviewers or as interviewers themselves. The first international training sessions for interviewers took place in Sydney (January 1995) and Paris (February 1995). In May 1995, the foundation organized a multinational training session in Amsterdam, which attracted participants from the Netherlands, Croatia, the

Above: Interviewers at a training session in Prague, c. 1995.

192

Czech Republic, Germany, Greece, Lithuania, the Russian Federation, and South Africa. In hindsight, recalls Kim Simon, "We learned that local training was a must. In the larger session, with so many individuals from disparate countries, we could not address local contexts and needs. It took a few more years for us to integrate what it means to be international, and that's really based on working locally."

As word spread throughout Europe about the Shoah Foundation, people working on post-Holocaust projects in their various countries were drawn into its orbit. One was Martin Šmok, a young documentary filmmaker in Prague. While trying to raise funds for a film about a little-known World War II Jewish rescue group active in what is now Slovakia, Šmok heard of the Amsterdam event and attended. There he was persuaded by Kim Simon to come to Los Angeles and work for the foundation. He eventually returned home to Prague but never left the organization, becoming its first interviewer in the Czech Republic. "Anything that we do in this part of Europe," he says, "is based on establishing relationships of mutual trust through local connections."

BEHIND THE INTERVIEW

The scale of the collection effort, coupled with the diverse experiences of both interviewers and interviewees, made it vital to develop a thoughtful and consistent methodology for the tapings. As with training, the foundation cooperated with and learned from other groups, adapting their approaches to its larger scope. For example, while they did not restrict the time allowed for interviews, they aimed for about two hours on average, as did the Fortunoff Archive and the Bay Area Oral History Project.

Two notable characteristics distinguish the testimonies recorded for the Shoah Foundation archive from those of other collections. These differences arose from the vision put forth by Steven Spielberg, and evolved over months of debate and comparison with proven models. One was the choice to interview subjects in their own homes whenever possible. The other was the three-part structure: about 20 percent of the interview covered the survivor's prewar life, about 60 percent his or her experiences during the war, and the remaining 20 percent on rebuilding a life postwar. Both principles departed from accepted practice. Some oral history experts insisted that home settings were distracting and prejudicial, maintaining that the best backdrop was a blank studio

> "We are committed to sharing resources and joining forces with important organizations engaged in documenting the Holocaust survivors."
> — Steven Spielberg

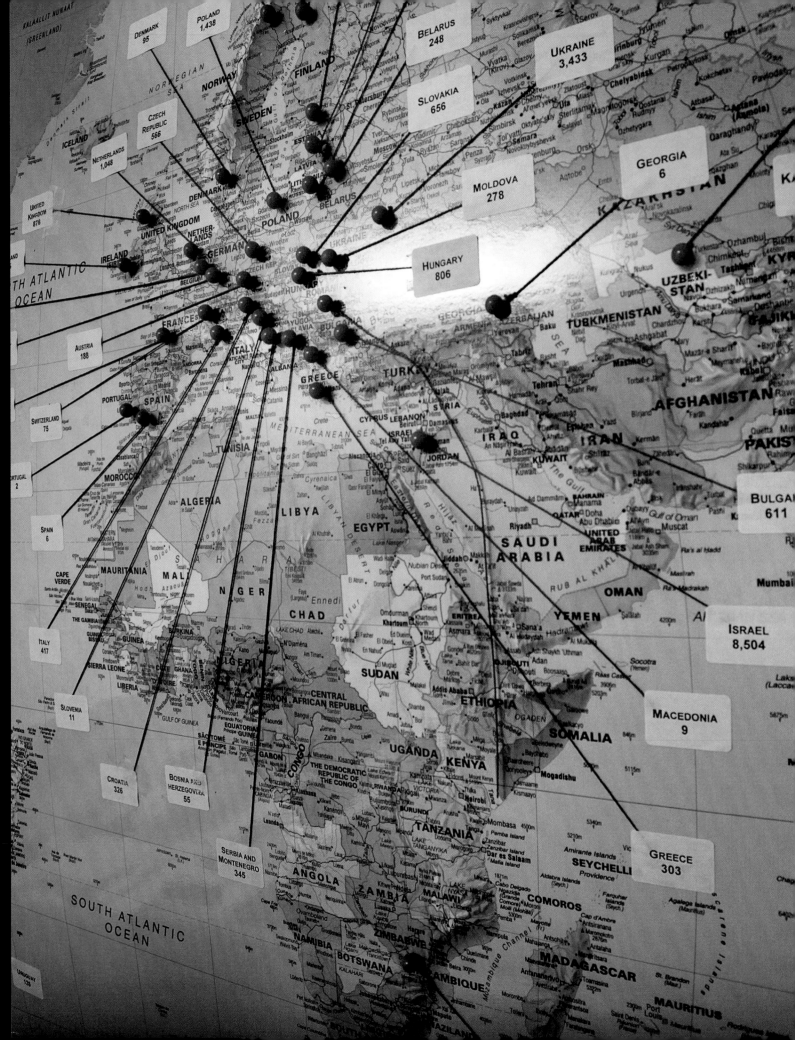

wall. And many similar projects were interested only in experience that directly concerned the events of the Holocaust.

The home environment was a big part of making survivors feel at ease. But it proved to have other benefits as well. "Filming in homes all over the world allowed us to catch a glimpse of each survivor's environment and to get a stronger sense of the person's life," says James Moll. "The furniture, the decor, and even the items in the background ultimately become a part of the historical record. In the future, those domestic backgrounds may provide valuable insights about how people lived in the mid-1990s."

Likewise, the pre- and postwar portions of the survivors' testimonies would turn out to be invaluable. In describing their prewar experiences, for instance, many survivors share memories of how they were affected by the Nuremberg Laws—the legislation that stripped Jews of their basic rights in prewar Nazi Germany and other countries. "The oral history from 1935 to 1939 is crucial, and the personal perspectives help us understand the slow and systematic way the Holocaust unfolded in a country as sophisticated as Germany was," says Ari Zev. "They speak of one day being turned away from school, of being required to sew a yellow badge on their jacket, of friends suddenly turning against them."

Starting off an interview by asking about the survivor's early life helped relieve anxiety about the more difficult topics ahead. An interview would never begin with "Tell us what happened at Auschwitz." Interviewer Nancy Fisher recalls, "After establishing names, places and dates of birth, family composition and such, I would ask 'If you and I were standing in front of your childhood home right now, what would I see?' By starting at the beginning, when childhood memories were influenced by family members, geography, religion, and culture, I would hear wonderful descriptions, often tinged with humor. Questions about food often brought sweet thoughts about everyday cooking in the kitchen as well as preparations for either the Sabbath or holidays."

How much time an interview spent on each of the three life phases—prewar, wartime, and postwar—was flexible, depending on the person's experience. No one was ever cut off after a preset amount of time, and some interviews did go

Opposite: This map in the foundation office showed where interviews were conducted and how many were done in that country, region, or city.
Above: Turning a Blind Eye, *by Hertz Allegrio, created for the 2009 Annual Holocaust Art and Writing Contest for students, sponsored by Chapman University. Student works are inspired by testimony from the Visual History Archive.*

on much longer than the standard two to three hours. Like most other organizations that interviewed survivors, the foundation stipulated that no other family be present during the main interview; this was known to inhibit interviewees from sharing as openly as they might otherwise, or at minimum, was distracting. While making *Schindler's List,* Spielberg had been shaken by the realization that each Holocaust victim who died or survived represented many future generations that would multiply—or never exist at all.

Taken together, these criteria reflected a clear intention that the survivor would offer a lifetime perspective—a self-portrait of a whole person rather than a life entirely dominated by the Holocaust. In this, we can see Spielberg's unerring instinct for how audiences connect with a story. Most viewers of any given testimony will not share the survivor's central trauma, whether that was living through imprisonment in a camp, deportation, flight, or going into hiding. But nearly everyone can relate to survivors' accounts of growing up on a farm or in a small town or city, of school and family life, of settling into a new home, building a marriage, becoming parents and grandparents.

There were exceptions to the rules, of course. Occasionally someone was reluctant to beinterviewed at home and would be accommodated. In parts of Europe where survivors hesitated to advertise their Jewish identity—even to their families—arrangements were made to hold interviews at a community center, a regional coordinator's office, or other location. "In some of these places, survivors and former Holocaust perpetrators lived as neighbors," says Anna Verkhovskaya, former regional production manager for the foundation in Eastern Europe. "That made coming forward more difficult." Another principle very rarely breached was that survivors received no compensation for giving testimony. But in remote rural areas, such as in Ukraine, where electricity was very expensive, an allowance might be offered for the power used by the lights and other video gear. A lack of reliable electrical power might also be a reason to interview someone outside the home. Even in the United States, poverty sometimes precluded conducting interviews in the home.

BEFORE, DURING, AFTER

I was often surprised by the happy memories that arose during the first part of the PIQ, when people described the warmth of family life, even if they had lived through difficult times or dealt with anti-Semitism. Revisiting this time gave life back to something lost forever. The part related to wartime was usually tense, as survivors tried to avoid "hurting" the interviewer with their stories. In talking about the postwar period, most Jewish survivors could not rejoice because they were confronting the emptiness, or sadness, of that time.

—*Viviane Teitelbaum Hirsch, former regional coordinator in Belgium, member of the Parliament of Brussels-Capital Region*

CAMP 2

Name of camp: KAUFERING (NEW CAMP) KAUFERING/BAVARIA GERMANY
(Name of camp) (Nearest large city or town) (Country)

3 AUGUST 1944 AUSCHWITZ EARLY SEPTEMBER 1944 LANDSBERG-K LAGER J
(Date arrived) (Arrived from) (Date departed) (Departed to)

Numbers or letters assigned to you (if known) 86711 Were the numbers or letters tattooed on your body? ☐ Yes ☑ No

Did you have a job, function, or assigned duty in the camp? (For example: blockaeltester, block clerk, body transport, burial detail, forest team, kitchen worker, laundry detail, hospital staff, platform worker, roll call clerk, etc.) ☑ Yes ☐ No Type of work

Type of work: FINISHING THE BUILDING WORK ON THIS NEW CAMP

Were you involved in religious, educational, and/or other cultural activities organized by prisoners in the camp? ☐ Yes ☑ No
Type of activities: NONE

Did you have any direct contact with Gypsies in the camp? ☐ Yes ☑ No

Did you have any direct contact with prisoners who were subjected to medical experiments in the camp? ☐ Yes ☑ No

Did you meet any prisoners who were persecuted for their alleged homosexuality? ☐ Yes ☑ No

---

4 F. DEATH MARCHES 4. Wartime Section F - Death Marches

This section applies to forced evacuations of inmates from camps and/or ghettos in response to the approach of liberating armies.

Were you on any death marches? ☑ Yes ☐ No (If no, please go to section "4 G".)

1. LANDSBERG-K 24 APRIL 1945 MUNICH
(Where did it begin [name of camp, ghetto, city, town, etc.]?) (Start date) (Nearest city or town)

DAUCHAU CAMP 26 APRIL 1945 MUNICH
(Where did it end?) (End date) (Nearest city or town)

2. WALKING TOWARD MOUNTAINS 27 APRIL 1945 GERMANY
(Where did it begin [name of camp, ghetto, city, town, etc.]?) (Start date) (Nearest city or town)

P.O.W CAMP - BUCHBERG 1st MAY 1945 GERMANY
(Where did it end?) (End date) (Nearest city or town)

3.
(Where did it begin [name of camp, ghetto, city, town, etc.]?) (Start date) (Nearest city or town)

Preparations for each interview began with the initial phone contact or a flyer returned by the prospective interviewee. Regional coordinators, guided by basic information about people in their region, assigned an interviewing team—aiming to choose the interviewer most knowledgeable about the kind of experience the survivor would bring.

A week or so before the scheduled interview, the interviewer arranged an in-person meeting to fill out the survivor's pre-interview questionnaire (or "PIQ" to foundation employees). This face-to-face conversation was a way to begin building rapport, describe the purpose and general shape of the interview, and field questions. But the PIQ itself was vital in many ways. It called for detailed biographical information, such as birthplace, family background and names, and religious and other affiliations, then asked about the survivor's prewar life, defining wartime experiences (such as the names of any ghettos or camps), and postwar life right up to the time of the meeting. The PIQ's main purpose was to make sure that the outline of the survivor's life was covered, with all dates filled in and names correctly spelled, so as not to let such details derail the narrative of the main interview.

Because interviews would be conducted in many countries, the PIQ had to be rendered in nineteen languages. Translation manager Jana Hillman quickly realized that professional translators could not translate the document properly due to its specialized vocabulary. "Even translating the seemingly simple word 'survivor' sparked a weeklong debate about the Slavic equivalents," Gustman says. "Each foreign-language version of the PIQ was the product of a painstaking process, involving extensive in-country review by the regional coordinators or other Holocaust experts around the world, followed by hours on the phone to discuss the edits."

ABOVE: Pages from a pre-interview questionnaire (PIQ) documenting a survivor's wartime experience in camps and forced marches.

THE TESTIMONY OF **ABRAHAM ZUCKERMAN**

Date of birth: . . . . .December 10, 1924
Place of birth: . . . . .Krakow, Poland
Date of interview:. . . . . .June 14, 1995
Location of interview: . . . . .Hillside,
New Jersey, USA
Language: . . . . English
Experience: . . . . .Jewish survivor

ABRAHAM ZUCKERMAN *was in the Krakow-Plaszow concentration camp in Poland when he was selected to work in Oskar Schindler's Emailwarenfabrik factory. Zuckerman had no idea who Schindler was or that his own fate had just taken a turn for the better. He has expressed his gratitude to Schindler for that life-saving opportunity in many ways, up to this day.*

One day, we were all called, and they cut away like a third of the people, and they told us to turn around and walk towards the gate. So we walked towards the gate. And at that time I didn't think about hiding, because the job I had was so bad, was so treacherous, so I figured whatever is going to

happen is going to be better than what I have now. So I went, and sure enough they started to talk, "We're going to Schindler." Going to Schindler.

I didn't know who Schindler was. And they were all ecstatic [because] he used to take people from the camp, used to take them to his factory. I guess he made a deal with [the Nazis] somehow that he built his own domain, he built his barracks, everything, where the factory was. I went there, and the minute I came into the camp, I saw that things are different, you know. First of all, there were potatoes . . . mountains of potatoes. [Also] the orders that he gave out to the guards and the policemen, they dare not shoot at random, in the towers, in the watchtowers, and the policemen, he said you dare not touch anybody. And that was his order.

I got the job in the pots and

pans [factory]. *Emalia* is the translation [of] "porcelainizing," you know. It was a factory . . . they were making pots and pans from a flat piece of metal. The machines brought it out, and then we were dipping it in porcelain, and after that it went to the ovens. The ovens on the outside had a rim. That rim was always red-hot. Just pure, red-hot. So I used to go, cut a few potatoes, put it in a pot, with water, and in ten minutes I had potatoes. So I was never hungry.

And [Schindler] tolerated all that. He could [not] care less what we were doing, you know? He watched over us, so one part was doing the pots and pans, one part was doing the shells for ammunition. The shells for ammuni-

FAR LEFT: Abraham with family in 1935. Left to right: his sister Dora, mother Anna, sister Hella, and Abraham. LEFT: Abraham and his wife Mina (Millie), at their wedding in 1947. OPPOSITE TOP: Oskar Schindler by Schindler Place street sign in New Jersey, c.1957. OPPOSITE BOTTOM: Abraham, Millie, and family, September 14, 2008.

tion were also done like make-believe . . . the whole thing was a fraud in a way. Because nothing ever went out of this factory for production. His excuse was, we're doing it all for the war effort, for the war effort, for the war effort. But when he needed ammunition, he bought it somewhere else, and sent it out. That was Schindler. You know, he said good morning to you, and never wore a uniform. He smiled to you, good morning. He was always around the factory. In there I regained my strength. I became a person again.

Later in his life, Zuckerman became a successful land developer in New Jersey, where he inaugurated a tradition of naming streets for his rescuer.

Yeah, we came here [New Jersey], and we started to build a house, two houses, and then in '52, we had our first development, first subdivision, that had thirty-two houses. And the first thing that we did was to name a street after Schindler. That was before we had anything in our pockets . . . because it's really mind-boggling what he did. It's really not to believe. You know, he did something that even [Raoul] Wallenberg didn't do. I mean, Wallenberg saved a lot of Jews, a hundred thousand Jews, by giving out passports, but he was a Swedish diplomat, the Germans could not do anything to him. Schindler was in the fire. He was surrounded by all these Germans. And he did what he did. He

could persuade, bribe, and do all these things, and [he] protected twelve hundred, thirteen hundred Jews. Protected. Nobody died in this place. One person died a natural death, and he was buried according to Jewish law.

Even the movie doesn't give [Schindler] enough credit for the little things that he used to do. He was a smoker, smoked constantly. So he used to take two puffs, and throw away the cigarette because he knew that some people smoked and needed a cigarette.

And of course, with every development, [we] had a Schindler Street. Today there are more than thirty streets. Schindler Drive, Schindler Place. And that we did before the movie came out. Even the movie doesn't give [Schindler] enough credit for the little things that

he used to do. He was a smoker, smoked constantly. So he used to take two puffs, and throw away the cigarette because he knew that some people smoked and needed a cigarette. ■

"The pre-interview questionnaire was a helpful tool in helping both the survivor and interviewer think about the chronology of the survivor's story," explained Ari Zev. This "discovery" process would determine the course of research that the interviewer would then conduct to ensure that he or she had a good understanding of the historical and geographical context of the particular survivor experience. This might be the case if the person had a rare or historically significant experience: had been a *Sonderkommando,* for instance, or had survived the Warsaw ghetto uprising. "Knowing this in advance, the interviewer could research those experiences within the historical context and prepare appropriate questions—with support from the foundation's team as needed," Zev adds

While the information was initially meant to help guide the interviewer in taking testimony, it also proved indispensable for the next stage of the project: cataloguing and indexing the testimonies. "What we discovered is that very often names, both place names and proper names, would be recorded on the PIQ but not mentioned in the video," says Karen Jungblut. "Since all these details became available to the archive along with the video, they can be used by scholars to fill in a picture, or cross-referenced with other testimonies containing the same names."

❝❝It is an awesome responsibility to sit across from a survivor and earn their trust so that they describe intimate patterns of their former life to you. It is ennobling to be in their presence—up three flights of stairs, or in a trailer park, or in a house with tennis courts and a swimming pool.❞❞ —Anne Bernard, interviewer

FACE TO FACE

The interviewer/videographer team aimed to arrive an hour or so before the taping start time, to share small talk with the interviewee, go through photos, and get set up. The pre-interview session would have already created a rapport between the interviewer and survivor, and this additional time, with the videographer present as well, increased the comfort level. A place in the home was chosen by mutual agreement—ideally in a room with a door that could be closed. Survivors often liked to sit in front of bookshelves, or sometimes beside a table of family photographs.

The start of the interview was "slated" with the date, survivor's and interviewer's names, and location and language of the interview. When the camera moves off the slate, we see the interviewer kneeling next to the seated survivor, reading aloud the information on the slate. The interviewer then takes a seat and asks a standard set of biographical questions to start things off. Interviewers usually brought notes and questions based on the pre-interview, but

they took no notes during the actual interview—believing that maintaining eye contact was important to building a connection and trust.

Interviewers were instructed not to express shock at the survivor's revelations, lest the survivor start to self-edit, nor to allow emotion to overcome them (the survivor might then want to comfort them). If a survivor broke down, the interviewer was simply to extend silent sympathy and wait for the person to regain composure. They were to wait out pauses while survivors gathered their thoughts. The tape was never stopped unless the survivor absolutely could not go on.

Interviewers tried not to interrupt unless the interview went way off course; they might ask for clarification on a key point and ask questions when appropriate without being intrusive. If the interviewee got lost in his story, the interviewer would unobtrusively help him pick up the thread. If he evinced discomfort about a difficult topic, the interviewer might help him open up or steer him back to the subject later, if it seemed important. If interviewers recognized errors in a person's story, they might probe with gentle questions, but they were never to challenge survivors or ask judgmental questions. Says James Moll, "The idea was to guide them to tell the story in their own way, not to impose any preconceived ideas of what their story should be. This technique is much harder than it sounds."

Similarly, the videographer's most important job, aside from making sure the

OPPOSITE: Survivor Eva Behar being interviewed in 2012. ABOVE: Interviewer Nancy Fisher works with an interviewee.

THE TESTIMONY OF **RICHARD ROZEN**

Date of birth: . . . . April 15, 1936
Place of birth: . . . . Radom (Kielce), Poland
Date of interview: . . . September 26, 1996
Place of interview: . . . . Brighton, Australia
Language: . . . . English
Experience: . . . . Jewish survivor

Richard Rozen remembers hiding with his parents for thirty months in what he describes as a small cabin in an attic on a farm in Luboml, Poland. The family lived in total darkness. At night when everyone was sleeping, Richard's father gave him lessons on how to read and write.

When the Germans invaded, my father had no problem understanding what was going to happen to us. We were taken by cart horse and some arrangement was made. And we [ended] up on a farm in an attic, hidden in a cabin about this size [Richard stretches out his arms], a meter high, about more than two meters long, and about a meter wide.

[My parents] couldn't walk. They could only crouch. It wasn't high enough. That cabin was behind a false wall. It was a commercial arrangement. My father was [paying] rent. We spent the next thirty months in that cabin. The three of us, my father, my mother, and I in total darkness—with never being out of the cabin.

My mother was always crying. She was very upset about the situation. She didn't like being there. My father was quite good. For the first time, I'd seen a lot of my father. I did my first year of school in the cabin. He taught me how to read and write on the palm of my hand, which I thought was good fun. And life for me became very normal.

[He was] always whispering in my ear because we had to be quiet. Most of the lessons were in the night so we slept during the day. We had to be quiet during the day. When everyone was asleep we used to work and clean and eat, and then the lessons started though the night and we would stop in the morning.

And I still remember today, if I see a number "3" I can feel it on my palm. I know what a letter feels like. Before I see what a *C* looks like, I feel the *C* [Richard draws a *C* on his palm]. It was good fun. It actually did me good because it improved my memory. I've been lucky as years went by and have had some reasonable success with chess and bridge. And I think it comes from there [he points to his palm]. It's not the conventional schooling, but it was quite okay. I have no complaints about that.

And [then] the money ran out and they kicked us out. ∎

ABOVE: Richard with his parents and aunt, 1938. LEFT: Richard, age twelve, among a group of boys in an orphanage in France, 1947; he is third from right in the top row.

tape was running, was to stay out of the way as much as possible. "We just wanted to see the faces and hear the voices clearly," says Moll. "We didn't want to interpret what was happening. So we didn't zoom in to a survivor's face while they were speaking, which would be, essentially, editorializing. The lighting was a very basic setup: natural, soft-key, not dramatic." A videographer's practical responsibilities included making sure that the interviewer was positioned near the camera and more or less at eye level with the lens, so the interviewee's gaze wouldn't shift, and to signal interviewers when the need to change tapes was imminent, so they could be alert for a natural break in the narrative or wind down the conversation.

Throughout the interview, the survivor had the opportunity to tell his personal life history in his own way. But from time to time—often toward the end—interviewers engaged more actively with their subjects. They might encourage an interviewee who wanted to sing, play an instrument, read a poem, or show a piece of art. This was also a time when the interviewer might ask general questions such

LISTENING

None of the interviews were easy, but one stands out in my memory as the most difficult and yet most rewarding. In 1996, I interviewed one of the few Greek *Sonderkommandos* who worked in the crematorium of Birkenau. This man was forced to assist in the burning of hundreds of thousands of innocent people. His story was incredibly difficult because of his emotional and graphic descriptions of what took place inside the gas chambers and the crematorium. He told me that he is haunted by the screams every night. At the end of his testimony, he thanked me and said that I helped him get a big load off his chest and that he had waited many years for someone who would listen to his testimony. — *Carol Stulberg, interviewer*

NEXT GENERATIONS

On an early interview, I met a survivor who described in graphic detail his imprisonment in Mauthausen, where he was forced to carry impossibly heavy rocks up the famous Mauthausen steps, and then down again, solely for the pleasure of his Nazi captors. He was then a strong, young man and he shared with me a dream he recalled that he frequently had while a prisoner in the camp. In the dream his father, who had been killed by the Nazis in the early days of the Holocaust, came to him at night and told him to stay strong, and that he must go on to have children and to tell his story so others would never forget. At the conclusion of his interview . . . his beautiful family huddled around him to offer thanks and to support to him. He looked right into the camera and proudly stated 'Hitler didn't win.' — *Fran Victor, interviewer*

RIGHT: Survivor Eva Behar with her family, July 2012.

as: What message would you like to leave for the future? Why did you want to tell your story? Is there anything else on your mind that you wish to share?

After the interview, family members were invited to join the interviewee on camera: usually spouses, children, and grandchildren. On one occasion a family of seventy-five gathered for the taping. They were introduced and sometimes spoke about the impact of the survivor's experience on their own lives. Nicola Gissing, the daughter of Vera Gissing (whose testimony is excerpted on page 290–293), recalls being so frightened by the stories as a child in the 1960s that she stockpiled an escape kit in her closet—they lived in London—against the possibility of another war. "I thought I would try to get to Switzerland," she says, smiling. Not surprisingly, most family members expressed great love and admiration for their survivor relative—most often a parent—and pride that he or she had chosen to come forward and

Top: Survivors' personal memorabilia captured on video during interviews. Left to right: A menorah that had been in Arlette Baker's family for centuries. A child's displaced person pass, or Kinderausweis, issued by the French in 1945 to Steven Adler. (The red J signified Jew, and the last name, Israel, was given to all Jewish males.) Yellow armband with star of David worn by Abraham Amaterstein. John Langwell's armband from Terezin (or Theresienstadt), the camp where nearly 100,000 Czech Jews perished. Doris Mannsbach's U.S. immigration card, 1940.
Above: Survivor George Weiss shows old family photographs.

THE TESTIMONY OF **SIDONIA LAX**

Date of birth . . . . .June 28, 1927
Place of birth . . . . Przemysl, Poland
Date of interview . . . . July 12, 1994
Location of interview. . . . .Sherman Oaks,
California, USA
Language. . . . . English
Experience. . . . . .Jewish survivor,
Shoah Foundation volunteer

SIDONIA LAX, *who immigrated to the United States in March 1947, remembers her first impressions of New York. After a short visit with a cousin in Chicago, Sidonia left for California. With the help of an uncle and aunt, she settled in Los Angeles.*

I t was March 1947 when I arrived in New York. I slept overnight in HIAS [Hebrew Immigration Aid Society]. I remember like today going [there] at two o'clock a.m. in the middle of New York. It looked like everyone was awake. Everything was open. These were the good times in New York.

[The next day] I went to Chicago by train [to meet] my cousin. It's amazing when I think about it today, the audac-ity, the nerve that I had at that time. I arrive in Chicago, I'm supposed to look for my cousin and his wife. They were going to hold a white handkerchief and I can't find one. I called for a taxi. I had three dollars in my pocket. I had an address in my hand and I arrived at their apartment. They were beside themselves because they couldn't find me at the train station. Finally they arrive at their apartment, and there I stand with my suitcase. They could not believe their eyes, that I found my way in a country without the language, without money, without knowledge of the habits of the country. I was not afraid. I couldn't do it today.

[The next] day I decided I wanted to see Chicago. They gave me a few dollars and I went on the subway and I went to Marshall Field's department store twelve floors high. I went from floor to floor, I spent hours there. After that I proceeded to launch into the nightclub. I didn't know it was a nightclub and they're laughing about it until today.

I was there for one week and proceeded to California. Here my uncle and my aunt had me registered in the local high school. I went to school and cried plenty because I didn't know enough English and I couldn't find my bus stop and I got an F on an assignment. I wrote on the wrong subject. But all of that is history now. ∎

LEFT: *Immigration document from 1947, when Sidonia entered the United States.*
ABOVE: *Speaking with students at Burbank High School, Burbank, California, in 2000.*

testify. Not always, though: some hesitantly voiced reservations about their father or mother reliving such painful times.

Survivors were also encouraged to assemble photographs and memorabilia—scrapbooks, clippings, awards, letters, official documents, clothing, or other artifacts from the period—to document on camera. These artifacts in themselves constitute an enormous, affecting, and valuable archive of the survivors' life and times, including family portraits dating to the nineteenth century. Many of those portraits depicted the survivors' own parents or other relatives and friends who did not survive—and so, like speaking their names aloud during the interview, capturing these images on tape was a way to memorialize the lost. This image archive, itself a significant historical resource, totals more than half a million items.

The Shoah Foundation's practice of including family members on camera came under some criticism. Some Holocaust experts felt that this improperly shifted the focus of Holocaust reflection away from death and toward survival; that the image of a happy family somehow did an injustice to the millions who perished. As a journalist from *Der Spiegel* wrote in a 1996 article, "Those who only want to see the traumatized and wish to hold on to the images of skeletons created from the misery of spring 1945 can only regard as frivolous the presentations of Holocaust victims as comfortable pensioners in the bosom of their family in Florida."

Foundation leaders find great injustice in this view, which they believe to be

ABOVE: Survivor Eva Behar being interviewed on July 26, 2012.

based on an inaccurate impression of the Shoah Foundation and its archive. "We have only those who lived," says Kim Simon. "But to imply that having children on camera presents just the happy families misrepresents the huge breadth of postwar experience contained in the testimonies."

For most viewers and users of the Visual History Archive, from high schoolers to Holocaust scholars, the final embedding of the survivor in the context of family and physical mementos adds rich layers of meaning. For those who gave testimony, it helped normalize and lend reassurance to what could undeniably be a difficult or frightening process. The presence of loved ones and life's artifacts at this climactic moment validated in a most profound way their decision to revisit terrible moments from their past.

FAMILY DYNAMICS

Some of the family moments at the end of testimonies reveal deeper family dynamics. I was astonished to find instances where the children of survivors spoke frankly to their parents—on camera or via audiotape or letters—about intensely ambivalent feelings of love and anger, or their difficult experiences of growing up with the legacy of the Holocaust etched into the minds, bodies, and behaviors of their parents. These moments are profoundly evocative and intellectually priceless: irreplaceable vistas into the lives of survivors and their families." —*Sean Fields, senior lecturer in historical studies, University of Cape Town*

OPENING HEARTS

Shoah Foundation guidelines instructed interviewers to be sure to document all the names and places mentioned, to obtain the survivor's signature on a release, and to follow up with a phone call a day or two after the taping. The guidelines remind interviewers, "They will certainly be thinking about you and the time you spent together."

Certainly they did. Survivors who gave testimony to the archive were deeply affected by the experience. Some suffered regret and a small few contacted the foundation asking to withdraw their testimony. One man, recalled regional coordinator Neelee Cymbal in the Los Angeles office, "had a nightmare because he thought the Ukrainians would come and harm his family." His interviewer managed to allay his concerns. As many survivors had never shared their stories, it's not surprising that such reluctance surfaced, either during or after the interview. To help ease the emotional impact, the Shoah Foundation made psychological resources available to survivors everywhere, through a variety of individuals and organizations.

As previously mentioned, each interviewee also received a letter of thanks from Steven Spielberg for contributing testimony and—most important—a copy

THE TESTIMONY OF **JACOB (JACK) ROSENBERG**

Date of birth: . . . . August 8, 1922
Place of birth: . . . . Lodz, Poland
Date of interview:. . . . . September 9, 1996
Location of interview: . . . . Melbourne, Australia
Language: . . . . English
Experience: . . . . Jewish survivor

JACK ROSENBERG *describes his arrival with his family members at Auschwitz-Birkenau. He remembers being separated from them. He shares a haunting poem he wrote about his loved ones who perished in the camp.*

The Germans knew how to create the chaos and the panic. [When] the doors were opened, [it was] *"Raus, raus, raus!"* ["Get out, get out, get out!"], and they had the dogs, and everybody was petrified. It was terrible. People were jumping from the trains . . . this was to terrorize, you know, not to give the people a chance to think what's taking place. They planned chaos. That's what they did. And it worked.

And then they lined up, men separate, women separate, and everybody had to stand and mention only your age. And according to this, you were given life or death. I describe [what happened] in my poem:

On the thirteenth date of the month,
after a journey of tears and sweat,
my family and I arrived
to Germany's kingdom of death.
I remember our last embrace,
mother breaking down.
What will happen to the children?
Will I ever see you, my son?
Oh, I know what happened to the
     children.
I know what became of them all,
but to keep what is left of my sanity,
there are scenes I refuse to recall.
The scenes in stony bunkers,
the last pleas for breath,
the smell of gas,
the eerie silence,
death.

But in the night,
there where the pit is still a flame,
I hear them calling my name,
my name, my shame.
I once had a mother and father,
two sisters in their prime of life,
Edith, the gentle dove,
and Pola, the rebel in strife.
I also had two nieces,
little girls of six and four,
one with a windowless basement,
the other with a lock on the door.
Now I have only ashes
and an everlasting sigh.
And in the twilight hours,
a mother's cry.

That's how it was. ■

And then they lined up, men separate, women separate, and everybody had to stand and mention only your age. And according to this, you were given life or death.

LEFT: *Jacob and his wife, Esther, in Marseille, 1945, just before immigrating to Australia.*

of the interview (first on VHS tape, later on DVD). "Nothing was more powerful in enlisting more survivors to give testimony," believes Kim Simon, "than this simple gesture of giving back to the people who had given so much of themselves."

In turn, the interview experience, and the follow-up, elicited an outpouring of thanks from survivors and their families. Hundreds of survivors sent letters of gratitude to Steven Spielberg. After videotaping their testimonies, Rita and Sam Starkman, both survivors of Auschwitz-Birkenau, wrote, "You opened hearts locked up for fifty years. We feel free again. We fulfilled promises we made when we were lying among the dead—that if we survived, we would tell what happened. Never again!"

> **"We fulfilled promises we made when we were lying among the dead—that if we survived, we would tell what happened."**
>
> —Rita and Sam Starkman, survivors of Auschwitz-Birkenau, in a letter to Steven Spielberg about giving testimony

Most of those interviewed—especially those who had held back their stories even from their families—felt afterward that a great weight had been lifted from them. In a letter to Spielberg, Harold Gordon, a survivor of Auschwitz-Birkenau and Dachau, wrote of how interviewer Renée Firestone (herself a survivor) and a cameraman spent nearly a full day at his home to record his testimony. "For many weeks I feared that day, knowing how painful it would be to stir up memories laid dormant for decades. Mrs. Firestone was as gentle as an angel . . . while leading me through the interview. . . . I felt a rush of release at the conclusion, feeling rejuvenated and restored."

Many survivors praised their interviewing team. Stefania Teichman, who survived three forced labor camps including Krakow-Plaszow, noted how well the process was organized, "but beyond that, I was taken aback by the extraordinary care they took for my comfort and sensibilities." Teichman also wrote to thank Spielberg "for the opportunity to fulfill a promise given over fifty years [ago] . . . to my cousin Sylvia to tell the world what happened if I survived the Holocaust. Until now . . . there was no avenue for someone like me to do so. With little formal education I didn't write books like some did and I didn't have the resources to build memorials like some did. So I thank you for opening this road to me and making this journey possible."

ABOVE: *Jack Welner, survivor of the Lodz ghetto, Auschwitz-Birkenau, Dachau, and a death march, with his interviewer, Lori Goldberg.*

Letters from the next generation were just as heartfelt. Tamara Gorosh described her sadness at having learned so little of her father's wartime experience before his death. But, she wrote, "My father's younger brother, Samuel Rosen, gave his oral testimony and . . . I recently watched the tape with my mother. We sat holding hands and letting our tears flow as we learned the tale of survival and loss. I was shocked to learn of how my grandmother, Rose Tamara, after whom I am named, was killed; I was amazed at the twists and turns of events that enabled the rest of my father's immediate family to survive; and I was so proud of my father's strength and heroism, without which no members of his family would have survived."

Leta Greenstein shared the story of seeing the tape of her parents' testimony at their fiftieth anniversary gathering (Polish Jews, they were married in a displaced persons camp in Germany), and thanks Spielberg "on behalf of our family and the thousands of other families who . . . have these cherished tapes to pass on to the following generations."

As in the latter two cases, the arrival of the taped interview proved a valuable facilitator for many families who could view it together. Others, however, placed the tape on the shelf to await a future occasion. Even today, many children of survivors are summoning the courage to watch their parents' testimonies.

Interviewers, too, were moved to write about the life-changing nature of their encounters with survivors. Jennifer Blum-Cronin, based in Minnesota, said that she echoed "every one of the survivors I have interviewed in expressing my

ABOVE: *Survivor Sara Shapiro and family members. Seated, left to right, Eddie Shapiro, Karen and Mickey Shapiro, Sara, and Sara's husband, Asa Shapiro; standing, Margie and Steven Shapiro.*

thanks. I cannot express fully enough what a blessing this project has been for me, and how it has changed my life. As a woman of half-German, half-Jewish descent, it has enabled me to learn more about one side of my background while providing an opportunity to atone for atrocities committed by the other. . . . The Shoah project allows people to meet on a spiritual plane that, in ordinary life, is rarely accessible. I cannot tell you how many times I have left survivors' homes after interviews, having been honored by being the recipient of their stories, their courage and generosity, and cried."

It was common for interviewers and regional coordinators to form enduring bonds with "their" survivors. Many kept in touch by mail, phone, and visits; the foundation helped this effort by holding periodic reunions of survivors, interviewers, and regional coordinators. A few romances were even kindled by the encounters. Interviewer Anne Bernard had a sixteen-year relationship with a man she interviewed.

> ## REMEMBER TO LAUGH
>
> Humor was an unexpected but necessary characteristic you needed for this job, because when you heard heart-wrenching stories about what adult and children had witnessed and survived all day everyday, you needed to remember to laugh. Survivors told us all the time that humor got them through the worst of days.
> —*Maura Minsky, regional coordinator, New York*

"We both found a new life together. I, a third-generation American and he, a yeshiva-trained former Belgian child survivor who, along with his twin brother, had been saved by a priest. He spoke four languages, I spoke English. He was courtly, I a fast-paced New Yorker. Though our offices were only four blocks from each other, our paths would not have crossed were it not for the foundation."

The impact of giving testimony tended to be profound and long-lasting. For some who told their stories, the effects remained private and personal, perhaps simply reshaping family relationships. Other survivors, though, found a sense of mission in continuing to share their experiences—in their communities, in the wider world of Holocaust remembrance, and especially in classrooms, which the foundation encouraged and facilitated. Historian Michael Berenbaum wrote about the "unique moral authority" the survivors carried, and the force of their ability to communicate their struggles against persecution.

■

By the end of 1995, the gathering of testimonies was nearing its peak of production, with some three hundred interviews being conducted each week around the world and almost nine thousand completed—on the way to an eventual 105,000 hours of testimony. In addition, the first testimonies had recently been taken from a political prisoner, and a homosexual survivor, expanding the range of experience represented in the collection.

“ Until I told my story, I was deeply and continuously worried that when I pass away there will be no record of what I saw and what I learned in the Holocaust. Now my children, grandchildren, and children of members of my family have my testimony. [This] relieved me of the heaviest psychological burden that I carried. ” —Adam Heller, survivor, Austin, Texas

While collecting testimonies was Spielberg's central focus, he was all too aware that it would be some years before technology could facilitate distribution of the archive in the way he envisioned. But he was committed to making sure that the testimonies weren't simply collected, but that they were seen by millions. The solution was a natural one: he was a filmmaker and the organization's founding directors had backgrounds in documentary filmmaking. So, with a growing archive of testimonies to work with, Moll and Beallor began to feature them in documentary films, fulfilling one of Spielberg's earliest aspirations for the foundation.

The copy of the videotape sent to the survivor was one of several made as soon as the original arrived in Los Angeles from the field office. Others were destined for use in making the archive broadly and deeply accessible. As early as 1996, the Los Angeles–based cataloguing team started to build a list of key terms around which the testimonies would be catalogued and indexed, and the technology team began to develop the computer software to make this possible. While the collecting of testimony would go on for another five years—to Branko Lustig's fifty thousandth and beyond—the foundation was preparing to move into its next major phase. ■

RIGHT: *Bill Steinberg in the Shoah Foundation production department, September 1998.*

212

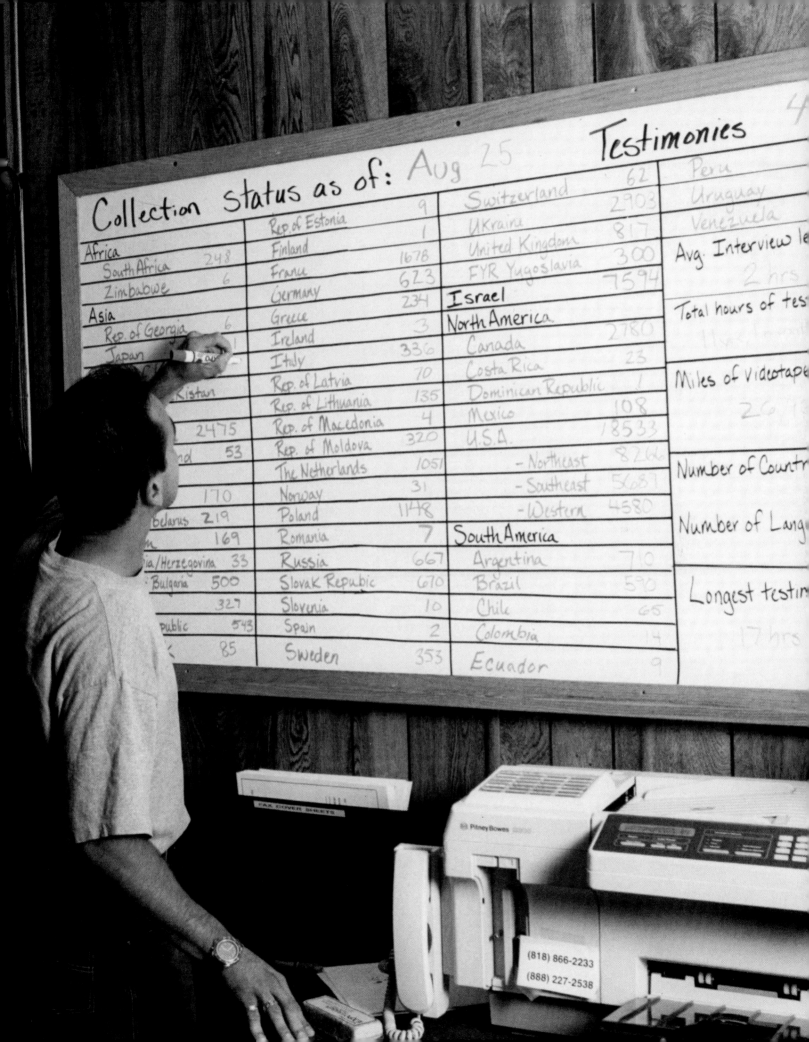

BUILDING AN INTELLIGENT ARCHIVE

They were precious cargo, the interview tapes that poured into the Shoah Foundation's Los Angeles headquarters starting in late 1994. Each represented many hours of intensive work by the field team and regional office. More important, each embodied the life history of a human being who had seen some of the worst and best aspects of our species—along with that person's hopes for and injunctions to future generations. They were the raw material and raison d'être of the organization. So what happened to them once they arrived?

"We had to think that all through very carefully," says June Beallor. "At one point we brought in people from the Rand Corporation to help us analyze the process, but they proposed a long-term study, which wasn't feasible. So James and I took the most direct approach. I remember saying, 'OK, I am the videotape—what happens to me?' These tapes were the heart of our work, and if they weren't properly handled and preserved at the beginning, we would have nothing today."

Beallor and James Moll devised a schematic to track each tape as it came in from a field office with its supporting documentation. It went first to a collection management area, where it was logged in and barcoded for future tracking—not only each set of interview tapes but every associated flyer, production report, interview summary, and release form, eventually adding up to more than a million pieces of media. The tape was copied for various destinations at the foundation—

LEFT: A foundation staff member moving videotapes into storage.

and for the survivor—then digitized using the technology of the day. No video was ever edited, as that would render it historically invalid. (Each original tape, by the way, still exists—held in secure storage on the East Coast, with multiple backup copies in different locations.)

Beyond the initial, important steps taken to safeguard and clearly identify each tape, many stops remained along the journey of each testimony. How it would be physically handled and preserved in perpetuity, how its content would be made accessible, in what form it would be distributed, and in what ways it would be used to advance the foundation's mission—all this remained to be discovered.

NEW MEDIA FOR THE MESSAGE

If the point of testimony is to individualize Holocaust history and make it personally meaningful for others (especially young people), it might seem paradoxical that technology—something that could be characterized as 'cold and lifeless'—would have an important part to play in bringing history to life. —SAM GUSTMAN, CHIEF TECHNOLOGY OFFICER

Every testimony was recorded on videotape stock in the Betacam SP format, chosen because it was the most widely available standard of the day for broadcast-quality video. The production experts at the Shoah Foundation, starting with Steven Spielberg, wanted to ensure that their interview footage would shine in any means of viewing. Beta SP came in thirty-minute cassettes, and videographers were directed to use them liberally—never allow the tape to run out mid-interview, always have a fresh tape ready to go.

Sam Gustman, who described the human network of field staff as the foundation's first "system," says that the second system was built to receive and process these tapes—235,000 of them by the end. (A 2.5-hour interview, the average length, consumed five tapes.) After being checked in on arrival, the next stop for each field tape was the tape transfer area, a custom-built video processing system. There, four copies of each master were created simultaneously on one of sixteen automated workstations; the operation could handle about sixty-four tape transfers daily. Each transfer was automatically tracked through an e-mail–based log

ABOVE: Videotapes of interviews waiting to be copied and digitized. OPPOSITE: One of the sixteen automated transfer stations.

THE TESTIMONY OF **PHILIP MARKOWICZ**

Date of birth . . . . March 15, 1924
Place of birth. . . . . Przerab, Poland
Date of interview . . . . . . January 29, 1998
Location of interview. . . . . .Aventura,
Florida, USA
Language. . . . . English
Experience. . . . . .Jewish survivor

PHILIP MARKOWICZ *recalls a miracle that happened while he and his brother Henry were being transported to the Flossenburg concentration camp in Germany. With his handmade knife, he was able to enlarge a hole on the floor of the train, through which a bystander placed a sandwich in his hand. He credits this sandwich with helping save their lives.*

We were going [on] the train . . . and people died in the train. A miracle happened [which] I would like to mention because this actually saved our lives. I had in Auschwitz made myself a piece of knife [though I was] not supposed to. I hid it in my jacket and I kept it with me . . . to have it. And then I cut out . . .

Interviewer: How did you make a knife?

By taking a piece of iron . . . you bend back and forth until it breaks. I had a short piece, no one can see it. I cut on the edge, over and over, day in and day out, day in and day out, sharpened it [on a stone] just so I could have something.

When I was in the train, there were openings that much [Philip gestures a

small space] at the bottom. I was laying on the floor and I kept cutting it. I was very good at wood cutting, and [with a hole] I just had more air to look out.

And then a miracle happened. Somehow the train stopped for a long, long time at night. At daybreak a passenger train came by and then stopped right in front of me, [and there was]

a door to go down. I saw people [go] down. I could only see their feet. I couldn't see anything else. I put my hand through [the hole], and somebody put a sandwich in my hand.

Me and my brother Henry survived because of that piece of bread. It was unbelievable such a thing should happen.

And I grabbed it. It was bread with fat, I don't know what kind of fat was smeared on—goose fat or chicken fat. But I hid it hard right away, and me and my brother Henry survived because of that piece of bread. I wish I could find who did it. This person must have been an angel sent from heaven to save me. I am choked now from what happened. It was unbelievable such a thing should happen. ∎

CENTER: Philip's great-grandfather, Herschel Litman, and great-grandmother, Rachel Litman, Belchatow, Poland, c. late 19th century. ABOVE: Philip's family in Toledo, Ohio, 1995. Left to right: Daniel Markowicz (grandson), Andrea Markowicz (granddaughter), Allen Markowicz (son), Hinda Markowicz (daughter-in-law). Nina Markowicz (granddaughter), Steven Markowicz (grandson).

and fault-reporting system. Because the workstations tapped into the foundation's main database, an operator could efficiently add the survivor's identifying information at the start of the tape.

The four copies included one on VHS for the survivor, another VHS copy for the cataloguing department, a digital Betacam version as a protection copy, and a digitally compressed version. This last one was destined for a 150-terabyte robotic retrieval system—essentially a pair of supercomputers—that took up two rooms. Designed in partnership with Silicon Graphics, these twin servers (dubbed Bubbe and Zayde by some staffers) formed a robotic digital library that initially enabled authorized users to access and navigate the archive.

"Our goal has always been to ensure that the testimonies of Holocaust survivors and other witnesses will still be available a hundred years from now," says Gustman. "All media degrades over time. Conservative estimates give shelf lives of fifty years for film, twenty years for videotape, five years for hard drives, three years for data tape, and only two years for DVDs before age-related 'data rot' causes visible damage." He was speaking at a later time, when DVDs had replaced CD-ROMs as the most popular "hard media" for storage, but he and his colleagues had to grapple with this reality from the start. The precious tapes would have a relatively short shelf life; they had to be backed up in multiple formats.

Any archive of film or videotape must concern itself with these issues, but they had a special urgency for the Shoah Foundation. Given the sensitivity of the mate-

rial, the sheer scale of the collection, and the promise that had been made to keep the testimonies in perpetuity, the staff knew that their archiving and preservation methods had to overcome many barriers to success. They had to work smart and fast, and right at the cutting edge of digital technology.

UNLOCKING THE TESTIMONIES

Protecting the integrity of the tapes and their content was always a paramount goal. But surpassing this—sometimes even clashing with it—was Spielberg's preeminent purpose for the Visual History Archive: making it broadly available worldwide as a means of educating people away from the forces that spawn prejudice and can lead to genocide. So, while the collecting of testimonies was moving into full production and the first tapes were being logged into the archive, an important copy made of each tape was the one provided to the foundation's staff of cataloguers.

Opposite: The tape robot in the Shoah Foundation offices, which provided users with access to testimonies stories on large servers, c. 2000.
Above: Sam Gustman, chief technology officer, shows visitors the technology behind the preservation and restoration of testimonies.

THE TESTIMONY OF **PHILIP MARKOWICZ**

Date of birth . . . . March 15, 1924
Place of birth . . . . Przerab, Poland
Date of interview . . . . . . January 29, 1998
Location of interview . . . . Aventura,
Florida, USA
Language . . . . English
Experience . . . . Jewish survivor

PHILIP MARKOWICZ *recalls a miracle that happened while he and his brother Henry were being transported to the Flossenburg concentration camp in Germany. With his handmade knife, he was able to enlarge a hole on the floor of the train, through which a bystander placed a sandwich in his hand. He credits this sandwich with helping save their lives.*

We were going [on] the train . . . and people died in the train. A miracle happened [which] I would like to mention because this actually saved our lives. I had in Auschwitz made myself a piece of knife [though I was] not supposed to. I hid it in my jacket and I kept it with me . . . to have it. And then I cut out . . .

Interviewer: How did you make a knife?

By taking a piece of iron . . . you bend back and forth until it breaks. I had a short piece, no one can see it. I cut on the edge, over and over, day in and day out, day in and day out, sharpened it [on a stone] just so I could have something.

When I was in the train, there were openings that much [Philip gestures a

small space] at the bottom. I was laying on the floor and I kept cutting it. I was very good at wood cutting, and [with a hole] I just had more air to look out.

And then a miracle happened. Somehow the train stopped for a long, long time at night. At daybreak a passenger train came by and then stopped right in front of me, [and there was]

a door to go down. I saw people [go] down. I could only see their feet. I couldn't see anything else. I put my hand through [the hole], and somebody put a sandwich in my hand.

Me and my brother Henry survived because of that piece of bread. It was unbelievable such a thing should happen.

And I grabbed it. It was bread with fat, I don't know what kind of fat was smeared on—goose fat or chicken fat. But I hid it hard right away, and me and my brother Henry survived because of that piece of bread. I wish I could find who did it. This person must have been an angel sent from heaven to save me. I am choked now from what happened. It was unbelievable such a thing should happen. ■

CENTER: *Philip's great-grandfather, Herschel Litman, and great-grandmother, Rachel Litman, Belchatow, Poland, c. late 19th century.* ABOVE: *Philip's family in Toledo, Ohio, 1995. Left to right: Daniel Markowicz (grandson), Andrea Markowicz (granddaughter), Allen Markowicz (son), Hinda Markowicz (daughter-in-law). Nina Markowicz (granddaughter), Steven Markowicz (grandson).*

Theirs was a task that had never before been undertaken on such a mammoth scale: how do you make 105,000 hours of personal testimony accessible, intelligible, and useful to end users at all levels of education and computer proficiency? How do you map a life story that touches on many topics and themes, lists scores of names, references major historical events—and discern how it relates to fifty thousand other such stories? If you're interested in, say, Jews from the Warsaw ghetto who escaped into hiding, or the fate of children sent to England by their parents in eastern Europe, where do you start looking in the testimonies? Unlike a book that's organized into readily accessible (that is, indexed) chapters and pages, a videotape is very difficult to search for particular information.

Transcribing every interview was not feasible—it would take far too long for the entire collection. A single two-hour interview would take several days to transcribe accurately. More to the point, the archive is intentionally visual: watching and listening to survivors tell their stories is a wholly different experience than reading a transcript. "By their nature, viewing the testimonies demands a commitment of time and energy to fully engage," notes Stephen Smith, who became the foundation's executive director in 2009. Adds Karen Jungblut, director of research and documentation, "There is so much nonverbal information communicated that gets lost on the printed page."

And so the foundation devoted extraordinary efforts to making the testimonies searchable through indexing and cataloguing. New indexing tools were developed by bringing together scholars of the Holocaust, oral history, and sociology, along with information management experts and software engineers. They drew on existing information management and library science protocols, as well as new approaches, to create a kind of searchable access unprecedented at the time. On the technical side, digitizing the tapes was essential, not only to preserve the information but as the first step toward making it searchable. Then the challenge, says Gustman, was finding a way to handle video as data, and marry it with other data. "Since there was nothing out there like this, we had to figure out step by step what it would look like, how to implement it," says Jungblut. "It was five steps ahead, three steps back."

Gustman describes how he got involved. "In 1994, when the founders were looking for the right kind of technology to drive this process, someone had the idea to

ABOVE: Karen Jungblut, director of research (in front) with, left to right: former educational programs project director Sherry Bard, visiting Italian archivists Lucilla Garofalo and Micaela Procaccia , and Kim Simon, managing director.

look at GIS [geographic information system] mapping, and it was the right idea," he says. "Databases work by associative relationships, and in this type of mapping you're looking at relationships among geographical features, so you can ask a question and get an answer. Putting it simply, we needed something that allowed us to treat video like maps." A mutual friend led the founders to Gustman, who had been working in mapping for the United States Army Corps of Engineers. "It took us a year to figure out how to apply the principles to video data, and another three years to develop and launch the system," he says.

Meanwhile the foundation was staffing up its cataloguing department with people who wanted a chance to contribute to this innovative project. An ad that ran in campus and other publications around Southern California sought "full-time cataloguers for both the day and night shifts . . . individuals with an undergraduate degree or a strong background in European history or Judaic studies . . . should possess strong writing and research skills and be prepared to make an extraordinary time commitment to the foundation."

Thus a team that grew to sixty people was assembled to comb through the testimonies, beginning in late 1995. They used a proprietary interface developed by Gustman and his team that enabled videotaped interviews to be indexed with great specificity, depth, and scope, reflecting the diversity and breadth of experience in each account. Some cataloguers proved adept at the work; others weren't meticulous enough—or were overly cautious and took too long. Some found the experience of viewing testimony hour after hour, day in and day out, too emotionally draining; others were inspired and energized. Some stayed a few months and then moved on; others stayed with the foundation and moved into larger roles—like Karen Jungblut, who started as a cataloguer and ended up running the department. Like their colleagues on the IT side, most went at their work with great passion, and found ways to leaven their long days or nights with camaraderie and humor.

KEYWORDS AND CATALOGUERS

Each cataloguer began the job with two weeks of intensive group training with seasoned staff and consulting historians. All new recruits attended lectures by historians and survivor volunteers, learned about the technology, watched documentaries, and got acquainted with the reference materials they would come to rely on, such as the

A NEW WAY TO DOCUMENT HISTORY

The organization brought together technology, library science, and academia. We had a once in a lifetime opportunity to develop a cataloguing methodology, a custom lexicon, and technology that would change the way historical events would be documented, indexed and shared in the future.

—*Kim Beauchamp, an early cataloguing department director*

THE TESTIMONY OF **ESTHER CLIFFORD**

Date of birth . . . . .December 5, 1920
Place of birth. . . . . Munich, Germany
Date of interview . . . . .November 3, 1996
Location of interview. . . . . Cranbury,
New Jersey, USA
Language: . . . . English
Experience: . . . . .Jewish survivor

After ESTHER CLIFFORD's father was denied his annual business permit to operate his shop in Germany, the family redoubled its efforts to emigrate. In her testimony, Esther describes how the family searched through a New York City phone book, spending precious time and money trying to find Jewish Americans to help them obtain immigration affidavits for America.

I remember that [my parents] started to take the situation seriously when my father couldn't continue working because times got very bad. They had a very hard time. They just didn't have enough money to pay the rent, to pay for food. We all pitched in, but it wasn't enough. And that's when they said that we have to go someplace. They started going to the American consulate to [obtain] a quota number because they wanted to go to America.

> I remember my mother saying, "I'll go to the jungle if I could just go anyplace and just live on bread and water." But we just couldn't go anyplace. We had no place to go to.

My brother once brought home a telephone book from New York. He came home with this heavy book. We had never seen a telephone book like that in our life. And we all sat around that book looking for Jewish names— Levy, Horowitz, all the Jewish names. And we spent most of the little money that  we had writing letters to Americans, begging them to give us an affidavit. You needed an affidavit in order to immigrate to America. And so we always said that we all had professions, that we can sew and do all kinds of things. We even enclosed a reply stamp, so it wouldn't cost them any money.

We had a few responses, but no affidavits. In 1937, you could get out of Germany, but it seemed that one country after the other closed their doors. I remember it was very hard to go anyplace. I remember my mother saying, "I'll go to the jungle if I could just go anyplace and just live on bread and water." But we just couldn't go anyplace. We had no place to go to. ■

LEFT: Esther (third from right) outside her father's store, c. 1923. ABOVE: Esther's brother, Leo, and sister, Rosa, on an outing in Frankfurt, 1935. TOP: Esther with her husband, Rudi.

66 Great things often happen as a result of many people doing the small but difficult jobs, and in our case it is the job of preserving history. 99 —Joshua Frey, cataloguer

THE TECHNO-SCRIBES

I am somewhat numb when I am here at work, listening to the interviews. The stories, though, follow me outside. When I see a freight train, I imagine the boxcars to be stuffed with people. Once, looking up at a hospital, I pictured soldiers throwing newborn babies out of the windows. And inside a synagogue, I [once] tried to imagine the doors being locked, the people trapped inside, and the building set on fire. . . . It is still hard for me to conceive that such horror is possible.
—*David Orenstein, cataloguer*

It's hard to know what to say about this place without being massively trivial on the one hand or massively melodramatic on the other. . . . You worry about the methodology, the keywords, the height of your chair, why it's too hot in the trailer, drinking too much coffee. . . . Underneath all of that and beyond it are those moments in the testimonies that remind you that all of the above is not important in any way, compared to what you are hearing." —*Crispin Brooks, cataloguer, later curator of the Visual History Archive within the USC Libraries*

Imagine if you could press on the page of a book about slavery and could then witness slaves talking about the moment in Africa they were torn from their families and taken to the Americas. . . . I think about other stories of inhumanity and destruction that have been passed down to us . . . through oral and written traditions. We are the techno-scribes using the tools of our age to document this extraordinary event of our time. —*Nadine Kadey, cataloguer*

ABOVE: Left to right, indexers Deborah Schlaff, Ita Gordon, and staff member Jessica Wiederhorn. BELOW: David Orenstein (left), Peter Ruskin (right), Zsuzsa Aradi (left rear), and Lauren Chevlen, indexing English-language testimonies, late 1990s.

Encyclopedia Judaica, Encyclopedia of the Holocaust, the International Tracing Service (which lists known Nazi camps and prisons), foreign language dictionaries, and map resources. Then, under close supervision, they were put to work.

To index each testimony, staffers took biographical information from the pre-interview questionnaire—birthplace, education, family members, prewar occupation, religious affiliation, ghetto and concentration camp experiences, resistance activities, and postwar life—and entered it in the main database. This entry would supplement the indexing of the videotaped testimony. Some information would be available right on the video; much remained in the background but was accessible to anyone searching the archive. This step was vital in making connections among survivors with similar experiences.

The painstaking work of indexing a video archive of this complexity and scale had not been done before and required careful thought. Indexing involves breaking down the entire interview by keywords, subjects, and phrases for later retrieval. The cataloguers (later called indexers) loaded the interview into a workstation, where the video appeared in one corner of the segmented screen.

INTIMATE HISTORY

With videotaped testimony, I'm moving away from the broad outlines and big cities of the history I studied in school and into the intimacy of oral history: small towns, family life, and amazing varieties of Holocaust experiences. Testimonies are very useful in the reconstruction of local history; often, few written records survive from small towns. And because the Nazis destroyed Yiddish culture and many of the towns in which the European Jews lived, the survivors' memories and photographs are often all that is left.

—*Kirsten Anderson, cataloguer*

They would watch the entire interview, mark off segments a few minutes long, and "tag" their content—key its place with digital time codes, like page numbers in a book—using an ever-evolving set of indexing terms. These "electronic hooks" would allow eventual users of the archive to locate and access precise moments in the video testimony. That set of keywords and phrases, based on names, geographic locations, experiences, and dates, grew in volume as ever more testimonies were indexed; ultimately the *USC Shoah Foundation Institute Thesaurus* would contain more than fifty thousand terms. (See sidebar, page 229.)

Deciding what constituted an indexable segment was primary. Originally, cataloguers would identify three- to five-minute segments—they looked for a coherent narrative or vignette, and then for crucial facts on which to "hook" the index terms. Where is the survivor at that point (a city, a ghetto, a transport)? What year is it? How is the person living (in hiding, imprisoned in a camp)? What

FOLLOWING PAGES: The cataloguing department in full production.

PERFECTIONISTS

It was a colossal, urgent mission. That realization informed every last detail of our work. Apprehending a flawed world, we became perfectionists at indexing it. Afterward the stories persist and reverberate, many with unutterable horrors, but plenty more with tenderness. —*Chaim Singer Frankes*

THE TESTIMONY OF **DAVID ABRAMS**

Date of birth . . . . December 8, 1928
Place of birth. . . . . Dej, Romania
Date of interview . . . . . .November 4, 1997
Location of interview. . . . . Brooklyn,
                                     New York, USA
Language . . . . English
Experience . . . . .Jewish survivor

When DAVID ABRAMS *shared his testimony with the Shoah Foundation, it was the first time in more than fifty years that he had spoken of his experience as a survivor. After he was liberated from Gunskirchen, a subcamp of Mauthausen, David (then sixteen) spent time in various displaced persons camps and finally returned home to Dej, Romania. He describes what he found on arriving there: that three of his sisters had also survived but that everyone else in his family had died in the camps.*

I finally got home to my hometown in the middle of the night after weeks of really going from one train to another, from one city to another. There was a welcoming committee from the town. Every night a train pulled in, they came to welcome survivors. Sure enough, they came and sang and were happy. And when they asked me to go on the wagon to go back to town, I refused to go with them, 'cause I wanted to walk on my own. I wanted to go to my house.

I start calling out names of my family, like I expected an answer. "I'm home! I'm home from school!" And it didn't take me long to realize there's no answer, nobody there.

So I walked until two o'clock in the morning. It was quite a distance in the dark. In the middle of the night, I [arrived at] my house where I lived— Number 9 Mihaly Street. I start calling out names of my family, like I expected

an answer. "I'm home! I'm home from school!" And it didn't take me long to realize there's no answer, nobody there.

So I woke up one of my neighbors. I asked him if he knew anything. I told him I just arrived and [asked if he knew] what happened to my family. So he told me that nobody came back, [except for one sister. He] told me where she stayed. So I went there and I knocked on the door. I yelled out my sister's name, Irene Hershkowitz. This was my favorite sister . . . [she] was three years older than me [and] took me everywhere. I adored [her]. I called up, "Irene! Irene!"

When she heard my voice, I heard screaming and crying. She came down to meet me and brought me upstairs for the night to stay there. It was really some reunion that I'll never forget. Then later on, I [found] two more sisters. So, me and my sisters [were all that was] left in the whole family. ■

ABOVE: *Clockwise from top: 1935 family photo, with David at far right; his paternal grandparents Sarah Abraham and Yeheskel Abraham, c. 1910; with his wife, Sheila, in 1981.*

is happening—something to do with food, or clothing, or a family interaction? Cataloguers were well trained in what to look for, yet choosing where to segment the interview could still be quite subjective. During training, says cataloguer Kirsten Anderson, "We practiced how to create segments and match up keywords with topics." They also learned about proposing keywords: if cataloguers couldn't find an appropriate keyword in the existing list, they would suggest a new one, which then went though a rigorous approval process before going into the thesaurus.

Cataloguers would also corroborate information in the testimony against that in the pre-interview questionnaire, adding relevant names and experience to the

MINUTE BY MINUTE

Through indexing hundreds of testimonies in Portuguese, Spanish, Yiddish, and English, I have had the rare privilege to see the breadth of humanity as well as the detail of each person's life. Minute by minute, the keywords provide a way for families, scholars, and students to find wonderful moments of insight and truth. — *Ita Gordon, cataloguer*

BUILDING THE THESAURUS

To most of us, a thesaurus simply means Roget's, the famous reference book that allows us to track down (if we're lucky) that perfect word we're seeking. But there are many kinds of thesauri—or "controlled vocabularies" —in many specialized fields; each attempts to render scientifically the profoundly subjective endeavor of describing something. "Creating keywords was our way to counterbalance the big human variable of having sixty-plus individuals doing the work of cataloguing and indexing," says Karen Jungblut.

Containing thousands of genocide-related concepts and experiences, the USC Shoah Foundation Thesaurus is one of the first of its kind. It lists the indexing terms used to describe the foundation's video testimonies and arranges them hierarchically under broad headings. These terms are assigned directly to digital time codes within testimonies where the specific topics are discussed, in much the same way that book index entries specify the page numbers where topics are covered.

The thesaurus evolved over time and grew in size as the testimonies were indexed. The great majority of indexing terms were geographic: cities, villages, and other locations—"Oswiecim (Poland)," for example—as well as place names such as "Treblinka (Poland: Concentration Camp)." Maintaining consistency was challenging because the spelling of European place names can vary widely.

While many terms were drawn from existing controlled vocabularies, the depth of content in the Visual History Archive meant that the team had to invent certain indexing terms to facilitate access more precisely. For example, they created experiential terms such as "corpse disposal forced labor" and "intergenerational Holocaust impact" to reflect the tragic commonality of experience brought forth in survivors' testimonies. In another case, a new term grew from an older one: cataloguing supervisor Brian Yates says that the term "reassertion of Jewish identity" (after the war) didn't fit the testimonies of many who had been children during the war and didn't even know they were Jews. "So we had to create the new term 'realization of Jewish identity.'"

Although the indexing of the Holocaust-related testimonies is complete, the thesaurus remains a work in progress and will continue to be refined and updated as needed.

database as needed. And, at the touch of a computer key, they created photo stills of the artifacts shown at the end of each testimony, and wrote captions for them. The result was an electronic scrapbook that researchers could access. This also allowed the reverse: the viewer can select an image, and the system would take him to the segment of video where that picture is talked about on video.

When finished working on an interview—which could take several days—the cataloguer would write a one-page summary of the testimony.

Cataloguing and indexing were guided by principles that aimed to minimize the unavoidable subjectivity of the deeply personal narratives in the archive. Although every act of description is in part subjective, the foundation aimed to leave the task of interpretation to the end user. So even if value judgments and emotionally loaded words may seem appropriate in a context of Nazi persecution, the index terms were meant to be neutral. Keywords were chosen to facilitate access to the testimonies' content, not as commentary on the events of the Holocaust. "Living conditions in the camps," for example, was the neutral phrase applied to survivors' descriptions of the often horrendous conditions they endured. "Keeping editorializing and interpretation to a minimum was partly to make

TOP: Bonnie Samotin, who led the quality assurance team, chooses tapes for her team to review. ABOVE: The indexing interface.

sure that the results would be acceptable for scholarly use," Jungblut explains.

Even while scrupulously following these guidelines, it was impossible for cataloguers not to become involved with the stories of the survivors. Like the interviewers, they would often speak of "my" survivor, and became attached even to the keywords they proposed to capture a survivor's unique experience. "I feel as though I'm on a journey through history from the inside out," wrote Anderson. "By watching and listening, I become each person I meet—from the mother in a ghetto who worries about her family to the child in hiding who waits for the war to end. I find that repeatedly listening to difficult segments . . . can result in sudden flashes of sadness or anger—and vivid dreams—but I accept this because the project is so unique an opportunity to educate the future."

Concurrently with indexing, a separate quality assurance team reviewed samples of testimonies from interviewers, to ensure consistency of method. Quality assurance notes were fed back to the interviewers and videographers, to support them and help them continually improve their work. This multilingual team, which included historian Michael Nutkiewicz and some of the most experienced foundation interviewers and trainers, watched interviews at the Los Angeles headquarters on day and night shifts. The goal was "to find the best and most consistent ways to communicate constructively with the interviewers," says Bonnie Samotin, who led the department. Regional coordinators also relied on the team for recommendations and information about the skills of interviewers in their region.

MOMENTS THAT TELL STORIES

Every minute of every testimony will be part of a segment in the archive. What a cataloguer is looking for are narrative moments that tell stories. Each segment is assigned a place where the survivor happens to be at the time—[for example,] Birkenau. We assign a year if we know it. ... We have experiential terms such as "camp intake procedures"—which refer to such events as the assignment of a camp uniform or the issuing of a tattoo.
— *Bryan Yates, cataloguing supervisor*

Early issues of *PastForward*, the foundation's newsletter, contained a feature called "Interviewer Tips & Techniques"—another way to communicate with the field teams. Its advice covered many bases: "When interviewing survivors from Hungary, remember that many were not affected by the war until 1944." For child survivors, "Questions should be adapted to the age and understanding of the survivor during the war. Evoke the senses—what did you see, hear, feel . . . ?" And, when asking about religious life, "Remember that people did not identify with the labels of today's Jewish movements. . . . For example, do not ask, 'Were you Orthodox?' Instead, begin by asking general questions, such as 'How would you describe your family's religious observance?'"

THE TESTIMONY OF **MIECZYSLAW (MIETEK) PEMPER**

Date of birth . . . . March 24, 1920
Place of birth. . . . . .Krakow, Poland
Date of interview . . . . September 13, 1997
Location of interview. . .Bavaria, Germany
Language. . . . . .German
Experience. . . . . Jewish survivor

MIETEK PEMPER *lived in the Krakow ghetto toward the end of the ghetto liquidation. He was sent to the Plaszow camp and selected by Amon Goeth, the commandant played by Ralph Fiennes in* Schindler's List, *to write his correspondence.*

The people Goeth asked mentioned me, and without being asked myself. I mean I couldn't tell Goeth, "Excuse me, I have to observe you first before I can accept you as my boss." I was completely unsettled [because] I was [immediately] asked to take dictation. Out of fear, I did not dare to interrupt the tyrant during the dictation. Afraid, I silently took stenographic notes, thinking, if something is unclear I will fix it within the letter somehow. But with this murderer I did not dare to say a word, because you never knew if you were allowed to speak.

At the end of the dictation, he then said to me, "Well, if you write as well as you record, then this might work out." This was the highest praise one could

ever get from him. I can remember, the first letters I began to write [for him] were dated March 18, 1943, because I have often thought about that.

I noticed in a letter to his father that he asked him if he was suffering from hay fever again this year. The name of his father was Amon Franz Goeth; the son, who was at our place, Amon Leopold Goeth; his dad's company's name was Franz Goeth and Son—publisher for military and technical literature, Mariahilferstrasse 105, in Vienna. I was in Vienna after the war and found no trace of that company at the address. I also found out that Goeth's father was regarded as a decent merchant, let's say old-school style, not striking in any way, and this son was an only child. He was raised by his aunt, if one could ever raise him. His mother died very early, and he had a special relationship with his father, and he inquired in letters [to him] later on, which I typed, about the well-being of the woman accountant, I be-

lieve her name was Miss Unger, about her health. So, quite ordinary letters, in which no one could ever believe, in what kind of murderous surroundings they were created. And so I started my job working for Goeth.

I did not dare to interrupt the tyrant during the dictation.

In another part of his testimony, Mietek describes how he gathered evidence against Goeth in an effort to protect himself from the commandant's unpredictable violence.

A German secretary, Miss Kochmann, came for two to three hours in the mornings. She was the wife of a much older public prosecutor of the special court in Krakow. Miss Kochmann knew Goeth from the work for an organization which dealt with the incorporation of Russian refugees and Germans from other countries.

And so it happened once, an accident. Miss Kochmann inserted the car-

bon paper upside-down while Goeth was waiting for it very urgently, since he had to attend a meeting in town. He scolded her harshly and she started crying.

So, I helped her by inserting a new stack of paper as soon as Goeth had finally left the office. And I said to her, "That won't happen again, I will help you by preparing full stacks of carbon paper with clips, and I will staple them together for you so that you cannot insert it wrong again!" But the thing I didn't tell her was that I always took a new stack of carbon paper and I read everything what she wrote down in mirror writing. But not because I believed

Opposite: Mietek in Krakow shortly after the war. Top left: Mietek records testimony during the trial against Amon Goeth in August 1946, Krakow. Top right: Mietek (with book) and translator Helena Gavlik at the trial of Nazis accused of crimes at Auschwitz, 1947. The witness (wearing headphones) is the accused Michael Krämer. Right: Mietek (right) with the actor Grzegorz Kwas, who plays him in Schindler's List (see page 132 for details.)

I could use it against Goeth in a trial, no, because I never thought about the fact that I will survive. Because I saw how he always furiously shot [people] and thought he might kill me one day without an excuse. It was connected to the following:

Goeth had an Austrian-Viennese accent, of course, but his was not quite clear, distorted a bit because he had,

I believe, once lived in Bavaria. He mumbled a bit and spoke not quite clearly, especially in the late evening around ten or eleven at night. He also was a diabetic, but he didn't rest, so that in turn he was very tired and spoke even more unclearly. Especially with family names, he never told me how they were spelled, and it really made it very hard for me, because I never knew how to spell them correctly, and one was not allowed to interrupt him during dictation. But with the help of this [mirror] trick I was able to figure out the spelling of those names. He did wonder how I could have known all of [the names] in the trial in 1946. But that's another story. ∎

ARNOLD SPIELBERG STEPS IN

As it approached the puzzle of cataloguing the testimonies, the foundation had a secret weapon: a recently retired computer engineering pioneer who now worked as a consultant to the industry. Among numerous career achievements, he held a patent on an electronic library system. And because he also happened to be the father of Steven Spielberg, he took a strong interest in the challenges the organization faced in making the testimonies searchable.

Arnold Spielberg served as a communications chief in a B-25 squadron in India during World War II, winning a Bronze Star Medal for his innovative contributions. Later he earned a degree in electrical engineering from the University of Cincinnati and in 1949 joined RCA, where he did early work on guidance systems, moving into computer technology when the company did. He went on to work for General Electric, IBM, and Scientific Data Systems in Cincinnati, Phoenix, Detroit, Orange County, San Jose, and elsewhere in the San Francisco Bay Area; his son well recalls the family's peripatetic lifestyle. In addition to designing and patenting the first electronic library system, which searched for data stored on an array of magnetic tapes, Arnold is credited with a number of breakthroughs during his professional career, among them early

guidance systems and computer circuit designs, leading the development of the first business computer (called the Bizmac), and designing the first computer-controlled "point of sale" cash register.

Spielberg senior began volunteering at the Shoah Foundation in 1995, working closely with Sam Gustman and Karen Jungblut as the cataloguing project ramped up. "He was instrumental on so many levels," says Jungblut, "from making sure the cataloguers had an ergonomically suitable work environment to helping figure out how to speed up the indexing. As it became clear that our process had to change, he focused on how to make it more scientific and less emotionally driven, creating spreadsheets and advising on restructuring. We met weekly for several years as he helped steer the shift in our methodology."

In April 2012, the foundation presented its first annual Inspiration Award to Arnold Spielberg, then aged ninety-five. He was recognized for his many years of mentorship and support, especially in the area of humanity through technology. Now known as the Arnold Spielberg Inspiration Award, the award honors friends who have supported and inspired the foundation, including community leaders, institute volunteers, teachers, scholars, and survivors. "Arnold's contribution ... through his pioneering work in the field of technology, has created a lasting legacy for current and future generations," said Stephen Smith at the award luncheon.

The honoree's son also spoke: "I am so pleased and touched to be able to recognize my father's vital contributions to the organization. With this Inspiration Award that will carry his name in perpetuity, my father will continue to be a beacon as we pursue our mission."

ABOVE: *Arnold Spielberg and Steven Spielberg at the event honoring Arnold with the first Inspiration Award.*

SHIFTING GEARS

The flip side to the cataloguers' high level of engagement was the slow rate of production: it took eight to twelve hours to index one hour of testimony. "At first we imagined that the cataloguing would proceed simultaneously with interviewing," Jungblut recalls. "It didn't take long to figure out that this wasn't realistic. By the time the indexing system was ready for us, we already had a backlog of several thousand interviews."

And with tapes flooding in from the field, the backlog grew day by day. In choosing the length and content of indexable segments, cataloguers were given considerable leeway—a key factor in why the cataloguing effort proceeded slowly at first. This approach to archiving involved a fairly elaborate process with multiple layers of staff. It was thorough but cumbersome, producing only about forty fully indexed testimonies a week for its first five years. "About two hundred interviews a week were coming in at that time," says Jungblut. At that rate "our grandchildren would be doing the work before all the interviews were completed."

Clearly the approach wasn't sustainable, and Jungblut and her colleagues began looking for ways to streamline it. One resource was standing by in the person of Arnold Spielberg, the filmmaker's father, who brought his computer engineering background to the task (see the sidebar). Then, in 2001, recently appointed president and CEO Douglas Greenberg brought in consultants from McKinsey to analyze the cataloguing operation. The key breakthrough turned out to be a conceptual shift in the indexable segments: rather than individual cataloguers selecting them, a computer would automatically time-code each interview into one-minute increments. And the indexer, almost in real time, would assign keywords from the established list while watching and listening.

Making this transition wasn't easy: some cataloguers couldn't help but feel that the decreased amount of time devoted to each indexing effort reflected a downgrading of the respect being accorded to the survivor. After a short trial period a number of cataloguers departed, while others adjusted well to the new, faster system. And the results were dramatic. Instead of several days to a week, it now took about four hours to index an average-length (2.5 hours) testimony.

> "Arnold was instrumental on so many levels, from making sure the cataloguers had an ergonomically suitable work environment to helping figure out how to speed up the indexing."
>
> — Karen Jungblut

In the years from late 1996 to mid-2001, the foundation produced about four thousand fully indexed testimonies; in the four years after that, indexing work was completed on nearly 46,000 of the testimonies. Concentrating first on the English-

1-excTESTIMONY

language tapes allowed the team to work out the kinks in the system before tackling the testimonies in thirty-one other languages, and hiring a new cadre of multilingual cataloguers (all of the indexing was done in English). By January 2006, 99 percent of the fifty-two thousand testimonies in the Visual History Archive had been catalogued and about 95 percent had been indexed. In the process, the foundation ended up with eleven patents and hundreds of inventions within those patents. Before long these technologies—for searching and distributing video and related systems engineering—were being licensed to governments and universities.

ACCESS: WALKING THE LINE

In parallel with developing the cataloguing and indexing system, the Shoah Foundation was also designing and engineering the multimedia interface that would enable the foundation to fulfill its core promise: making the testimonies available worldwide. But not all at once, and not on the Internet as we know it today.

As far back as the original six-month pilot program, the foundation had established partnerships with five major Holocaust remembrance and educational institutions, which would become satellite locations where authorized users could

access the collection. These repositories—the Museum of Jewish Heritage in New York, the Simon Wiesenthal Center in Los Angeles, the United States Holocaust Memorial Museum in Washington, the Fortunoff Video Archive for Holocaust Testimonies at Yale, and Yad Vashem in Jerusalem—would decide who could view the testimonies and exactly how. In this way, starting in 1998, the relatively small number of testimonies that had already been digitized and catalogued were made available—starting with the nearby Simon Wiesenthal Center's Museum of Tolerance.

"The repositories won't have copies of the tapes," wrote Beallor and Moll in a 1995 preview of the plan. "They will access our multimedia database and be able to pull up information in many different ways, depending on the design of their interface (the program that decides how the user will be able to see and use the testimonies in our archive). Each repository's interface will be different, and we're working individually with them to design for their needs and goals."

"Our ultimate goal," the report went on, "is to make this archive available to people who may never visit a museum or university, over the 'information superhighway.'" Reaching that goal took some time, however. Even the now-quaint term "information superhighway" suggests how early this was in the general embrace

236

of information sharing on the World Wide Web. And the foundation was treading very cautiously around issues of security and privacy before releasing any testimonies on the wild and woolly Internet of the mid-1990s. Survivors feared that the detailed personal information they'd provided could find its way into the wrong hands—even to people actively hostile to Holocaust remembrance. In November 1996, the foundation had "no plans to make the testimonies of the survivors available through the Internet."

That would eventually change. The foundation took a basically techno-optimist line that the information revolution was a good thing; clearly it could extend their mission's reach. The organization's first website was launched in 1996, and plans were laid to start making a limited number of interviews available on the Web. Even that couldn't happen right away, as 1990s technology didn't offer enough bandwidth to handle high-resolution video signals. "For that we had to wait for Internet2," says Gustman—that is, the high-speed, secure service used by institutions such as universities.

Word of the Visual History Archive spread quickly through the community of people interested in Holocaust issues, and by late 1999 the foundation had responded to 161 unsolicited early access requests from scholars, museums, documentary filmmakers, and community organizations worldwide. The foundation also invited well-known Holocaust scholars such as Christopher Browning and Yehuda Bauer to Los Angeles to test the system, confident that they would quickly realize its value to their work. Whether at the foundation's headquarters or at one of the remote repositories, interested parties could experience the testimonies via the interactive user interface connected to the robot-driven digital storage library. It worked like this:

"Suppose you want to watch an entire testimony or just a particular segment from it," wrote Yale's Geoffrey Hartman in 2000. "If the computer cache at the repository already contains that particular testimony, your access will be instantaneous. If the material is not on the cache, your request will activate the robot—which is like a huge computer drive—via a fiber-optic connection. The robot will spin around, locate the testimony (or segment) and load it up for high-speed fiber-optic transition to the remote terminal. Total waiting time will be only about five minutes."

Opposite: The "Tree of Testimony," using interviews from the Visual History Archive, at the Los Angeles Museum of the Holocaust. Above: Students at the Voices of Liberty exhibition at the Museum of Jewish Heritage, which features Holocaust survivor testimony from the archive.

THE TESTIMONY OF **ÉVA SZÉKELY**

Date of birth . . . . April 3, 1927
Place of birth . . . . . Budapest, Hungary
Date of interview . . . . . August 5, 1999
Location of interview . . . . . . Budapest,
Hungary
Language . . . . Hungarian
Experience . . . . .Jewish survivor

In the 1940s ÉVA SZÉKELY was already a very talented swimmer, winner of many championships. In the winter of 1944, Hungarian Nazis raided in Budapest, rounding up Jews and shooting them on the banks of the Danube. A young Hungarian Nazi came for Éva but spared her thanks to her father's pleas; years later she recognized the man as a high-ranking Communist officer. Eva spent the war years in Hungarian forced labor battalions as well as in protected houses in Budapest. After the war she went on to win a gold medal at the Helsinki Summer Olympics (1952) and a silver medal at the Melbourne Summer Olympics (1956).

They were shooting people into the Danube. The raid came. A kind of young Arrow Cross man came in. [The fascist *Nyilaskeresztes Part* or Arrow Cross party controlled Hungary from 1944 to 1945.] My sister was immediately hidden. They always hid her. I was told to lay down and tell him I was sick. And I laid down and the Arrow Cross man came in and right away [he] started with me. They mainly wanted young people. "Come on, get going!" Then Dad told him, "Don't take her, she is sick, can't you see how she cannot walk?" He said: "She does not have to walk far." Meaning only to the Danube nearby. Then Dad said, "But she cannot walk!" "Doesn't matter, she should come!"

And then, by some heavenly influence, my father said, "Don't take her. She is the swimming champion of Hungary and you will be happy you saved her life!" "Say your name!" He looked at me and I looked at him, and I said my name, and saw that one of his eyes was gray and the other one was brown. And this stayed with me, as never before had I seen a man with different-colored eyes.

This is how I stayed alive. And in 1950 there was a great international swimming championship in Margaret Island, and I swam very, very well there. And they announced "100 meters freestyle" and I stood up and they said that the medal would be given to me by the chairman of the Swimming Association, and the special prize of the State Security will be given by the major of the State Security Authority. And imagine—there I stand up on top of the podium with a vase in my hands, and the man looks at me and it was that Arrow Cross man! With his different-colored eyes. I thought I would fall off the podium. ■

Top: Éva in the pool in 1954. Above: Hungarian Olympic team after the Helsinki Games, with the women swimmers in the front row, Eva second from right.

Through the 1990s and early 2000s, the foundation continued to provide access to testimonies in this and other limited ways. Some, for instance, were incorporated into museum exhibits in Los Angeles, New York, Paris, Amsterdam, Rome, and at the Auschwitz Jewish Center in Oswiecim, Poland. They were quoted in publications and used in scholarship, documentary films, and educational projects; small collections were assembled for regional institutions. (See the next chapter for details.) With the completion of cataloguing and indexing drawing near, the prospects for sharing the archive would soon blossom. "Far into the future," wrote Beallor and Moll in a 1995 document, "distribution and educational applications of the archive will continue to evolve, limited only by the emergence of new technology."

> **History is normally recorded by elites who acted in history. What we have here are the collective testimonies of eyewitnesses to an historical event.**
>
> —Michael Berenbaum, president and CEO of the Shoah Foundation from 1997 to 1999

■

Through the late 1990s the Shoah Foundation was maturing and finding its identity as an organization. As the focus shifted from collecting survivor and witness testimonies to disseminating them, the foundation's gifted and dedicated staff continued to imagine new ways to use technology: to preserve the Visual History Archive, to map the testimonies via cataloguing and indexing, to mine them for other media, and to share them with the world.

To facilitate this shift, the Shoah Foundation expanded its leadership, continuing to add staff members with experience in history and education. Among them was the Holocaust scholar and writer Michael Berenbaum, who had been project director and director of the Historical Research Institute at the United States Holocaust Memorial Museum. Berenbaum served as president and CEO of the Shoah Foundation from 1997 to 1999, consolidating and deepening the organization's relationships in the Holocaust remembrance community worldwide. During his tenure, the fifty-thousandth testimony was taken; in marking that milestone Berenbaum said, "We have in our possession the most powerful narratives by the most extraordinary ordinary people about the most powerful, the most frightening, the most awesome and the most evil event in human history. Imagine the power of fifty thousand narratives." ■

ABOVE: Steven Spielberg and Michael Berenbaum.

SHARING THE LEGACY

At the turn of the millennium, the Shoah Foundation was poised for a momentous shift. The lion's share of the fifty-two thousand Holocaust-era interviews had been recorded, and were steadily being catalogued and indexed. The foundation's leaders knew they were in possession of a matchless resource in the Visual History Archive, whose power was manifest in its impact on their own staff and on all who had been granted access to the testimonies so far.

Now it was time to change the primary focus from collecting and cataloguing to sharing the testimonies, as Steven Spielberg had envisioned. The new emphasis was timely, as the 1990s had seen a sharp rise in the public's consciousness about the Holocaust. This was due in part to the impact of *Schindler's List* but also to other important factors, such as the opening of the United States Holocaust Memorial Museum in 1993, the 1990 publication by Yad Vashem of the seminal *Encyclopedia of the Holocaust,* and the fiftieth anniversary of the end of World War II. Events in Rwanda and Bosnia inevitably gave rise to comparisons with the vaster genocide a half-century earlier.

"Our goal is clear," wrote Ari Zev, then serving as interim CEO, in a letter to the foundation's supporters in 2000. "The survivors and witnesses who have so generously given testimony will now become teachers, providing moving personal lessons in cultural, religious, and racial harmony today and for generations to come." To help guide this transition, another distinguished historian, Douglas

OPPOSITE: Filming a scene from The Last Days *documentary in Hungary with survivor Tom Lantos and four of his grandchildren, on the bridge where he had been forced to work in a labor battalion during the German occupation.*

Greenberg, joined the foundation that same year as its next president and CEO. Long associated with Princeton and Rutgers Universities, Greenberg was also the former head of the Chicago Historical Society (now the Chicago History Museum).

"Since my arrival," Greenberg wrote later in 2000, "I have been immersed in the complex yet hugely rewarding task of determining how best to use our archive . . . to ensure that the twenty-first century does not repeat the greatest horror of the twentieth. To do that, we must make the archive available to scholars, students, and the general public, not only in this country but around the world."

> "Each of us has an obligation of memory. At the Shoah Foundation the preservation of memory is what we do." —Douglas Greenberg, past president and CEO

THE IMPACT OF TESTIMONY

Greenberg valued the Visual History Archive so highly because he knew that the experience of viewing testimony is multilayered and uniquely powerful. It starts with whom the speaker is addressing: Family members? Future generations? The world? Steven Spielberg? (Some do speak directly to him on the tapes.) And it varies according to the viewer, who might be a close relative of the survivor, a teenager studying the Holocaust in school, a present-day resident of the town where the survivor grew up, a scholar investigating a particular corner of wartime history, or a victim of prejudice on the other side of the globe.

ABOVE: Douglas Greenberg, past president and CEO, in the transfer room, 2005. OPPOSITE: Students in Philadelphia pilot-test IWitness, 2011.

But common to all encounters with testimony is the close engagement that takes hold purely because the interviewees share of themselves so deeply. Viewers respond with such empathy and respect that even young students are inspired to watch entire two-hour interviews. The interviewees open up, make themselves vulnerable, forge a personal connection with viewers they will likely never meet. They make eye contact and give an accounting of themselves, finding meaning in their own stories as they tell them. Oral history expert Geoffrey Hartman, who directs the Yale Fortunoff archive, says, "There is a conservation of narrative, of life experience, which you get in video testimony which restores to [survivors] their identity. You see them embodied—there is a great deal of intensity which comes from the video testimony."

> **I am inspired when I hear Holocaust survivors speak about miracles. To be able to describe something as miraculous, in the midst of such suffering, is amazing.**
>
> —Raheem Parpia, a student in a USC seminar on Memory and History

In her testimony, Polish survivor Itka Zygmuntowicz speaks to Hartman's point about the recovery of personal identity, and what that means to her: "The Nazis did everything in their power to dehumanize and destroy. This is the reason why, when they called me Number 25673, I said, I am not a number. . . . My family taught me that who I am—my *mentshlekhkeyt,* my humane-ness—does not depend on how others treat me but on how I treat others."

We as viewers find our own meanings in the stories. A Hungarian college student, Andrea Scheili, shared her thoughts about watching testimony with the Shoah Foundation's regional consultant in 2007: "When a living person is telling me that this happened to him, that this is how he survived or was rescued, it has an elemental strength. These people could walk on the street with me, and I would not know what they have been through. This says to me that this can happen to anybody, to ordinary people. These people could have been my grandmother or grandfather."

These examples barely hint at the wealth of learning held in the foundation's testimonies. "We always knew that the archive would hold layer upon layer of recollections combined with a mosaic of data that would be tremendously valuable and exciting to discover," says Ari Zev. "From so many perspectives—personal, historical, cultural, psychological—and across so many disciplines—history, art history, anthropology, law, language studies, and more—the archive is a treasure trove for learning and understanding." All that was to come. At the dawn of the new century, the testimonies' journey into the world was just beginning.

WHY WE TAKE TESTIMONY

Many survivors have reported that in the camps, they wanted to survive to "tell the world." This might seem easy to say after the fact; but the diaries and notes of the *Sonderkommando* in Birkenau, and the testimony of other Jewish survivors, attest to the fact that even under seemingly hopeless conditions, people were determined to survive to bear witness for those who could not. The testimonies fulfill that promise and provide the eyewitness accounts they said they would give.

When the Holocaust survivor says "beware of the dangers of hatred," they are challenging the viewer to be self-reflective. It's interesting to note that in their testimonies, the survivors are not always direct in their challenge. Rather, they share episodes from their lives that have a point or moral to which they expect the viewer to respond. Their point may be about the importance of family, or security, or resistance, or hope. They may want us to consider the dangers of making a hasty judgment; they may challenge us to think about choices. Testimony is as much about the response of the viewer as it is about the content of the testimony itself.

Holocaust survivor testimony is not primarily about death, but rather about overcoming the Nazis' attempt to murder them. The very fact that

the survivor is in front of the camera indicates that they overcame the odds. Testimony, then, is about living through. The Yiddish term for survival, *iberleben*—to live over—takes that literally. The very presence of survivors onscreen attests to the resilience of the human spirit, the basic ability to endure unimaginable suffering and loss, and then continue to create homes and families and new generations, to set new goals and aspirations. The fact that survivors testify is in itself a form of hope—despite humanity's huge failing.

Testimony is never one thing. It gives the chance for each individual to remember the past as an eyewitness. It provides much-needed historical data about what actually happened to individuals, and how those experiences changed the course of their lives and shaped their perspectives. It also challenges us as human beings, to give us the hope we need to continue our work.

—STEPHEN D. SMITH

ON THE SCREEN . . .

Even before the foundation began to share the Visual History Archive directly, it was mining the testimonies for use in documentary films and educational CD-ROMs—the digital publishing medium of the day. As of its twentieth anniversary, the Shoah Foundation had produced eleven documentary films using the testimonies in its collection. Collectively, the films have been broadcast in fifty countries and subtitled in twenty-eight languages.

First to appear was *Survivors of the Holocaust,* directed by Allan Holzman, which wove together archival images and clips from the foundation's first four hundred testimonies to explore life in prewar Europe, the rise and fall of the Third Reich, the devastating impact of Nazism on European Jewry, the liberation of the camps, and postwar life. Its evocative score was composed by Cantor Meir Finkelstein—the son of a survivor—as an expression of the composer's lifelong connection to Jewish music. The film earned numerous accolades when it was released in 1996 by Turner Broadcasting: two Emmy Awards, the CableACE Award for a Documentary Special, and the prestigious Peabody Award. It also served as a call to action: when the film aired with an appeal and a toll-free number at the end, calls poured in. Says June Beallor, "Reaching such a large audience with the testimonies was a defining moment." Furthermore, the film's success proved the value of sponsorship (in this case by Chrysler), which allowed the foundation to conserve resources for its primary mission. "We also held a benefit screening to raise funds, a model we would continue to use," says Beallor.

Following the next year was *The Lost Children of Berlin,* directed by Elizabeth McIntyre and narrated by Anthony Hopkins. In the dark days of the Third Reich, Jewish schools were shut down in every major city the Nazis invaded. This film tells the story of the last Jewish school in Berlin to be shut down, in 1942, and follows the lives of fifty students who survived the war to meet again at a 1996 reunion in the newly reopened Grosse Hamburgerstrasse School. The actress and producer Sally Field brought the idea for the documentary to the Shoah Foundation's attention and served as executive producer.

BODY LANGUAGE

As an intern, I watched many testimonies. In some, the interviewees expressed emotions such as shame, anger, love, or guilt. I understood these emotions not only through their spoken words, but also from the expressions on their faces or the movement of their hands—something I never got from reading about these tragic events. Each person had a different way of expressing the same emotion; while watching some interviews, I felt a sense of anger through a look in the interviewee's eyes; in others, it was a grand gesture of tight fists in the air. —*Shoah Foundation intern Caitlin Koford*

THE TESTIMONY OF **WALTER SCHWARZE**

Date of birth . . . . December 24, 1914
Place of birth . . . . Leipzig, Germany
Date of interview . . . . . November 11, 1997
Location of interview . . . Leipzig, Germany
Language . . . . German
Experience . . . . Homosexual survivor

In 1940, WALTER SCHWARZE *was arrested and convicted according to Paragraph 175, a provision of the German Criminal Code that made homosexual acts between males a crime. In his testimony, Walter describes his arrest and imprisonment in the Moabit prison and the brutal treatment he received as an inmate at the Sachsenhausen concentration camp.*

The name of the judge was Freisler. The district judge said that according to jurisprudence and law, there was no paragraph to convict [me], until the Gestapo officer said, "There is one law for the conviction, Paragraph 175. That's the *Schwulenparagraphen* [anti-homosexuality paragraph]."

I was [in prison] in Moabit, and then we were transported to Sachsenhausen. What did I know about concentration camps? We were all pulled out of the bus, and then we saw the SS standing there with German Shepherds on the leash. So, then

the names were called out in alphabetical order, and we were either hit on the head or the stomach. We also had to crawl and roll around on the roll-call square.

A lot of dirt was there, and I was wearing a very nice suit, and in my side pocket there was a picture of me with a very beautiful girl, Margret; she was a hairdresser in the Haidenstrasse, in Leipzig. I never had sexual contact with her, but nevertheless we really liked each other. So, then my name was called and [one of the SS] grabbed the picture from my side pocket, took it out, and shook his head. I was the only one who did not get beaten.

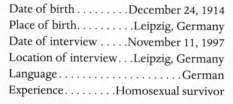

And then there was the worst part, the *Stehkommando* [being forced to stand for long periods of time]. We had to stand the entire day in one place [outside]. My lower body hurt so much; they just passed around a bucket if you needed to go.

In 1940 and 1941, we had a bitter cold [winter]. [Our] pockets were stitched up; there weren't any gloves and we only had some rags for our feet, and some wooden shoes. Above us, the crows from the trees around us could smell the dead people lying around. And, while watching the smoke coming out of the crematory, one always thought: "When is my time going to come?"

But the worst of it all was when someone escaped. We had to run around the square all day long; or during winter, we had to shovel the snow from one place to another, and then again back to the same place, back and forth, all day long. ∎

CENTER: *Walter at about age twenty.* ABOVE: *Walter (right) with his brother, Gerhart (left) and sister, Gerda, who died shortly after this photo was taken, c. 1918.*

The foundation's first feature-length documentary, and the most acclaimed film built around testimonies, was *The Last Days,* which won the 1998 Academy Award for Best Documentary Feature. Director James Moll and producer June Beallor focused on five Hungarian Jews who return from the United States to their hometowns and to the ghettos and camps where they were imprisoned. These survivors—who include artist Alice Lok Cahana and former U.S. congressman Tom Lantos—tell their stories with no framing narration. *The Last Days* was enriched by the discovery of rare footage and photographs never previously used in a film, and a powerful score by Academy Award–winning composer Hans Zimmer.

The filmmakers realized that illuminating this single chapter of the Holocaust could convey its overall magnitude. "I had never considered the fact that World War II was essentially over for the Nazis when they invaded Hungary in 1944 and, with the support of their Hungarian accomplices, launched a full-scale genocide," says Moll, "even to some extent sacrificing their own war efforts to carry out their 'Final Solution.'"

As Steven Spielberg sought to broaden the foundation's international presence, Moll enlisted talented film directors in five countries for ambitious series of one-hour documentaries collectively titled *Broken Silence* (see the sidebar on page 248). Completed in 2001, the films were screened widely

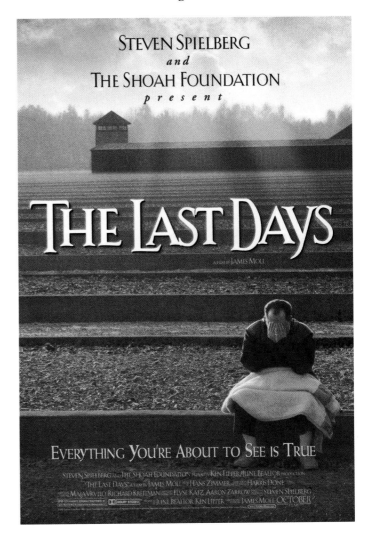

in their countries of origin—Argentina, Hungary, Russia, Poland, and the Czech Republic—and ultimately in eighteen countries around the world. The films were especially targeted to schools: the foundation partnered with national and local groups to build educational programs around them. The whole series aired on HBO's Cinemax channel in 2002.

The impact of *Broken Silence* may be impossible to measure but can be inferred from viewers' comments, like that of Dmitrii Suvorov, a sixteen-year-old student from Moscow who wrote a prizewinning essay about one of the films in the series, *Children from the Abyss*. "This film tells how sixty-five years ago, millions of Jews perished: old people and children, women and men, talented and average. They rejoiced in the sun and wind, fell in love and argued, expected and raised children—in short, lived. Maybe they even dreamt of leaving their legacy in history. None of them thought, however, this legacy would be one of a Holocaust victim."

For the tenth anniversary of *Schindler's List* in 2004, Spielberg and his colleagues produced a documentary that

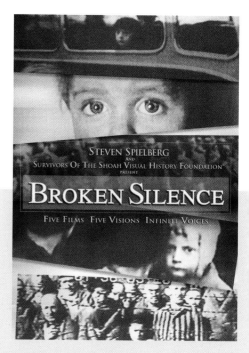

BROKEN SILENCE

Broken Silence is a foreign-language documentary series of five one-hour films representing the Holocaust as experienced by survivors now living in Argentina, the Czech Republic, Hungary, Poland, and Russia. Distinguished filmmakers from each country worked with Shoah Foundation researchers and historians to build a documentary that would resonate most effectively in each country, language, and culture.

EYES OF THE HOLOCAUST, (A Holocaust szemei) directed by Janos Szasz
Hungarian filmmaker Janos Szasz, the son of Holocaust survivors, focuses on the experiences of survivors who were children during the Holocaust.

SOME WHO LIVED, (Algunos que vivieron), directed by Luis Puenzo
Argentine filmmaker Luis Puenzo wove together testimonies from Holocaust survivors now living in Argentina and Uruguay with archival and modern-day footage; the film also explores the connections between Nazism and the darker chapters in Argentine history.

CHILDREN FROM THE ABYSS, (Дети из бездны) directed by Pavel Chukhraj
Holocaust survivors detail their experience of resistance, betrayal, rescue, and the desire for revenge in this film from Russian filmmaker Pavel Chukhraj.

I REMEMBER, (Pamiętam) directed by Andrzej Wajda
Academy Award honoree Andrzej Wajda directed this Polish-language documentary about four survivors who were either helped or betrayed by their Polish neighbors.

HELL ON EARTH (Peklo na Zemi), directed by Vojtech Jasny
Renowned Czech filmmaker Vojtech Jasny directed this look at Theresienstadt, the "model" Czech ghetto set up by the Nazis to deceive the world about how well the Jews were treated.

TOP: *Poster for the* Broken Silence *films.* LEFT: *Steven Spielberg with Argentine director Luis Puenzo.*

focused on Oskar Schindler's legacy; *Voices from the List* was included on the film's DVD. Following an on-screen introduction by Spielberg, a dozen of the *Schindlerjuden* relate their experiences in and around Krakow before and during the war, their testimonies skillfully intercut with archival footage and still photos. Leopold and Ludmila Page (Poldek and Mila Pfefferberg), Leon Leyson, Rina Finder, Leopold Rosner, Helena Jonas-Rosenzweig, and others share their memories of the German army marching into Krakow, the increasingly intense persecution of Jews, the death camp transports, the Plaszow camp and its horrible conditions—and of Oskar Schindler in all his complex humanity.

In 2006, the foundation released two more films: In *Nazvy svoie im'ia (Spell Your Name)*, Ukrainian director Sergey Bukovsky takes a group of Ukrainian students on a journey of discovery into their history, exploring the ethnic stereotypes that persist in Ukraine and efforts to memorialize the sites where tens of thousands of Jewish families and others were executed and thrown into mass graves. The film uses Ukrainian and Russian-language testimonies from the Visual History Archive and new footage shot on location. And in *Volevo solo vivere (I Only Wanted to Live)*, director Mimmo Calopresti follows nine Italian citizens (chosen from several hundred Italian testimonies in the archive) who survived Italy's descent into fascism and their own deportation and internment in the Auschwitz death camps.

> **"**When the dictatorship took place in Argentina, it was much like it was in Europe. This is something we are all subject to, no matter where we live.**"**
>
> — Survivor Pedro Boschan, in the film *Some Who Lived*

. . . AND ON DISK

In the decades before DVDs, memory sticks, and digital information storage and retrieval in the cloud, CD-ROMs were the medium of choice to distribute software as well as other kinds of content long confined to the printed page, such as illustrated

Steven Spielberg in association with Survivors of the Shoah Visual History Foundation and Fogwood Films present

the Lost Children of Berlin

Original Score by   Piano Concerto by

ABOVE: Poster for the documentary film The Lost Children of Berlin.

books and encyclopedias. The production and IT experts at the Shoah Foundation were quick to see the medium's potential for their nascent efforts to share the testimonies. "We knew this would be a great way to get the interviews out there in a multimedia format, especially to the schools, as a tool for promoting tolerance and supplementing Holocaust history," says Moll.

In 1999, the foundation released *Survivors: Testimonies of the Holocaust,* its first CD-ROM based on the Visual History Archive and featuring the testimonies of Bert Strauss, Paula Lebovics, Silvia Grohs-Martin, and Sol Weider. As viewers proceed through "chapters" told by each survivor and illustrated with images from the survivors' personal collections, they can follow their curiosity by clicking on supporting materials: historical overviews and sidelights, archival photographs, maps, timelines, and a comprehensive reference library. Thus the survivor's personal experience and reflections are embedded in a broader historical context of World War II and the Holocaust.

Beyond the intricacies of assembling this multimedia package (its production was led by art director and IT team member Stephanie Barish), the real challenge was making sure it reached a wide audience. Aiming to connect with high school students, the narration was provided by Leonardo DiCaprio and Winona Ryder.

66 That CD-ROM will tell your children and grandchildren. Long after I'm gone, you're going to see my face. **99** — Silvia Grohs-Martin

A study guide was developed in collaboration with the Boston-based education organization Facing History and Ourselves, and the CD-ROM was promoted through county and state education boards for use in American classrooms, where students are separated from the events of the Holocaust by an ocean and more than a half-century. After the launch of *Survivors* in the States, the foundation went to work on making it available to teachers and curricula in other English-speaking countries. In 2005, it found new form—and a new audience—as an interactive exhibit on the Web.

Steven Spielberg lent a hand with outreach, as did the survivors featured on the disk: at emotionally charged launch events at schools in Chicago, New York, and Los Angeles, Strauss, Lebovics, Grohs-Martin, and Weider had the profound

ABOVE: One of the disks for Survivors: Testimonies of the Holocaust, *the foundation's first CD-ROM. OPPOSITE: Survivor Bert Strauss and Steven Spielberg with a student at the New York City launch of* Survivors.

experience of seeing students react to their testimonies. In New York, students who had lived with discrimination recognized parallels between the survivors' experiences and their own. Speaking to the *New York Times,* Silvia Grohs-Martin said, "That CD-ROM will tell your children and grandchildren. Long after I'm gone, you're going to see my face."

The next CD-ROM project was truly international: the German arm of the Shoah Foundation, known as Shoah GmbH, produced *Erinnern für Gegenwart und Zukunft (Remembering for the Present and the Future),* which was developed with student focus groups across Germany and debuted in 2001. After viewing *Erinnern,* German students spoke of how it had raised their empathy and awareness: as one said, "You have to read it, hear it, and see it to even begin to understand these events."

A third educational CD-ROM, *Voices of the Holocaust: Children Speak,* explores perspectives and themes unique to the experience of child survivors, using four such testimonies from the Visual History Archive. Designed for students aged eleven to fourteen and narrated by Elijah Wood and Natalie Portman, it found wide distribution throughout the United States in public, private, and religious schools.

The films and CD-ROMs represented the Shoah Foundation's efforts to bring the testimonies into the educational sphere via the technology of the time. Much was learned in producing them, and they were incorporated into the foundation's expanding educational initiatives.

THE TESTIMONY OF **ELIZABETH HOLTZMAN**

Date of birth . . . . .August 11, 1941
Place of birth. . .New York, New York, USA
Date of interview . . . . . . .August 23, 2000
Location of interview. . . . . Brooklyn,
New York, USA
Language. English
Experience. . . . War crimes trial participant

Elizabeth Holtzman was a member of the United States House of Representatives in the mid-1970s, serving on the Immigration Subcommittee. She helped pass legislation to expel Nazi war criminals who had immigrated to the United States. The suspects had been included on a list kept by the Immigration and Naturalization Service. In her interview she stresses her intent to bring Nazi criminals to justice.

I believe it was 1974, a man asked to see me. I don't remember his title now. He was somehow connected with the immigration service. I don't remember if [he was] a government employee or with a group associated with it. I was on the Immigration Subcommittee, so I agreed to see him. He came to see me

and said, "You know, the U.S. government has a list of Nazi war criminals living in the United States and is doing nothing about it." He said it in a very calm way—was not screaming or yelling or agitated. And the way he handled himself up to that point suggested that he was not a crazy person.

I didn't care how many people were supporting me on this, as I didn't take a poll before I started this. This is a wrong that had to be righted and justice had to be done here.

But the allegation to me was shocking, was inconceivable, and was outrageous. I thanked him for the information and I said to myself: How can this be true? The U.S. government has a list of Nazi war criminals! Nazi war criminals living in the U.S.! How can that happen? We fought Hitler in World War II. What the Nazis believe in is antithetical to our whole society, to our democracy: inclusion and human

rights. So I thanked him and I sent him on his way. And then I couldn't quite forget what he said. I did not know how to begin to investigate it. But I couldn't let that idea go out of my mind.

My own experience with the Holocaust was, you know, my father had some family members, probably remote family members, who were killed in Pinsk; most Jews did not survive who lived in Pinsk. But probably my own reading of the Holocaust started with the [Adolf] Eichmann trial. So I knew a little about it. I wouldn't say I was particularly knowledgeable but, as a Jew, it was horrifying to know that there was an effort to wipe out from the face of the earth my people, and if I lived in Europe, the same would have happened to me.

Holtzman went to the immigration commissioner and asked to see all of the files of the people on the list. She was amazed by what she found.

I don't know if I had a right to see all the files, but I wanted to find out

what was going on. For some reason, the files were in New York, and so I came back from Washington and an appointment was made for me to go to see these files, Federal Building, downtown Manhattan.

I looked through file number one and it started, allegation by XYZ, So-and-So was a police official, I think in one of the Baltic countries during World War II, where he was responsible for the execution of the Jewish population of a certain area. And then I go on and I read what the immigration service does about it. They send somebody to the person's house. They knock on the door, according to the files, and they say, how is Mr. So-and-So's health? He's very well. Thank you very much. They close the door. They go home and put that in the files.

You have the allegations. Someone is responsible for the mass murder of the Jews and what does the immigration service do in response? They go to check on this person's health. This

Opposite: Holtzman at congressional hearings on the issue of Nazis living in the United States. Above: President Gerald R. Ford signs a proclamation marking Women's Equality Day on August 26, 1974. Present are a group of congresswomen including Elizabeth Holtzman (at left, wearing glasses), as well as activist Bella Abzug, at right in hat.

is file number one. This [must be] an aberration. I go to file number two. The same thing. Different allegations. Different person. Same response by the immigration service. They go knocking on the door. How's this person's health? That's it. I went through about ten, fifteen files. Basically, the same thing. In other words, the allegations were there and the immigration service was doing nothing to interrogate them. Nothing.

Well, I realized what had to be done. I sat down and said now what? How should the government handle it? There's got to be a special unit created, with people with the expertise to conduct an investigation. They have to go all over the world and find evidence. And so I had a press conference and I laid out a plan that I thought the government should follow in terms of bringing those Nazi war criminals to

justice. That was in 1974, in April. Of course it made me think about Watergate because I was working very hard on Watergate at the same time. We held our hearing in July. This was just a few months before the final hearing on the impeachment of Richard Nixon. This was another government cover-up.

So many things occurred to me at the time. Why did this happen? Why did the government allow them to come here? Who was responsible for this? But I said to myself, the most important thing now was to find out how many Nazis there are and bring them to justice. What can we do now with the Nazis living among us? That was my first and primary objective. I didn't care how many people were supporting me on this, as I didn't take a poll before I started this. This is a wrong that had to be righted and justice had to be done here. ∎

OPENING THE ARCHIVE

Steven Spielberg knew that the documentary film medium would be an effective way to reach large audiences until technological advances—and a completely catalogued archive—made it possible to provide direct access to the testimonies. Meanwhile, varied constituencies were waiting to search the archive for themselves or to gain access to testimonies specific to their own aims and needs. In general terms, these audiences have been:

- survivors and their families
- the homeland communities where survivors hailed from, and the communities they came to call home
- scholars from many disciplines who rightly saw the potential of so much important and untapped data
- institutions (museums, libraries, other archives) around the world that focused on the Holocaust or other genocides
- documentarians, authors, curators, and other creative professionals who wished to make use of video footage in their own or institutional projects
- teachers and educators at all levels, in every part of the world

Serving these diverse constituencies as effectively as possible—with care, imagination, and state-of-the-art technology—has been at the core of the foundation's work in the current millennium. The requests began to come in well before the organization was equipped to fulfill most of them. There were systems to be set up—especially building the interface and connecting the repositories—and

issues of security and privacy to resolve, as discussed in the preceding chapter. "It got to a point where we had to say to people, 'Not yet,'" says Kim Simon. "We so wanted to offer access, but the systems and infrastructure still had to be built. That tension between the mission to provide the broadest possible access and the desire to care for the testimonies ethically and responsibly is at the heart of who we are.

It would still be years before the complete archive of fifty-two thousand testimonies could be accessed at universities and research institutions worldwide. In the meantime, the foundation began to as-

semble compilations of testimonies to be made available for research, education, and general use at libraries, museums, universities, and other institutions. The various compilations might include some or all of the testimonies collected in a particular city, country, or language, or representing a specific set of experiences. One "client" might request all interviews conducted in the Midwest; another wanted all the testimonies conducted in Italian. These subsets of the archive might contain as few as a half-dozen interviews or as many as a few thousand.

Between 1999 and 2002, the foundation fielded more than six hundred requests for access from museums, universities, documentary filmmakers, researchers, students, governments, and educators; by mid-2002, about half of those had been fulfilled. As more detailed information became available through cataloguing, that number rose quickly. The requests fell into these categories:

Geography-based collections. Some institutions wanted to establish collections of testimonies from a particular region for public viewing. For example, the Jevrejske Zajednice Bosne i Hercegovine (Jewish Community of Bosnia and Herzegovina) in Sarajevo created a collection of forty testimonies from Bosnian Holocaust survivors. Other examples include the Charleston County (South Carolina) Public Library and the Joods Historisch Museum in Amsterdam (see sidebar, page 260).

Experience-based collections. Other collections were defined by a common experience, such as the one at Dokumentations und Kulturzentrum Deutscher Sinti und Roma (Documentation and Cultural Center for German Sinti and Roma) in Heidelberg, Germany. In May 2002, the center unveiled a collection of twelve testimonies from the foundation's archive of German and Austrian Sinti and Roma survivors.

Opposite: Educators watching testimony. Top: Ten of the survivors whose video testimonies are included in the foundation's Visual History Collection at the Sherwin Miller Museum of Jewish Art, Tulsa, Oklahoma, with executive director of advancement Steven Klappholz.
Above: Joods Historisch Museum in Amsterdam.

THE TESTIMONY OF **LINA JACKSON**

Date of birth: . . . . December 10, 1929
Place of birth: . . . . . . Papenrode, Germany
Date of interview: . . . . . December 8, 1997
Location of interview: . . . Wheeler, Texas, USA
Language: . . . . English
Experience: . . . . . Sinti and Roma survivor

LINA JACKSON *remembers the unexpected rounding up of her family members because they were Sinti and Roma, and their subsequent deportation to Auschwitz. She describes the difficult conditions on the freight train.*

ABOVE: Lina holding her daughter, Rosemarie, with her two sons, William and James, on the ship SS Washington, en route from Germany to New York in the 1950s. CENTER: With her husband, Richard Jackson, at their wedding. RIGHT: Lina's younger brother, Walter, who died in a camp at age five.

I t was early, early in the morning. Maybe two or three. They came in and they didn't just knock on the door. They slammed the door open. They said, "Get your clothes on and let's go." And my grandmother said, "Can we pack a suitcase?" "No! Just what you [have] on." So that's what we did. We got our clothes on and [went]. I was happy. I thought that something exciting happened. What did I know?

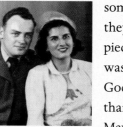

They took us to the train station. It wasn't a train station where you sit, you know. There was a whole bunch of people there. It was just like where you put the cows and horses . . . and that's where they put us. There were a lot of

people in there. And everyone asked, "Where [are] we going?"

They gave us something to eat sometimes. And sometimes they didn't. A small, small piece of bread. Water. I was glad for that. I thanked God for everything I got. I thanked them for everything. Maybe that's why I'm here.

When Lina's interviewer asks her if her captors ever opened the door of the train, she replies, "We were just a bunch of cows."

They had us go to the bathroom in there. The little kids [were] screaming for hunger. I don't know how people could do that. Really, how can they do that? To little children. Little children got deadly sick. ∎

They came in and they didn't just knock on the door. They slammed the door open. They said, "Get your clothes on and let's go."

Publications. Many writers quoted directly from testimonies, or viewed testimonies as research for their work. Svetlana Danilova's 2000 book on the "Mountain Jews" of the Nalchik region of Russia's Caucasus Mountains included transcripts of testimonies of eleven survivors from this community.

Scholarly research. Suzanne Kaplan, the foundation's regional consultant in Sweden, was one of the first scholars to base her doctoral research on Shoah Foundation testimonies. Kaplan used forty interviews with child survivors for her thesis on children's reaction to trauma and loss.

Documentary films. Aside from the foundation's own documentaries, the makers of *Paragraph 175,* a film about the Nazi persecution of homosexuals, viewed eleven interviews as research and included portions of homosexual Holocaust survivor testimonies on the DVD version of the film.

> **"** That tension between the mission to offer access and the desire to care for the testimonies responsibly is at the heart of who we are. **"** — Kim Simon, managing director

Exhibits. When the Auschwitz Jewish Center in Poland opened in 2000, visitors to Auschwitz for the first time could get a sense of prewar Jewish life in the vanished community of Oswiecim; testimonies from the Shoah Foundation Visual History Archive were central to the visitors' experience. In 2001, the Sydney Jewish Museum opened the exhibition *Crossroads: Shanghai and the Jews of China,* which chronicled Shanghai's Jewish communities before, during, and after World War II. A video in the exhibit featured segments from five interviews, conducted with survivors who fled to China from Nazi-occupied Europe and eventually immigrated to Australia. And the BBC in 2003 put portions of four testimonies on its website as part of an online exhibit about child survivors of the Holocaust.

Sharing methodology. Organizations undertaking video history projects, small or large, came to the Shoah Foundation for help. "We welcomed opportunities to leverage our experience by helping others who are trying to document important histories," says Ari Zev. The opportunities were many and diverse: testimonies about the American civil rights movement for the National Center for Civil and Human Rights, a project for the Go For Broke Foundation documenting Japanese Americans who fought in the US Army in World War II, testimonies documenting the lives of contemporary women in Korean society for the Ewha Womans University in Seoul, and the Stolen Generations' Testimonies for children of Australian Aborigines.

ABOVE: A 1942 Chinese identification document for Piotr (Peter) Sapir, then seven years old. Polish-born Peter fled with his family to Shanghai and later immigrated to Australia, where he recorded his testimony with the Shoah Foundation in 1995.

The US Latino and Latina World War II Oral History Project at the University of Texas at Austin adapted the foundation's pre-interview questionnaire for its project of interviewing Latino veterans. In 2003, the foundation offered the PIQ to history professor James Spee in Redlands, California, who was conducting interviews with survivors of Bangladesh's 1971 war for independence, in which millions died. In 2007, Italy's National Audio Visual State Archives licensed the foundation's methodology to index its own audiovisual collections.

Over its second decade, the foundation built on its experience of serving these "early adopters" of the archive. It also continued to explore and enlarge its role in the greater Holocaust community; for example, staff members took part in a major international conference in London and Oxford, *Remembering for the Future in 2000: The Holocaust in the Age of Genocide,* and made a presentation on cataloguing (another case of sharing methodology). In that same year, the foundation launched a nationwide Testimony to Tolerance initiative in partnership with the American Association of School Administrators with a three-day conference for educators in Los Angeles—an early foray into the educational arena that would become so important later.

In all its endeavors to share the Visual History Archive, working in partnership became the foundation's guiding principle. In 2005, Douglas Greenberg wrote, "As the scope and reach of our work broadens, we are fortunate to have as partners a growing support system of educators, librarians, scholars, and curators at institutions around the globe. These partnerships are key to our effectiveness, and we will develop them even further to accomplish together what none of us could do alone."

For the first few years of the new century, foundation staff traveled widely in search of new partnerships to disseminate the Visual History Archive in various forms, meeting and establishing relationships with institutions in the Netherlands, United Kingdom, Germany, Hungary, France, Russia, Ukraine, Romania, Slovakia, Lithuania, Italy, Sweden, and Australia. With Yad Vashem, the foundation planned a new project to provide access to testimonies in Israel.

Top: One of the eleven foreign-language portals—in Czech, Croatian, French, German, Hungarian, Italian, Polish, Russian, Slovak, Spanish, and Ukrainian—on the foundation's website. Above: Premiere of the documentary Spell Your Name *in Kyiv, 2006.*

Throughout this era of transition, the touchstone remained the survivors: sharing their stories, giving back to them and their communities, informing them about how their testimonies were being used, recruiting the willing and able for in-person appearances, and above all, staying faithful to their directive to use the testimonies to teach tolerance.

BRINGING THE TESTIMONIES HOME

Just as the Shoah Foundation sent a copy of the interview tape to each person who gave testimony, it aspired to give back on a larger scale almost from the start. Both in the United States and abroad, local and regional entities such as libraries, museums, synagogues, and state archives had helped to make interviews possible. Now they wanted copies for their own use—even if they didn't always know at first what that might be. Where feasible, the foundation created customized collections, drawing up licensing agreements and notifying the interviewees. These interview packages were provided first as VHS tapes and later as DVDs; larger collections were put on a stand-alone server. The requesting organizations paid for these collections, just enough to cover the foundation's cost; this was sometimes a sensitive point, as groups with scant resources thought they should be provided gratis. As a functioning nonprofit, though, the foundation had to exercise fiduciary responsibility.

Community organizations and institutions in the United States and western Europe—France, Germany, the Netherlands, Italy—were the first to make such requests. "They had the means and the organizational structures in place; they were proactive in working to make the interviews accessible in their countries,"

Above: Kim Simon (center) at the launch of the Italian Central State Archives' website portal providing access to the Shoah Foundation's Italian testimonies, 2012.

says Kim Simon, who oversaw the foundation's international activities for many years. "In the mid to late 1990s, in central and eastern Europe, new governments were emerging after the fall of communism, and the field of Holocaust memorializing and education was still nascent. Local communities were hungry to form partnerships, but formal structures for educations and commemoration had yet to be developed.

"So we began to develop relationships and programs incrementally. We'd find partners and, with our colleague Martin Šmok and a few committed donors, develop a pilot program for a specific country or region, beginning with a small collection: five to thirty testimonies. We would work with local educators and partner organizations on classroom resources that incorporated local testimonies in the local language, and that addressed the historical context and social landscape. In some ways, these efforts formed the bedrock for where we are today."

The testimonies were the core resource, but this kind of grassroots effort wouldn't have worked without people on the ground. As Simon describes the foundation at the turn of the millennium, "We were evolving as an organization while doing the work. We didn't realize when we started the interviews how extended

TESTIMONY COMING HOME

More than one thousand Holocaust survivors and other witnesses who were born or lived in the Netherlands gave testimony to the Shoah Foundation. Their videotaped interviews (conducted by some eighty local Dutch interviewers and videographers) compose the Shoah Foundation Visual History Collection at the Joods Historisch Museum (JHM) in Amsterdam, which opened to the public in 2002.

This collection was a milestone: it was the first time the foundation returned testimonies to the country where they were gathered. With support from the Dutch government and in partnership with the Joods Historisch Museum, the foundation cre-

ated its first testimony catalogue, a "biographical search tool" that allows museum visitors to identify interviews they wish to watch, based on biographical information."

The Shoah Foundation Visual History Collection at the JHM contains:

- 1,035 testimonies
- 926 Jewish survivors
- 76 rescuers and aid providers
- 27 Jehovah's Witness survivors
- 4 political prisoners
- 1 Sinti and Roma survivor
- 1 homosexual survivor

Most of the interviews are in Dutch, with some testimonies in English, French, German, Hungarian, and Flemish.

our involvement would become in some places. We were working in some countries for four or five years." Although the foundation realized it had to bring the collection phase to a close, and do so on a clearly defined schedule, Simon and others were determined to preserve the continuity of these relationships during the transition.

Although many regional offices closed, Simon and the regional coordinators in France and the Netherlands (Mark Edwards and Denise Citroen, respectively) worked out a way for some of the foundation's representatives to continue part-time as regional or national liaisons. Today these individuals (called "consultants") organize and deliver many of the foundation's educational programs internationally.

The foundation was thus able to sustain an international presence and, in so doing, help guide its future identity. "We are based in Los Angeles," says Simon, "but with a commitment to working internationally. It shapes us in small and large ways. Over the years some have questioned, why do this, why maintain that network of representatives? I think it comes down to the ethic of being local, of serving diverse cultures and communities in ways best suited to them. And that applies within the United States as well as overseas."

Regional collections in the United States continued to proliferate. The foundation's second public collection of testimonies opened in 2003 at the Holocaust Memorial of San Antonio, Texas: twenty testimonies had been videotaped in that city. In 2004, the foundation returned eight testimonies given by Holocaust survivors and witnesses from Greenwich, Connecticut, to that community. And a Testimony to Tolerance program, designed to bring anti-bias and Holocaust education to mid-sized communities around the country, began in Des Moines, Iowa, and Jackson, Mississippi, where public libraries hosted small collections of testimonies. "The fact that our collection features testimonies of Iowa residents is very humanizing," said Jan Kaiser of the Des Moines Public Library. "Everybody in the community knows these survivors. [And] today, Des Moines has a large population of immigrants from Latin America, as well as refugees from Sudan. As our city becomes aware of this great diversity . . . a lot of people can benefit from this project."

ABOVE: Artwork created by student Alison Rodriguez in response to viewing testimonies at the Holocaust Memorial of San Antonio.

THE TESTIMONY OF **JACOB (JAAP) VAN PROOSDIJ**

Date of birth . . . . April 15, 1921
Place of birth. . . . . Amsterdam,
the Netherlands
Date of interview . . . . .June 28, 1998
Location of interview. . . . . Pretoria,
South Africa
Language. . . . . English
Experience. . . . . . Rescuer and aid provider

JAAP VAN PROOSDIJ *reflects on his role as a rescuer—he worked in the Westerbork transit camp in the Netherlands with Dr. Hans Calmeyer, who helped save lives by changing the classification of Jews—and on the potential risks one faces when making decisions to help others. He explains that decisions to rescue are sometimes made in the moment, not planned ahead of time.*

I am not after recognition. I just acted normally as far as I'm concerned. And if people wanted to name that as heroism, or whatever it is, it's not. It's just what one does. I can't think that I would not have done it.

It wasn't always easy. We were vulnerable, of course. Once we had a Jew who was staying with us for a while,

because we had not found another place for him. He was there upstairs, and on the Sabbath, he was a bit loud in his prayers, and we asked him to tune down a bit, because we were afraid. You never know what the neighbors will do, you see.

I am not after recognition. I just acted normally as far as I'm concerned. And if people wanted to name that as heroism, or whatever it is, it's not. It's just what one does.

The general population was not unsympathetic. But most people didn't go out of their way to do something. I think that's normal in any country. It's difficult to say. For instance, the, spying organization once asked me whether they could use my office for meetings, and I

said, no, you can't because there's too much at risk because of my other connections. And luckily it was, because a month later, there was a traitor and the whole thing was rolled up. So, that's it. You had to separate those things.

But I can't have any judgment on other people. I don't know their circumstances. It's difficult, for instance, if you are married and you have a child. Can you put them at risk? I don't know. You can only decide when it happens. If you were to ask me, "Would you do it again tomorrow?" I probably, I would say yes, because I handled [it]. What I did was my normal way of doing it. But if you ask me if I see that someone is in danger, would I go and rescue him if I would be in danger, I don't know. When it happens, you decide, or you do it automatically. But you can't say beforehand. ∎

LEFT: *Certificate that permitted Jacob to "walk freely in camp" to assist Dr. Calmeyer.* ABOVE: *Medal of the Righteous among the Nations, awarded to Jacob by Yad Vashem in 1997.*

SCHOLARSHIP AND THE ARCHIVE

"The importance of video testimonies . . . is the emotional aspect of it; it's one thing to read powerful words, but it's not anything near seeing the reaction in the person's face."

This was how Simon Payaslian, professor of Armenian history and genocide studies at Clark University, responded to viewing visual history testimonies at the Shoah Foundation's Tapper Research and Testing Center, which opened in 2002 at the foundation's headquarters. Payaslian was one of the first scholars to have direct access to the foundation's archive—in his case, to research a comparative study of armed resistance during the Armenian genocide and the Holocaust.

In the years when the full archive was still available at very few locations, the Tapper Center was a place where students, researchers, and educators could connect with its rich resources. Housing six computer workstations, the Tapper Center became home to the Visual History Archive, which enabled visiting scholars and educators to search through the fifty-two thousand testimonies and to identify and view the interviews most pertinent to their work. In addition to being a research facility, the center also served as an on-site classroom open to teachers and students, often for workshops on using the archive.

The next big step in expanding the reach of the Visual History Archive to scholars came in 2003, when the Andrew W. Mellon Foundation awarded a $1 million grant and the National Science Foundation awarded $300,000 to support an Internet2 connection and software development, to provide access for scholars at the University of Southern California (USC), Yale University, and Rice University. The grant

enabled the foundation to provide its digitized archive via Internet2 to the three universities. (Internet2, the more secure, higher-speed version of the Web designed to serve academia, had been introduced in the late 1990s and was as yet in use at only a few institutions.) The Mellon grant also supported a pilot project to explore research and classroom uses of the testimonies.

"This was really what it took to start providing widespread access for scholarship," says Karen Jungblut. "All three universities began to integrate testimonies

ABOVE: Left to right, Daisy Miller, Al Tapper, Deborah Dwork, and Douglas Greenberg at the dedication of the Tapper Research Center, 2002.

into classes as diverse as history, languages, art, anthropology, and computer science." Over the ensuing years, more and more universities in the United States and abroad gained access to the archive, and a lively milieu of critical thought and discourse emerged around it. Scholars in many fields became aware of its breadth of content: not just about the Holocaust period but—because of how the interviews were structured—about details of life in hundreds of Jewish communities before the war, and about the huge range of survivor experience through the end of the twentieth century. They could flesh out the historical record in countless ways,

adding the perspective of how people behaved, responded, made decisions.

As Stephen Smith wrote in 2011, when scholarly use of the archive had flowered fully, "With testimonies in thirty-two languages and from fifty-six countries, there is much comparative data about how the story [of European Jewish life in the twentieth century] is experienced and told differently in different contexts. For example, there are testimonies given by Holocaust survivors who had just lived through the 1990s Balkan wars; Yiddishists have hundreds of hours of testimony to watch and listen to; visual historians have hundreds of thousands of images to review; genealogists have 1.2 million names to work with. Public health professionals could search on the keyword *typhus* and yield results from 4,098 testimonies; if psychologists search on the keyword *trauma,* they too have thousands of testimonies at their fingertips."

The range of scholarly inquiry was remarkable. Dr. Egon Mayer, professor of sociology at Brooklyn College, viewed more than thirty testimonies as research for a book on the Kasztner transport. (Mayer's family was among the more than 1,600 Hungarian Jews saved by Reszo Kasztner's efforts.) Regina Kecht, professor of German and Slavic studies at Rice University, taught a seminar that examined individuals' responses to totalitarianism in Nazi Germany and the factors that create an "altruistic personality." Thanks to the Mellon pilot project, Kecht and her students gained direct access to foundation testimonies in their classrooms and on their personal computers, enriching their understanding of what nurtures altruism.

ABOVE: *Jewish refugees from the Kasztner transport on their way to Palestine.* OPPOSITE: *Mark Harris of the USC School of Cinematic Arts using the Visual History Archive with students.*

At Yale, courses making use of testimonies have focused on contemporary fiction, the modern history of Italy, and "visuality and violence." At USC, a professor of business ethics had his students view testimonies of survivors who had worked as slave labor in the Nazi industrial complex IG Farben. Courses at USC's School of Cinematic Arts have also made use of testimonies, such as one on media representations of the Holocaust. (See the essay by Jeffrey Shandler exploring a related topic, page 276–277.)

Over time, the expanding reach of the Visual History Archive has transformed the very place of testimony in scholarly research. Traditionally, oral history had not been considered a reliable primary source; most historians used testimony mainly to illustrate events they were reconstructing from official documents—"a practice that has impoverished our understanding of the Holocaust," according to Omer Bartov, professor of European history at Brown University. Bartov and others make a strong case for integrating testimonies into Holocaust history on an equal footing with other forms of documentation, many of which were "written by perpetrators and organizers of genocide." Eyewitness accounts can bring to light perspectives on events that would otherwise remain unknown, saving them from oblivion and providing "a richer and more complex reconstruction" of history. They offer historians new perspectives and allow them to correct "official" versions of events. And because of their very subjectivity, "Personal testimonies provide insight into the lives and minds of the men, women, and children" who experienced persecution and genocide, and thus "can tell us much about the period's mental landscape, the protagonists' psychology, and others' views and perceptions."

SURVIVORS AND *SCHINDLER'S LIST*
A Scholar Examines the Shaping of Memory
by Jeffrey Shandler

The USC Shoah Foundation's Visual History Archive (VHA) provides rich resources for scholars—and not only on those topics that the archive's creators first had in mind. Indeed, the test of any archive lies in what researchers discover within its holdings beyond the original vision of their value.

As part of my ongoing interest in memory practices—especially the roles played by various media in the ways that narratives about the past are created and shared—I have turned to the VHA to study how Holocaust survivors relate their life stories. I've long been curious about how survivors' personal histories are informed by other Holocaust narratives that these men and women have encountered over the years in history books, memoirs, films, museum exhibitions, and other sources. The VHA provides singular opportunities to pursue this question. I found an especially revealing example in the dozens of Holocaust survivors who mention the film *Schindler's List* at some point during their interviews. Most of them—65 interviews, all with Jewish survivors—were conducted in English; they include 15 of the hundreds of Jews helped by Oskar Schindler during World War II, who came to be known as "Schindler Jews." Watching these videos reveals many surprising, thought-provoking insights.

Survivors mention *Schindler's List* at various points in the course of being interviewed. Sometimes they invoke the film as a point of comparison; knowing that their interviewers had recently seen *Schindler's List*, these survivors describe their wartime experiences in relation to what appears in the film. For example, Sia Hertsberg describes witnessing deportations of children in Riga: "When they were taking the children, I remember in *Schindler's List* he showed that the children were taken by a truck, but an open truck, and ours was a closed one."

Schindler Jews make more pointed comparisons between their recollections of events and how they are portrayed in *Schindler's List*. Thus, Roman Ferber claims that he was the boy shown in the film hiding in the sewer during the liquidation of the Cracow ghetto ("You're looking at him right now," he tells his interviewer) but then differs with the film's account: "There were two of us and three girls. But we didn't ever jump in…, we just hid in the toilet. . . . Had we jumped in, like it's shown in the movie, . . . I would have been dead today, because it was about sixteen, eighteen feet deep."

Some Schindler Jews grapple with disparities between their own story and the film's narrative. They rationalize these differences by explaining how the film came to be made or by considering the limits of the medium. During her interview, Helena Jonas-Rosenzweig reports that her family was upset that she was not mentioned in Thomas Keneally's novel, on which the film is based. Rosenzweig rationalizes that everyone involved in the actual events could not be included as a character, "otherwise the book would never end and the story would never end." Of her absence from the book and film, she remarks, "It doesn't matter, the story is there." Several Schindler Jews comment that the film does not portray the full extent of the horrors that they witnessed during the war and wonder whether any film could—or should—do so.

Toward the end of their interviews, a number of survivors recall going to see *Schindler's List* as a memorable event in their lives. George Hartman, for example, recalls crying when he saw the film and describes this as a "curious" response. "When . . . seeing the reality you don't cry, there's nothing to cry about, you know you're going to die tomorrow probably, you see all this horror. . . . It's only when I see it now, when . . . everything is normal . . . it's much more emotional than actually being there."

Several survivors claim that seeing *Schindler's List* motivated their decision to talk publicly about their wartime experiences. For others, reflecting on the film prompts them to consider the implications of transforming an experience into a narrative, such as the challenge of relating in a few hours events that had happened over the course of several years. Israel Arbeiter explains that *Schindler's List* was the "closest that I have ever seen to the truth of what happened in Auschwitz, [but] it gives you only five, ten minutes—I went through this five years. . . . How can this be shown?"

Survivors' discussions of *Schindler's List* variously affirm, elaborate, or question its narrative. The film inspired some survivors to tell their own stories, others to ponder the challenges of doing so. And *Schindler's List* is not the only work about the Holocaust that survivors mention during their VHA interviews. They also refer to other feature films, documentaries, telecasts, and books, as well as museums and other institutions dedicated to remembering the Holocaust. Some of these survivors clearly paid great attention to the many public presentations of Holo-

caust narratives made over the course of the half-century between the end of World War II and the time when the interviews were made.

Given that they were recorded in the mid-1990s, the life histories in the VHA may be, in comparison to all Holocaust survivors' personal narratives, among the most extensively informed by other such accounts, whether of other individuals' wartime experiences or of the Holocaust writ large. This in no way undermines the significance of these interviews, though it challenges expectations that they offer "pure" or "unmediated" memory. Rather, it points up the value of the VHA's recordings as richly layered palimpsests of memory. These videos reveal how Holocaust survivors have reflected—in some cases, for decades—on what it means to recall this harrowing chapter of their lives, knowing that it is part of

one of the most extensively represented episodes of modern history.

My study of survivors discussing *Schindler's List* is but one of many such possibilities that the VHA provides for scholars interested in the workings of memory. I'm also looking at other sets of interviews, including those that were conducted in Yiddish, as well as interviews in which survivors reveal injuries they received during the Holocaust, recite their own literary compositions, or talk about religious items they had during the war—and often still have, displaying them during the video. Each of these interviews offers new insights not only into how survivors recall the past but also into how media both shape the way survivors relate their life stories and enable researchers to explore new questions about the Holocaust and its remembrance.

———

JEFFREY SHANDLER is Professor of Jewish Studies at Rutgers University. His books include *While America Watches: Televising the Holocaust*; *Awakening Lives: Autobiographies of Jewish Youth in Poland before the Holocaust*; and *Anne Frank Unbound: Media, Imagination, Memory*, among other titles. His translations from Yiddish include Yankev Glatshteyn's *Emil and Karl*, the first Holocaust novel for young readers.

TEACHING WITH TESTIMONY

"Testimonies give students a very human, real experience. It transcends the cultural and linguistic barriers that I constantly face. With the students that I teach, I need to get to their hearts before they'll let me into their heads."

—High school teacher Sharon Hine (Miami, Florida)

In 2001, the Shoah Foundation adopted a new mission statement: "To overcome prejudice, intolerance, bigotry—and the suffering they cause—through the educational use of the foundation's visual history testimonies." Education was the driving motive behind everything the foundation was already doing, but this explicit commitment to an educational mission mapped its path into the future.

"Why did you choose to give testimony? Do you have a message for future generations?" Interviewees were often asked to respond to one or both of these questions. Most survivors or witnesses express the hope that, by speaking out, they will be remembered and will help prevent future tragedies by educating others about the consequences of hatred. The foundation's leaders intended to fulfill that hope for all who gave testimony. Doug Greenberg considered this fervent wish "as compelling as the original mission to collect fifty thousand testimonies, and it must also be pursued relentlessly."

With the wrapping up of interviewing, the foundation was free to shift resources to its education department, which was expanded in 2002. Carrying out the newly formalized mission would be a global effort, with considerable focus on students who had not been exposed to Holocaust education, especially in the countries directly affected. As with all the foundation's efforts, educational outreach would be undertaken through partnerships and oriented to local cultures and ways of learning—whether carried out in Miami or Munich.

Key resources for bringing visual history into the classroom were the products the foundation developed using the eyewitness testimonies, such as CD-ROMs and documentary films. They were used in many ways. For example, by late 2002, the five films in the *Broken Silence* series of documentaries (see page 248) were being screened for teachers and students in Russia, Hungary, and Italy; adoption in other countries followed. After a screening for high school students in Budapest of *Eyes of the Holocaust,* the Hungarian-

Above: Young Hungarians watch the Broken Silence *documentaries at the Szeged Film Festival, 2002. Opposite: Teacher Garry Barnette brings lessons from the Visual History Archive into his classroom at Fort Dorchester High School in Charleston, South Carolina, 2002.*

language documentary, one teacher noted how "the Holocaust is seen from children's perspective . . . [and it] captivates students' attention."

These visual tools were typically used in a framework of programs the foundation built and supported, with the help of educational partners. Among the earliest was a joint initiative with the American Association of School Administrators, aiming to answer two questions: How do you make the history of the Holocaust part of schoolchildren's broader education in tolerance? And how do you prepare administrators and educators to convey this information? What emerged was a three-year pilot program to explore strategies for teaching tolerance at five public school systems representing a diverse student population: Sarasota, Florida; Long Beach, California; Chicago; Fairfax County, Virginia; and Portland, Oregon. Steven Spielberg shared his hopes for the effort at its launch: "Ultimately, what we're going to do is build a more tolerant and humane generation of students—by providing students with the skills that allow them to deal constructively with prejudice and hatred." Toward that end, more than one hundred educators collaborated to develop curricula that used the foundation's films, CD-ROMs, and teacher training materials.

Students and teachers in one of the participating school districts, Long Beach, had the chance to meet face to face with survivor Paula Lebovics—chosen because she was close to the students' own age at the time she went through the war and camp incarceration. Students in eighth-grade history classes wrote essays about her experience. Educator Laurie Shaw noted that the program connected the survivors' imperiled sense of personal identity during their wartime traumas with the students' efforts to define who they are—a theme that would surface again and again in the foundation's educational programs.

"The question is," said Shaw, "are teachers just teaching facts or are they getting to a deeper level? That's why the foundation materials are so powerful—because they get down to that deep emotional level where you begin to feel a sense of outrage. That's when kids really start to internalize what it means to treat people in a respectful, tolerant fashion."

> ❝ We hope to give future generations the tools to do what ours has failed to do: to abolish intolerance and genocidal violence from the human landscape.❞ —Douglas Greenberg

THE TESTIMONY OF **PAULA LEBOVICS**

Date of birth . . . . September 25, 1933
Place of birth . . . . Ostrowiec, Poland
Date of interview . . . . March 16, 1995
Location of interview . . . . Encino,
California, USA
Language . . . . English
Experience . . . . Jewish survivor

As PAULA LEBOVICS *describes, most of the prisoners at Auschwitz-Birkenau were marched out of the camp by the German guards when Soviet armed forces neared the camp in January 1945. She was among the few who remained in the camp, and she remembers searching for food and warm boots. Paula was liberated by Soviet soldiers on January 27, 1945. She was eleven years old at the time.*

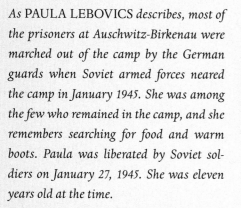

December 1940

All through January, the people were just marching out. And the camp next to us—my brother's camp—was completely empty. But about ten days before liberation, the last patrol, they came on motorcycles with an attached little wagon. And they pulled up in front of our block. I don't remember if they took some of our children. They might have taken some but they did not take me. And they took my mother. And they marched them away.

After they went, we had no Germans, nothing. We were all free. We were by ourselves. No electricity, no nothing. The first thing we all did was to go to the storeroom and got bread. And I remember holding my bread under whatever I was wearing. I had bread, bread wherever you touched me. I was completely insulated.

The second thing we did was to go to the storerooms and got ourselves dressed warmly. This was heaven. I remember that I wanted to have boots and I couldn't find boots. I found one boot in a brownish luggage-color leather with cocoa-color felt. But I couldn't find the mate. I was so frustrated and the kids all wanted to leave, [but then] I found another boot. It was black leather with white felt and it was much bigger. I remember there was nothing happier in my life than finding these boots at that time and putting on warm shoes. But little did I realize, I went outside in the snow and they soaked right through. But it was heaven.

And, on the twenty-seventh of January, the Russians came in. And they liberated us. A lot of people have bad memories from it, but I have good ones. I am very grateful. I had a particular wonderful story about a soldier picking me up, sitting me down, and rocking me in his arms and the tears were flowing down his face. And I can never forget that as long as I live. Just to look at him and figuring in my head, "Somebody out there really cares about me?" It was the first time I had that kind of feeling. It was overwhelming. ∎

OPPOSITE: Still photo from a Soviet film made just after the liberation of Auschwitz, 1945; Paula is the shortest child, second row center, with headscarf. ABOVE: Paula, aged about seven, with her family in Ostrowiec, Poland, late 1940; she is seated in front.

270

Expanding access to the Visual History Archive itself was another key strategy in rolling out the education mission. In 2000, foundation staff and volunteers worked with researchers and teachers under the auspices of the National Writing Project to explore how teachers could learn to mine the archive directly—and gain the technical and historical knowledge to then share its resources with their students. Similar efforts proliferated over the years: in 2003, the foundation hosted a week-long workshop at the Tapper Center, funded by the National Science Foundation, for teachers from geographically and culturally diverse cities across the United States.

> ❝ You build the technology, and we'll learn how to talk to it . . . and then we'll teach others how to use it so that these memories can be shared throughout the world. ❞
>
> —Cathy Pettijohn, high school teacher, Oklahoma City

Educational efforts went international, too, as more communities outside the United States gained local access to the Visual History Archive. In 2002, the foundation participated in the European Council of Jewish Communities educators' conference in London—an important step in nurturing dialogue with European teachers and students. Educators from all over Europe attended screenings of the *Broken Silence* films, and Luca Illy, the foundation's regional consultant in Hungary, conducted a workshop on using visual history testimony in the classroom. As Illy explained, "Teaching European students about the Holocaust requires going beyond a theoretical approach. For

A HUNGARIAN STUDENT RESPONDS TO TESTIMONY

Melinda Orosz, a student at Barczi Gusztav College, took a course about prejudice and diversity called Racism-Antiracism, which uses Hungarian-language materials from the Shoah Foundation. She spoke about it with regional consultant Luca Illy.

Q. How did watching *Eyes of the Holocaust* and Shoah Foundation testimonies affect you?

A. I have always been interested in World War II and have read many books about it. But what was new for me is that survivors could make us, the viewers, feel how they felt when these things happened to them. The way they recount their experiences [is echoed] in their eyes and makes a deep impression on me.

My friends . . . think that the Holocaust is exhausted, it is "gnawed bones" . . . they are tired of it and [want to] forget about it. Through this course, I realized that survivors did not really have the opportunity to speak, either because they were not ready or because nobody wanted to hear them.

Q. How do you feel about the Racism-Antiracism course?

A. For me, what I feel when I leave the classroom is important. Each time I leave the racism course, my heart is throbbing. The entire lesson just stays in me. There is a special atmosphere during the lessons: I feel that what I say really counts.

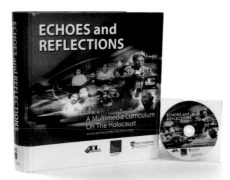

instance, there is a high school in Budapest where two thousand Jews hid during the war. The challenge is to teach beyond the facts and connect students to personal perspectives of events that occurred in their own towns, in their own backyards."

The *Broken Silence* films, as well as the German-language CD-ROM, were important outreach tools throughout this early period. Higher education became a target as well: in 2003, *Racism-Antiracism,* the first college course based on the foundation's Visual History Archive, was offered to students at Barczi Gusztav College in Hungary. With a new partnership begun in 2003, testimonies from the foundation's collection were paired with the renowned educational programs of the Holocaust Educational Trust in the United Kingdom. And in 2004, the foundation established the Central and Eastern European Education Fund to develop partnerships and provide access to the testimonies and related products for educators and scholars.

For its most ambitious educational program of the pre-USC years, the foundation in 2003 partnered with the Anti-Defamation League—and later with Yad Vashem—to develop a multimedia curriculum that would integrate testimonies from the archive with the robust teaching materials of the partner organizations. *Echoes and Reflections,* which ultimately came into use in every state in the nation, was a complete ten-lesson package that high school educators could use to teach the complex issues of the Holocaust—topics including anti-Semitism, Nazi Germany, the ghettos, the Final Solution, and resistance—and also support the study of world history, English, Holocaust studies, fine arts, and character education.

One of the program's chief aims was to connect the study of history to contemporary issues of diversity, prejudice, and violence. "I see a lot of connections . . . ways that I can bring in current genocides," commented a ninth-grade teacher in Washington. "It serves as a great stepping stone to talk about those issues, because students need to know that this is something that is still going on right now—not

KIDS GET THAT

When students see a testimony, they almost always say, "That person reminds me of my uncle, or my grandmother. . . ." It really helps them personalize their perception of the Holocaust. Also, testimonies speak to the strength of the human spirit, [demonstrating] that people are resilient and able to forgive. They present a challenge to the rest of us: tragedies are part of life and we must find the strength and resolve to get on with life. And kids get that. One of my students said, "If the people hadn't recovered after the Holocaust then Hitler and the Nazis would have won completely." —*Garry Barnette, a teacher at Fort Dorchester High School, Charleston, South Carolina*

ABOVE: Echoes and Reflections *program package*

THE TESTIMONY OF **MURRAY PANTIRER**

Date of birth . . . . .June 15, 1925
Place of birth. . . . . .Krakow, Poland
Date of interview . . . . . September 6, 1995
Location of interview. . . . . .Hillside,
New Jersey, USA
Language. English
Experience. . . . . .Jewish survivor

MURRRAY PANTIRER *was transferred from the Krakow-Plaszow concentration camp in Poland to the Gross-Rosen camp in Germany. In Gross-Rosen, living conditions for Murray became increasingly difficult, and the future looked bleak until he learned that his name was on Oskar Schindler's list. As a result, he was transferred to the Brunnlitz camp in Czechoslovakia, where he was eventually liberated.*

In October I was put on a train because they started liquidating Plaszow. When we got to Gross-Rosen, there were no beds. We sat on the floor. If one guy had to go to the bathroom, the whole row [turned], like sardines. We were getting showers, we were getting new clothing. They took all our old clothing away, because they were thinking maybe we have some stuff, maybe some money, some [valuables].

We were told that they don't keep people more than five days. After five days in Gross-Rosen, if they don't call you out to some camp to work, or some factory, they liquidate you. They kill you.

If I was a [religious] fanatic, I would say that [an] angel flew down to Gross-Rosen and wrote down my name, and Oskar Schindler was sent from God.

After three days, rumors had it Oskar Schindler was coming with a list. We were thinking it's wishful thinking, maybe somebody dreamed up a story. On the fourth day, we were called out on the *Appellplatz* [roll-call area], and we were told, every name that will be called [should] go to the side. One of the Jewish police, Master Goldberg, was reading the list. At number 205, they call out: "Pantirer, Moses!" And the Germans were yelling, *"Beruf! Beruf!"* [job or trade]. What's my trade? I didn't know what to

say, but somebody else who was with Master Goldberg was saying, "sheet metal worker." To this day I don't know who put me on the list, and who put "sheet metal worker."

I was nineteen years old then, I was already a few years in camp. I was a kid of fourteen years old when the war broke out—I had no opportunity to learn a trade. But somebody lied for me so I could survive.

If I was a [religious] fanatic, I would say that [an] angel flew down to Gross-Rosen and wrote down my name, and Oskar Schindler was sent from God. Maybe someday we will find out. Maybe the skies are not empty after all. ■

ABOVE: Murray and his family standing with his partner and fellow survivor, Abraham Zuckerman, at the dedication of Schindler Terrace in West Orange, New Jersey, 1995.
LEFT: Murray's younger brother, Chaim, in 1940, age thirteen.

something that's fixed in history. And we need to talk about it today." *Echoes and Reflections* remains the foundation's chief curriculum to teach about the Holocaust.

Another project developed during this period was *Giving Voice*—a comprehensive classroom kit containing two videos and a teacher's guide. Inspired by the dynamic style of reality TV, the first video intercut survivor testimonies with the video diaries of seven Southern California teenagers, following them through a one-day workshop as they responded to watching the testimonies. The second video featured seven interviews from the archive that high school students could view with their teacher. *Giving Voice* allowed students to tell their own stories via video testimony, in parallel to the survivors' eyewitness accounts of the Holocaust, thus making connections between history and their own lives. It was

a powerful experience for the young people involved and for those who later used the videos in their classrooms. "You never really know how judgmental you are, until you stop being judgmental," said seventeen-year-old Roxanne, a student from Venice, California, who took part in the filming. "A single experience can help you make that change. For me, it was *Giving Voice*." Roxanne's friend, Nikki, who is also featured on the video, adds, "I expect people my age to have the same values, but to realize that we shared so many values with Holocaust survivors, such as the importance of family, or standing up for one's rights—that was unbelievable!"

■

"Our dream, our goal for the decade hence is that children in schools throughout the world will be able to see the face, hear the voice of a survivor, and realize that a society free of racial hatred is theirs to build."

When Douglas Greenberg wrote this vision statement in 2005, he added, "Our work of the last ten years, though focused on the past, has built a foundation for the future." The Shoah Foundation had just marked its tenth anniversary the pre-

Top: Left to right, Shoah Foundation board of councilors member Yossie Hollander, and wife Dana Hollander; Avner Shalev, chairman of the directorate Yad Vashem; Douglas Greenberg; Abraham Foxman, director of Anti-Defamation League. Above: Participants in the Giving Voice project.

AMBASSADORS FOR HUMANITY

Recognizing its kinship with people everywhere who share its aims and values, the Shoah Foundation in 2000 inaugurated its Ambassadors for Humanity award, which honors "individuals who embody the Shoah Foundation's goals of promoting tolerance, cultural understanding, and mutual respect around the world." The presentation gala for the award soon became the organization's chief fundraising event. Recipients have included Jeffrey Katzenberg, chairman and CEO of DreamWorks Animation; Robert A. Iger, chairman and CEO of the Walt Disney Company; legendary actor and humanitarian Kirk Douglas; philanthropist Wallis Annenberg; and artist and humanitarian George Clooney.

In 2005, when the foundation hon-

ored President Bill Clinton with the award, more than 750 guests gathered in Los Angeles to pay tribute to the former president's commitment to fighting racial, ethnic, and religious discrimination. Clinton was president during a time of genocide and ethnic violence; his humility in acknowledging how daunting this challenge was made his message all the more powerful. Referring to Clinton's activist role, Steven Spielberg said, "This is a story that proves, like the story of Oskar Schindler, that one person can make a difference." In accepting the award, Clinton said, "Let us never be guilty of teaching our children to categorize others by the color of their skin, the source of their creed, the nature of

their politics, or their ethnic, tribal, or clan background." He also returned a compliment to Spielberg, saying about *Schindler's List*, "It is a tribute to his insight that he understood the power of the true stories of the real people who survived could do even more."

Top LEFT: Wallis Annenberg speaks at the 2010 gala. TOP RIGHT: Jeffrey Katzenberg, who received the award in 2010, with Steven Spielberg. LEFT: Steven Spielberg and Bill Clinton at the 2005 gala. ABOVE: George Clooney, the 2013 awardee.

vious year. During its first decade, the foundation met and surpassed its original goals, collecting fifty-two thousand testimonies of survivors of the Holocaust and other eyewitnesses in fifty-six countries and in thirty-two languages. Half of the testimonies had been indexed and digitized, with the remainder of that task slated for completion within two years.

The entire Visual History Archive could be accessed at three universities in the United States and would soon be available at universities and libraries around the world. Parts of the archive, in the form of national and state collections, were available in fourteen countries. The foundation's documentary films had been broadcast and screened in forty countries, and subtitled into nineteen languages. Its educational products were in use in eleven thousand schools nationally and internationally—and many would soon be available on a new website, reaching hundreds of thousands of schools in virtually every country on the globe.

Yet the foundation's leaders could not feel complacent about their accomplishments, with hate crimes on the rise in the United States and in other countries. To cite just two pieces of evidence: during 2003, the Southern Poverty Law Center monitored the activities of 708 hate groups in the United States. And in November of that year, bombers attacked two synagogues in Istanbul, Turkey, killing sixty-two people. In a disturbing new trend, hate speech and images were enter-

ing youth culture through the veins of popular music and video games. As the power of the Internet grew exponentially, it became clear that it was a two-edged sword; it could help promote tolerance—or the reverse. The Shoah Foundation intended to be a force for tolerance to prevail.

On the minds of Steven Spielberg and his colleagues were some urgent priorities: to extend the organization's educational reach, to find a secure and appropriate lifetime home for the archive, and to make sure that the videotaped testimonies, whose shelf life in their original form was waning, would be forever preserved so that they could go on speaking to successive generations, into the far future. A unique opportunity to fulfill those goals was on the horizon. ■

ABOVE: cast members Caroline Goodall, Sir Ben Kingsley, Embeth Davidtz, and Ralph Fiennes, with Steven Spielberg and Sid Sheinberg, mark the tenth anniversary DVD release of the film and the tenth anniversary of the Shoah Foundation, 2004.

NEW FRONTIERS
FOR TESTIMONY

On a Friday in December 2005, half a dozen moving vans pulled up to the trailers on the Universal Studios lot, and began loading the contents of the Shoah Foundation offices for a momentous move. A few months earlier, in a joint press release, the foundation and the University of Southern California had announced the foundation would become part of USC, effective January 1. By the end of that December day, the organization was housed in the Leavey Library on USC's Los Angeles campus, in preparation for its reopening as the USC Shoah Foundation—The Institute for Visual History and Education. Its home at the university would be the Dana and David Dornsife College of Letters, Arts and Sciences.

Under the landmark agreement that preceded the physical move, not only did USC guarantee the perpetual preservation of the Visual History Archive's fifty-two thousand testimonies, but it also made a commitment to expanding the foundation's educational mission along with access to the archive for scholarship and research. The rebirth of the foundation as an institute at USC made it possible to accomplish a profound transition in the focus of its work and, in a very real sense, enabled the organization to continue to exist.

LEFT: *Steven Spielberg with students at the launch of the IWitness Video Challenge at Chandler School, Pasadena, February 2013.*

This news climaxed five years' worth of careful planning for the future of the foundation and its priceless archive—a process led by president and CEO Douglas Greenberg and the board of directors with the support of Steven Spielberg at every step. In fact, the move to USC was a natural, perhaps inevitable, outcome of the vision Spielberg had always held for the testimonies: that they would be preserved in perpetuity and used for education far into the future. Even before Greenberg was hired, he and Spielberg had agreed that they should work together with an expanded board—and its energetic new chair, Susan Crown—to find an academic home for the archive.

Among the first fruits of that planning process was a new mission statement, crafted in 2001. The core task it described was "to overcome prejudice, intolerance and bigotry— and the suffering they cause—through the educational use of the testimonies." This became the touchstone for all the work of the following years, as educational outreach—undertaken with a vigorous new education department, with active partners, and internationally—took center stage. Emphasizing education meant finding new ways to involve students and teachers at the secondary level; it also meant strengthening ties with institutions of higher learning and museums around the world. "We turned the collection of testimonies into an internationally available resource for scholarship and teaching," says Greenberg. They found partner sites for the testimonies around Europe; worked with governments and NGO partners throughout Europe and in Israel and Australia to create educational products and projects that had real impact; and, with Internet2 connections, they partnered with Rice and Yale Universities and USC to encourage scholarship. The budding relationship with USC proved to be pivotal.

Preservation issues, always front and center, were becoming urgent. As Sam Gustman frequently reminded his colleagues, "Tape rots." Preserving the testimonies was another race against time, as Greenberg saw it. "It is our moral obligation and our most challenging responsibility." In the first years of the new millennium, the foundation's leaders also began to think hard about building new collections beyond the Shoah testimonies, and some traveled to Rwanda as a first step toward that end.

Finally, it was no accident that the arrival of the moving vans at the close of 2005 exactly coincided with the completion of indexing on all fifty-two thousand testimonies. Another outcome of the planning process begun in 2000 was the shift into a faster indexing gear. This was vital, because until the indexing was accomplished and preservation was assured, none of the planned rollout of new programs in education and scholarship could happen. Along with the move to USC, the last indexed testimony thus represented a true turning point for the organization.

FINDING A HOME AT USC

"USC is where the Shoah Foundation belongs. It is where the Shoah Foundation will be in guaranteed perpetuity. This is the anchor that the Shoah Foundation needs, even more than symbolically, to reach out to other institutions all across the world, to disseminate fifty-two thousand voices that will never be silenced." —Steven Spielberg

Spielberg and his fellow leaders saw clearly that the Visual History Archive could make its greatest contributions in the context of a major research and educational establishment. They needed the support and resources of such an institution to fulfill the goals to which they were so passionately committed. USC in turn recognized the enormous potential of the Visual History Archive, not only to further the study of the Holocaust and other genocides on its own campus but also as a resource for scholars around the world. Douglas Greenberg, who would become the first executive director of the institute at USC, describes the move as "very much like a great collection of manuscripts" arriving at the university.

USC, of course, was one of the first universities to make use of the collec-

> " No matter how our civilization advances, certain values define us as individuals and as a society. The content of the Visual History Archive is priceless material to teach those core values to our students. "
>
> —C.L. Max Nikias, president, University of Southern California

Above: Ari Zev in the lobby of the USC Shoah Foundation Institute 2007.

tion—by 2003, all its students and faculty had a direct link, from their classrooms and on their computers, to the digitized testimonies in the archive. Connections also had grown up between faculty members and foundation staff; for example, in exploring testimony from Rwanda. Discussions about establishing a more permanent relationship went back to 2001. But it would be a complex and wrenching undertaking for both sides. By 2005, despite plenty of good faith and hard work, the obstacles were beginning to seem insurmountable.

The key figure in turning the tide was the university's newly appointed provost, C. L. Max Nikias, who made clear his intent to ensure that the marriage took place and began intensive negotiations toward that end. It all came down to one final meeting that autumn among Nikias, Greenberg, the foundation's board, and their respective attorneys in the provost's office. At day's end, as Nikias tells it, he paced the floor nervously as the foundation board stood in a circle outside his window, speaking by phone with someone he presumed to be Steven Spielberg. (At least up to that point, Spielberg had kept apart from the discussions, wanting to make sure that USC truly recognized the scholarly and educa-

Top: C. L. Max Nikias, president of the University of Southern California. Above: Members of the USC Shoah Foundation Board of Councilors in 2012. Seated, left to right: Tad Taube, Erna Viterbi, Robert J. Katz (chair), Lee Lieberman, Stephen A. Cozen. Standing, left to right: Eric Greenberg, Yossie Hollander, David Eisman, Jerome L. Coben, Joel Citron, Dr. Anita Friedman, Phyllis Epstein, Mickey Shapiro, Harry L. Robinson

tion value of the archive.) After the final details had been hammered out, founding board member and longtime Spielberg counselor Jerry Breslauer returned to the office and embraced Nikias. "We have a deal!" he said.

Although very complicated in its details, the deal boiled down to a simple exchange: the foundation conveyed its intellectual property in the archive to USC in return for USC's guarantee of perpetual preservation. "Without USC, it is not too much to say, the archive was in danger of disappearing altogether," Greenberg believes. Instead, the world's largest video archive—and the unique technologies Gustman had devised to access it—found a permanent home at USC. Not only would the archive be preserved, but its reach would be vastly extended.

"By combining the strengths of the Shoah Foundation and USC," said USC President Steven Sample when the agreement was made, "we can work together to help eliminate the attitudes and prejudices that divide societies around the world." Max Nikias, who succeeded Sample as president, understood that USC is an ideal home for an organization with a global mission, with an enthusiastic community of scholars and teachers prepared to mine the testimonies for the good of humanity. He spoke eloquently for his university about the responsibility of holding the archive: "I am honored and humbled to be the custodian of the USC Shoah Foundation's archive. The testimonials of more than fifty thousand survivors of the Holocaust give voice to the voiceless and life to the lifeless in the kingdom of memory."

IN PERPETUITY: PRESERVING VISUAL HISTORY BIT BY BIT

"By capturing the human condition digitally, the USC Shoah Foundation has made one of the most significant contributions toward understanding and improving our world."

—STEVE KAY, DEAN, USC DORNSIFE COLLEGE

Three years after the foundation joined USC, its combined IT teams led by Chief Technology Officer Sam Gustman initiated the next-generation preservation effort so urgently required—an endeavor that would produce exact digital replicas of the aging videotaped testimonies, and in the process turn USC into a world leader in visual archiving. First up was actually transferring the archive to USC. In May 2009, the first 15,000 of a total of 235,000 videotapes made a cross-country journey by truck from a vault in the eastern United States, where the masters were securely stored, to the institute. The rest would follow over a period of three years.

Then began a massive, multiyear initiative to copy all the testimonies in an advanced digital format. In figuring out how to convey 235,000 videotaped master recordings to state-of-the-art digital storage, Gustman first had to set some criteria. The system would need to maintain the original, ultra-high quality of picture and sound for these preservation copies. The team would need to make additional copies in a variety of formats and resolutions to accommodate all imaginable uses. And they would tolerate zero errors in the transfer from tape to digital: a high bar and costly bar indeed.

"With nondigital items—books, for example—errors such as torn pages and water damage can't be assigned a numerical value. But in the digital world, degradation is absolutely measurable," Gustman said in 2010. "The institute's 'bit by bit' preservation system will keep the archive's digital degradation to zero, including minute changes that would take centuries even to detect with the human eye."

To design the system, Gustman turned first to the US government—specifically the Library of Congress and its Packard Campus of the National Audio-Visual Conservation Center in Culpepper, Virginia. This little-known center, supported by taxpayers and the Packard Humanities Institute, stores the nation's largest collection of film, television, and video—more than 1.1 million items—and boasts state-of the-art facilities for the acquisition, cataloging and preservation of all audiovisual formats. "They had the resources to do the upfront engineering," says Gustman.

In the system ultimately built at the university's new data center, a robotic device takes the analog tapes and automatically creates files as fast as it can, then

LINKS THROUGH TIME

Our mission . . . depends upon the preservation of the archive; the life stories it holds are the links through which generations of people, ever more distant in time and space from the Holocaust, will come to understand its historical significance and human consequences. —*Douglas Greenberg*

"writes" them to a large file server. "We check all the way, step by step," says Gustman, "to make sure the quality of the signal taken off the tape is unchanged by the time it arrives at the storage systems." The archive now totals four petabytes in size—the equivalent of 959,795 DVDs. The institute's IT team checks the whole archive every three months for any evidence of lost data.

The preservation copies were recorded in an electronic format called Motion JPEG 2000, which captures a lossless copy of the original signal from the videotape. "This is becoming the format of choice used to store moving images," Gustman says, "and

the institute is one of the largest early adopters." That copy is then automatically "migrated," avoiding loss of quality over time. Migration, the most reliable approach to preservation, entails constantly copying a video file from one piece of media to another before it starts to degrade or when it shows signs of doing so. Long-term success requires keeping multiple copies, preferably in different locations. Two complete copies of the Visual History Archive exist in the United States, with another planned in the Netherlands and a fourth at Charles University in Prague. Ultimately, says Gustman, the safest situation will be to have one on every major land mass.

Beyond monitoring the data constantly, the IT team is working on restoring some of the interviews. Glitches or variations in the quality of the original video sometimes resulted from dirty or broken cameras, or operator error; some 12,000 of the 235,000 original videotapes acquired an imperfection of some kind during the production process. With proprietary technology they developed, technicians are restoring those damaged tapes, one at a time.

In June 2012, a milestone was reached when all 51,694 testimonies in the archive had undergone the preservation process. It's easy to get carried away by the sheer technological sophistication of the work, but it's all in the service of the institute's mission. Making sure that the testimonies are safeguarded in their wholly original, authentic form; that none of the information or the impact of "seeing and hearing" the survivors is lost because of degraded quality; that formats are available for every use currently imaginable—all of this matters critically in optimizing the impact of the Visual History Archive for the next generation.

THE ARCHIVE UNBOUND

When electronic access to the Visual History Archive via Internet2 was piloted in 2002, the foundation was able to connect with only a few universities, due in

Opposite: Shoah Foundation information technology staff move original videotapes from storage to prepare for the preservation effort.
Above: Brian Roberts, chairman and CEO of Comcast, with Sam Gustman, right, at the IT systems facility in 2011, the year Roberts was named the foundation's Ambassador for Humanity.

part to network and server limitations. As Karen Jungblut explains, "We had to limit the initial number of participating institutions so we could identify the technical requirements, logistical challenges, and financial resources needed to host the archive electronically." Joining forces with USC enabled the institute to turbocharge its capacity to provide access for scholarship and research at many more sites around the world.

"The university's High-Performance Computing and Communications (HPCC) supercomputer cluster is one of the fastest supercomputers in academia," notes Gustman. "At seventy-two teraflops, it's super fast and therefore capable of transforming the entire archive into almost any digital video format in weeks."

In December 2006, Freie Universität Berlin became the first institution outside the United States to provide access to the entire Visual History Archive via Internet2. By 2007, "thanks to the HPCC," said Gustman, "we [could] deliver content to institutions as far away as Monash University in Melbourne, Australia ... connected to the archive at 400 megabits per second." And beginning in 2008, any university, archive, museum, or other site with Internet2 or equivalent connectivity could offer electronic access to the complete Visual History Archive.

> 66 Thanks to advancements in telecommunications, the rapid evolution of digital video technology, and our full integration into a leading university, there has never been greater opportunity to share the testimonies with the world. 99 —Kim Simon, managing director

ABOVE: Video archive and post-production specialist Jeremy Morelock works on digitally restoring a testimony.

By late 2013, users at forty-four institutions on every continent except Antarctica—from Aristotle University of Thessaloniki (Greece) to the Zentrum für Antisemitismusforschung in Germany—could access the Visual History Archive. Most institutions are universities but the list also includes the United States Holocaust Memorial Museum in Washington, D.C., and Yad Vashem in Jerusalem. A redesigned user interface, introduced in 2010 and regularly updated, enables users to navigate through multiple web pages, bookmark search results and video segments for future use, share searches, and password-protect projects.

A not-quite-final frontier was making testimonies available on the open Internet—a prospect the organization had always approached with great care and caution (see page 236). In 2007, the institute worked with developers to design and build a new website; it included an Online Testimony Viewer with which users could access carefully selected clips from interviews. In 2009 the institute launched its YouTube channel, part of USC's educational network of channels, offering content ranging from scholarly lectures and other informative videos to short clips of testimony and more than one hundred full-length testimonies. It was obvious to institute leaders that the then-new Web 2.0 had great potential as a platform to raise awareness of the testimonies and encourage their educational use. Stephen Smith said at the time, "Online access is the key to fulfilling our obligation to disseminate these memories responsibly throughout the world."

> ""Imagine a place where great minds with access to powerful resources can help all of us—children, adults, families, and decision makers around the world—frame our sense of who we are as humans. That place is the USC Shoah Foundation.""
>
> —Peter M. Siegel, CIO and vice provost for information technology services, USC

PARTNERS IN REMEMBRANCE

Yad Vashem has partnered with the Shoah Foundation since its establishment by Steven Spielberg in 1994. From the start, we shared the foundation's understanding of the need to preserve for posterity accessible visual testimonies of Holocaust survivors. It is indeed appropriate that Yad Vashem's own vast databases provide access to [the] institute's collection at USC, for the benefit of meaningful Shoah remembrance worldwide.

—*Avner Shalev, chairman, Yad Vashem Directorate*

Starting in 2012, the online version of the Visual History Archive delivered one thousand English-language testimonies over the Web. Today users can search all of the metadata of all fifty-two thousand testimonies, and play thirteen hundred testimonies online, at vhaonline.usc.edu.

THE TESTIMONY OF **IURII PINCHUK**

Date of birth . . . . .November 23, 1930
Place of birth. . . . . Shpola, Ukraine
Date of interview . . . . .June 21, 1998
Location of interview. . .Vinnytsia, Ukraine
Language. Russian
Experience. . . . . .Jewish survivor

In 1941, when the Germans invaded Shpola (in the former Soviet Union, now Ukraine), IURII PINCHUK's family home was taken over by the German administration, and the family was forced into a local ghetto. In July 1942, all Jews remaining in the Shpola ghetto were marched to a concentration camp in Dar'evka, where they were executed a few days after arriving. Iurii, aged eleven, managed to escape from the camp. He describes the last day with his mother.

I don't know much about [my mother's] life. She perished just when I was eleven. But I can tell you that she was a good mother. Her fate was just not to be.

One day [she] told me, "Iura, you're getting out of here tomorrow." I cried, "What about you and my brother and sister?" She said, "Don't worry, we will all get out one by one." She told me

what to do, who would meet me and where. She said, "You will go out of here and you will follow the path."

I don't know much about [my mother's] life. She perished just when I was eleven. But I can tell you that she was a good mother. Her fate was just not to be.

The area was surrounded by a barbed-wire fence. At the end, behind the bushes, there was a gate used by police and the Germans. A guard stood there. There were guards on all corners of the camp. Policemen walked up

and down, too.

She told me, "There's the path. Stick to the path. Follow it to the pond by the sugar refinery and you'll get to the bridge. There'll be a young woman waiting for you on the bridge. She'll know you, but you won't know her. She will not approach you. She will be standing there, looking at the water. You will walk past her, and she will call your name. You must keep walking. She will catch up with you and you will follow her."

And that is what happened. I did not want to leave. I hung on to my mom and cried. The policeman at the gate shouted, "What's the holdup? Is he coming or not?" And she literally pushed me, opened the gate, and pushed me through. And she turned around and walked away. I started walking down the path. This was the last time I saw my mother. ∎

ABOVE LEFT: Iurii and his wife, Liudmila Pinchuk, during his interview. ABOVE RIGHT: Iurii's maternal grandparents and great-aunt, c. 1930s. LEFT: Identification document verifying Iurii's wartime ghetto experience.

IN THE UNIVERSITIES

"One can argue . . . that oral witnessing stood at the cradle of historical writing, with Herodotus and Thucydides. It is very much alive today."

— Yehuda Bauer, dean of Holocaust scholars, professor emeritus of Holocaust studies at Hebrew University of Jerusalem

Not surprisingly, being based on a campus and becoming integrated into the university environment at USC greatly enhanced the possibilities for promoting the use of visual history in college classrooms. And as access to the VHA proliferated, students on more and more campuses could be exposed to testimony in courses from many disciplines, from anthropology to film, law, and psychology. By the middle of 2013, a total of 371 courses at forty-four universities drew upon the institute's testimonies in more than twenty-five disciplines and fields. Steven Spielberg puts it simply: "Being on a university campus allows academics to look at the archive differently than when we were in trailers on the back lot of a major Hollywood motion picture studio."

> ❝I want to help the students see that when we see intolerance—that when we see bigotry and racism—not doing something is simply not an option.❞
>
> —Paige Leven, Edward R. Roybal Learning Center, Los Angeles

The institute's close relationship with USC's School of Cinematic Arts (with which Steven Spielberg has long been involved) has given rise to several courses at the undergraduate and graduate levels. The Student Voices Film Contest challenges USC students to "join the conversation about genocide and human rights" by producing a five- to seven-minute film using testimony from the Visual History Archive. Winner of the third annual contest in 2013 was Cecilia de Jesus, an MFA candidate in the School of Cinematic Arts. Her first place entry, *Where Is My Home?*, used sand animation to tell the compelling story of Vera Gissing's journey from peril into the unknown, based on Gissing's testimony.

USC's School of Dramatic Arts has used the testimonies to explore

CREATIVE COLLABORATION

Over the years, the U.S. Holocaust Memorial Museum has partnered with the Shoah Foundation on many projects. Together we have imagined and built new ways to educate young people. The museum's Collaboration & Complicity exhibition, for example, uses testimonies to explore the human behavior, motivations, and decision making of the ordinary individuals often called "bystanders." The institute's powerful research tools enabled us to locate the compelling stories at the heart of this exhibition. The access those tools provide will be vitally important when there are no eyewitnesses left to speak for themselves.

—Sara J. Bloomfield, director, U.S. Holocaust Memorial Museum

how performance and storytelling may be able to transform perception, raise awareness and understanding of genocide, and bring about real change. In April 2013, the institute partnered with the school in a series of events for the university's Genocide Awareness Week. One evening featured the presentation of short plays about the Cambodian and Rwandan genocides, and a discussion among the playwrights and performers with Stephen Smith and USC dramatic arts professor Stacie Chaiken, who leads the institute's Witness and Responsibility program.

SPEAKING THE UNSPEAKABLE

It is deeply difficult for most humans to engage fully with testimony related to catastrophe or mass atrocity. We cannot breathe in the face of them. Artists—by virtue of their training—are able to stand in the face of unspeakable things and breathe, in order to make works with which a broad audience *can* engage.
—*Stacie Chaiken, Witness and Responsibility program*

The institute also partners with USC Dornsife College's Problems Without Passports program, which combines problem-based learning research exercises with study abroad. The institute has offered courses in both Rwanda and Cambodia on conflict resolution and peace research. In both, students receive extensive background knowledge and also training in the institute's interviewing methodology. When they travel to those countries the aim is to explore the complex task of post-genocide reconstruction from many sides.

ABOVE: Actors perform playwright Catherine Filloux's short play, Photographs from S-21, *about the Cambodian genocide during USC's Genocide Awareness Week, April 2013. OPPOSITE TOP: USC students who traveled to Rwanda in 2013, as part of the Problems Without Passports program, at the site of a former mass grave at the Murambi Genocide Memorial Center.*

TESTIMONY IN ACADEMIA

Nearly 4,000 university students have enrolled in 137 university courses worldwide that have incorporated testimony from the Visual History Archive. The testimonies have been used in a variety of disciplines, including history, human rights, genocide studies, sociology, psychology, anthropology, business, and film.

These few examples demonstrate the range of topics and themes that the institute's archive of video testimonies can help illuminate.

French IV: Paris as Seen by Writers, Filmmakers, and Photographers

Professor Colin Keaveney's upper-level French course at USC explores themes of love, loss, collective and personal memory, and modernity through readings of French literary texts, theoretical readings, films, poems, and songs. Professor Keaveney contends that "the VHA can provide factual and emotionally powerful information to allow students to better understand those who experienced the German occupation of France in the 1940s."

Animation, Simulation, and Performance

Emily Roxworthy is a member of the theater and dance faculty at the University of California, San Diego. Her course using the archive focuses on graphic representations of war, such as comic books, animated films, and video games about World War II and the global war on terror. "Despite the fact that their generation was practically raised on graphic novels and the comics medium . . . the majority of these students decided that the VHA interviews provoked more empathy and participation than [Art] Spiegelman's *Maus* did," says Roxworthy.

Communicating Grief, Loss, and Trauma

Carolyn Ellis, a professor of communication and sociology at the University of South Florida, leads a graduate seminar that cultivates students' ability to consider testimonies of loss, trauma, and disruption within the dialectic of intimacy and distance. "Listening to [the testimonies from the VHA] prepares students for meeting and listening to survivors and helps them anticipate issues that arise in their interviews," Ellis says.

LEFT: *Professor Carolyn Ellis of the University of South Florida.*

THE TESTIMONY OF **VERA GISSING**

Date of birth . . . . July 4, 1928
Place of birth . . . . .Prague, Czechoslovakia
Date of interview . . . . . . .October 25, 1996
Location of interview . . .Wargave, England
Language . . . . English
Experience . . . . .Jewish survivor

VERA GISSING *remembers her parents discussing and eventually deciding to send her and her sister Eva on a "Kindertransport" from Czechoslovakia to England in May 1939. She describes their farewell at the train station in Prague, and the journey.*

In May, I think, May 1939, we were sitting at the table having dinner, and my mother's plate remained untouched. She suddenly pushed her plate away and looked at Father and said, "I heard today that both Eva and Vera can go to England." And there was a deathly silence. My father suddenly looked very pale and drawn, and he buried his face in his hands, and then he sighed and said, "All right, let them go." It was a very, very strange moment, and after that, I was filled with excitement and apprehension. I didn't know anyone from our town who had ever been to England.

"There may be times when we can't write to one another. But even while we can't, let the stars of the night and the sun of the day be the messengers of our thoughts and love. And in that way, we'll always remain close."

Suddenly, my sister and I assumed great importance, and it seemed like a big, big adventure. And yet we were both going to different places—I to a family in Liverpool I knew nothing about and my parents knew nothing about, and my sister to a school in Dorset. We were going to be separated, the two of us.

Saying goodbye [to my parents] at the Wilson station in Prague in the middle of the night was very hard. The platform was filled with anxious parents and German soldiers, and Mother and Father bravely smiled at us until the time came for the train to leave, and I cried impulsively, "See you again in a free Czechoslovakia!" And suddenly everybody looked horrified and frightened. And as the train chanted from the station, my parents were crying, though they still tried to smile, you know, as they waved us goodbye. And suddenly, I was so glad when my sister's hand reached for mine, and I realized I

Above left: Vera and her older sister, Eva Hayman (right), shortly after departing for England from Celakovice, Czechoslovakia, June 1939.
Above right: Vera (left) and childhood friend Marta Pavlickova in Celakovice, 1995.

still had her. And she confirmed this in the same very words, she said, "You'll always have me, come what may, you can always turn to me to be there for you." And this sister, who I didn't particularly like, being the elder, bossy sister, suddenly changed into a guardian angel, and she remained so, all through the years of the war.

When we went through Germany and Holland, the Dutch people gave us cocoa, I remember, and some chocolate bars at the station, and of course our parents had packed rucksacks full of food for us. And then we got on a boat, and it was nighttime, and I could just hear the sea, I couldn't even see it. But early in the morning I woke up, and through the little cubbyhole I could see the sun rising, and my sister woke up as well, and she sat there with me, and put her arms around me. And we saw this glorious sun shining over the sea, our first sight of the sea, and our first conversation with our mother and father, through the sun.

Later in her interview, Vera recalls the leather-bound diary she received from her parents as a gift just prior to departing for England.

It was a leather-bound book full of empty pages, and [my father] told me to write in it when I was lonely or homesick, or when I was happy, when I had something of interest to say, so that when I came back home, we could all sit round the table and read the diary together. And my mother, she carried me on that last night at home to an open window, and I remember the night sky was full of stars, and she said,

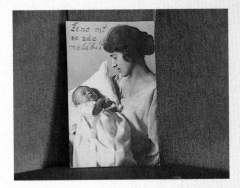

"There may be times when we can't write to one another. But even while we can't, let the stars of the night and the sun of the day be the messengers of our thoughts and love. And in that way, we'll always remain close."

They couldn't have guessed what a godsend those thoughtful gestures would be. Not just to me but to my sister, too, because when war started and all correspondence ceased, we both poured our hearts into our diaries, and I as a little girl every night prayed to God and talked to Mother and Father through the stars. And if a falling star suddenly appeared, I thought, "That must be a special messenger from Mother," you know, and it made all the difference. I never felt abandoned by them, I always felt close to them. ■

Top: Vera's mother with the infant Eva, 1924. Center: Vera's foster parents, Gladys and Robert Rainford, Liverpool, 1941. Above: Vera with her husband, Michael Gissing, and her aunt Berta Kestner (right), Celakovice, 1968.

THE TESTIMONIES ARE ALIVE

The institute's testimonies are alive in a way memoirs are not. You can see survivors struggle with their memories and with the inability to describe sexual violence, which was invaluable for my research on the language of sexual violence—how survivors describe and explain what happened. Memoirs, although they may be beautifully written, are static. ... there is no struggle to articulate the meaning of rape. That is not the case with the institute's testimonies, wherein I can see the physical and linguistic manifestations of traumatic memory.

—*Monika Flaska, history instructor at Kent State University who used testimonies in doctoral research on sexual violence by Nazi soldiers*

The institute continues to encourage scholarship that mines the archive. Using the more than fifty thousand indexed keywords in the thesaurus, scholars can look at topics in detail and find interesting intersections with more traditional sources. What people saw, how they felt, what language they were speaking, who they were related to, where they were and in what time frame—all these provide many data points. Because the material is so rich, the institute has developed several paths by which scholars from many disciplines can discover new understanding in testimony, including teaching and research fellowships and scholars-in-residence.

More resonant than any single course or research project are the discoveries that continue to arise from ever-deeper explorations of the testimonies by scholars. As Stephen

RESISTING THE PATH TO GENOCIDE

This interdisciplinary research group, established at USC in partnership with the institute, tackles a crucial question for today's world: What enables people to oppose or resist racist ideologies, state discrimination practices or the active participation in mass atrocities? Led by professor of history Wolf Gruner and Stephen Smith—and involving faculty from history, anthropology, political science, languages, and psychology—it focuses on how individuals, groups, or indeed whole so-

cieties have resisted the path to genocide. The aim is to learn from those who have attempted to resist in different ways during times of violent crisis, such as the networks of people who worked to undermine the Nazis' attempts to murder. Participants investigate social and political conditions as well as human behavior—which testimony provides— in search of clues to better understanding. "As a Holocaust historian, I was amazed to discover in the Visual History Archive just how many Jews

engaged in acts of resistance to the Nazis in the 1930s," says Gruner. "There are many episodes of individual opposition that add up to significant defiance when taken collectively. This changes our understanding tremendously!"

Smith observed in 2011, "As themes are explored and comparative studies done between single testimonies or groups of testimonies, insights that we did not expect emerge. As researchers from the humanities, social sciences, and life sciences mine the information, new questions are raised on topics that vary widely, such as experiences related to resistance, gender, geography, or religious belief. Often we find that the witnesses in the archive have answered questions they were not directly asked. The archive is actually much greater than the sum of its parts; the many themes it addresses are an interdisciplinary treasure trove for researchers and students alike."

> **"The Visual History Archive provides an invaluable resource for undergraduate and graduate teaching. Every one of my students receives an extensive introduction to the archive."**
>
> —Wolf Gruner, Shappell-Guerin chair of Jewish studies and professor of history, USC

INTERNING AT THE INSTITUTE

As many as forty students each year take part in the institute's mission through its intern program at USC. They often describe the lasting effects of survivors' stories. "Caitlin Koford, who visited the institute for a history class, says, "As a historian, the diversity of the testimonies reminds me to try to understand the many smaller, detailed stories that form the basis for a much larger and more general historical event."

Some students come to the Institute to fulfill a course requirement. Others, such as Brennan Wise, begin with a more personal interest. "My grandparents are survivors who don't talk about their experiences," says Wise, a freshman majoring in business administration. "Hearing the personal stories has helped me feel closer to them."

Leticia Villasenor began as an intern in 2013. Villasenor is working toward her PhD in French from USC, and holds a master's in international studies at the University of Denver; she held a summer student fellowship at the institute in 2013. "I'm looking at the testimonies of survivors of the Vel d'Hiv roundup in France in 1942. I want to see what survivors say about French police.'

ABOVE: Steven Spielberg with USC student interns in 2012. With them are Disney CEO Robert Iger and his wife, Willow Bay, visiting the institute before the Ambassadors for Humanity gala where Iger was honored.

WITNESSES FOR HUMANITY

The Shoah Foundation essentially stopped taking testimony from Holocaust survivors and witnesses in 2000. After that, no new testimonies were added to the Visual History Archive until 2009. These were interviews with survivors of the 1994 genocide in Rwanda, in which nearly a million people were murdered in just one hundred days. The decision to resume taking testimonies was a momentous one, but it was also a natural evolutionary step. Sad to say, the world had experienced new genocides even since the foundation's birth: in Rwanda, in the Balkans, in Darfur. And the late 1970s slaughter of 1.7 million Cambodians by the Khmer Rouge regime—the largest genocide since the Holocaust—was still fresh in memory. Said Douglas Greenberg in 2005, "Too many men, women, and children bearing witness to the horrors of the last century and this one are yearning for their stories to be told."

Steven Spielberg's vision for the foundation had always reached beyond the Holocaust. Speaking to the *New York Times* in 2005, Spielberg said that the foundation planned to turn the Visual History Archive into a resource for people who want to chronicle other tragedies around the world, past or present. "Ten years

Above: Holocaust survivor Renée Firestone at the Kigali Genocide Memorial Centre in Kigali, Rwanda, 2013.

TEACHING THE RWANDAN GENOCIDE

"Each genocide is unique, but we can understand the cycle, the patterns, and the warning signs," says Carla Garapedian of the Armenian Film Foundation. Thanks to Rwandan survivors who gave testimony, teachers can guide their students through a study of the stages of genocide and its aftermath using a new lesson available on the institute's website. Authored by Rob Hadley and Kelly Watson, two graduates of the institute's Master Teacher Program,

"If You Survive, Be a Man: Teaching the 1994 Rwandan Tutsi Genocide" explores four aspects of genocide—warning signs, acts of violence, response, and legacy—from the perspectives of two survivors and a rescuer who remember the hundred days in 1994 when as many as one million Tutsis lost their lives.

Opposite and above: Josette Umutoni, murdered in the 1994 Rwandan Tutsi Genocide, is depicted in the "Tomorrow Lost" exhibit at the Kigali Genocide Memorial Centre.

from now, I see it as the hub of a wheel with many spokes," each one the visual history of a world-changing event. "We would hope to find lines of connectivity from the events in Rwanda to the events at Auschwitz," he said, or find witnesses to ethnic cleansing in Bosnia. As Greenberg described, "[We] have plans to use our expertise to support the documentation of other genocides, and to work collaboratively with organizations and individuals who collect oral and video history."

In 2007 and ensuing years, foundation leaders traveled to Rwanda to meet with survivor organizations and government agencies that wished to record survivor testimony. They formed a relationship with IBUKA—the umbrella organization representing Rwandan Tutsi survivors—that led to the pilot interviews as well as interviews on site in Rwanda, sometimes on the very ground where massacres took place.

It was important both to the institute and the Rwandans that they conduct the interviews themselves, for their own archive at the Kigali Genocide Memorial Centre (KGMC). The USC Shoah Foundation offered support on many levels. Karen Jungblut worked with KGMC director Freddy Mutanguha to design a pre-interview questionnaire based on the one used in taking Holocaust testimonies, and KGMC staff later traveled to Los Angeles to learn indexing techniques. In 2010 the institute hosted a public panel discussion "Rwanda: Confronting a Painful Past," on the role of testimony in the process of national mourning, transitional justice, and memorialization.

Indexing of the Rwandan genocide testimonies proceeded in the same careful and nuanced way as with the Holocaust testimonies. Index terms or keywords were always based on the content to be indexed, and could be tailored to different kinds of experience. Karen Jungblut's staff held discussions with the Rwan-

66 From each testimony the children of Rwanda will understand exactly what happened to their families, their parents, their sisters, and their brothers. And not only the children of Rwanda but also the children of the world. 99

—Freddy Mutanguha, Rwandan survivor and director of Aegis Rwanda

ABOVE: Above: List of massacres in Darfur, compiled by refugees at the Touloum refugee camp in Chad.

GENERATIONS OF SURVIVORS

When I look at Holocaust survivors, I realize that they suffered before I was born. I am listening to another generation of survivors as a survivor myself. I hope no other generation will have to listen to us as survivors."—*Rwandan survivor Yves Kamuronsi, deputy director, Kigali Genocide Memorial*

dans who came to work at USC about keywords, descriptions, and narratives. Says Jungblut, "We came to appreciate how many keywords describing the experiences of Holocaust survivors and witnesses also resonated for the experiences of the Rwandan genocide." Thus they could use the existing thesaurus as a starting point, adding keywords specific to Rwandan geography, history, and culture.

A total of sixty-five Rwandan survivor interviews formed the first new collection to become part of the VHA, made available in early 2013. Eventually, the Rwanda Archive and Education Program, a partnership between the institute and KGMC, aspires to record and preserve some five hundred Rwandan testimonies.

Around the same time as the Rwandan effort, staff from the Documentation Center of Cambodia (DC-Cam) began working with the institute to support DC-Cam's ongoing effort to collect testimony from survivors of the genocide perpetrated in Cambodia by the Khmer Rouge regime. The first few testimonies they recorded—again with the institute's help in designing protocols—constitute another new collection in the VHA.

THE ARMENIAN COLLECTION

What did you see with your own eyes?" That was the question filmmaker J. Michael Hagopian asked every eyewitness he interviewed about the Armenian genocide, the first major genocide of the twentieth century. For 40 years, Hagopian traveled the world to record survivors' stories on film, dedicating his life to preserving visual evidence of the tragedy. His was a unique challenge: to find survivors from 85 year earlier and persuade them to describe their experiences of seeing people thrown from cliffs into the Euphrates, or of having escaped being burned alive

in desert caves. In May 2010, Michael and Antoinette Hagopian signed an agreement to include Michael's priceless films in the Visual History Archive, so they could be shared with universities around the world.

ABOVE: Armenian refugees on a forced march, c. 1915. Right: Dr. J. Michael Hagopian in his studio.

THE TESTIMONY OF **FREDDY MUTANGUHA**

Date of birth 1976
Place of birth. . . . Bujumbura, Burundi
Date of interview . . . September 1, 2010
Location of interview. . . . Los Angeles,
California, USA
Language: . . . . English
Experience . . . . .Rwandan Tutsi
genocide survivor

At the outbreak of the genocide in Rwanda on April 7, 1994, FREDDY MUTAN-GUHA's parents put him into hiding near the family home. For a week he stayed there while his parents negotiated with the In-terahamwe militia, using the little money and food they had to stay alive. Freddy de-scribes how his mother would come every night to bring him food.

My family were not first to be killed, because they had some money, and then they were giving money for life. [My friend] Jean Pierre, he was coming to tell me what is going on. I didn't like to hear those stories, how they are raping the girls and the women you knew before. Telling you how they have cut in pieces of your friend you went to school together. He say that your father and your mom they have given them money, and they are not going to kill them today. But I don't know tomorrow what [will] hap-pen.

Each and every night, [my mom] was coming to see me with food . . . from the night of seventh [April], eighth, ninth, tenth, eleventh, twelfth, she kept doing the same thing. I had some hope, because each and every night my mom see me. And every day, Jean Pierre was telling me the stories of what is going on, and the bodies start to have smell around us, around all the village. On the twelfth all the Tutsis were killed. I was waiting when they will come and kill my family. I didn't think about myself, because I thought,

OPPOSITE: Left to right, Paul Rukesha, Yves Kamuronsi, Martin Niwenshuti, Freddy Mutanguha, Consolée Uwamariya, Diogene Mwizerwa. The men work with the Kigali Genocide Memorial Centre; Uwamariya is an institute staff member.

EVERY SURVIVOR HAS A STORY TO TELL

probably I am safe here, but my family's not safe, they're still at home, they don't know what to do.

On the night of [the] thirteenth my mom came to see me and she said that probably [this] is [her] last day. The food was finished because she had to feed the militia, she had to give money out each and every day. She brought me beans and vegetables. She knew that I didn't like those kinds of food [so] she [also] brought me passion fruits, two of them, and [said] "I know you like fruits."

She was different. Her face was very different. She was so quiet. She told me how they were harassed by the militia.

She told me that there was no food, no money, nowhere to go. [She said,] "We don't have hope [for] tomorrow." I think she [said] that it was not possible to live [much longer] "because we don't have anything to give to the militias."

The passion fruit became my memory of my mom.

I ask her and say, "What will happen if you die and I don't die? Because of you hiding me here, you were exposed."

She [said], "If you survive, be a man." This is the last word I heard

from her. She didn't even say goodbye. She just disappeared. The passion fruit became my memory of my mom. And the last word, I would never forget it.

The following day at about eleven, I heard a very big group of people come to my house. They took everybody from the house and they killed them. I could hear the screaming of people being beaten and killed. It took about fifteen minutes. Then I realized that everybody had died. It [was] so hard to listen to that. Sometimes I have nightmares and I listen . . . exactly, exactly the same noises come to me. It's so hard to live with.

But, life [has] to continue. ∎

In addition to new testimonies, the institute is keenly interested in bringing existing collections of oral and visual history into its archive. In this category is an extraordinary group of more than four hundred interviews with Armenians who survived the 1915–1917 genocide during which an estimated 1.5 million Armenians were murdered. The interviews were conducted by the late Dr. J. Michael Hagopian, a documentary filmmaker and himself a genocide survivor. The Armenian Genocide collection is the third collection being integrated into the Visual History Archive. A collection of interviews with refugees from Darfur conducted between 2007 and 2008 will join the archive as well.

In 2012, the institute recorded interviews with twelve survivors of the 1937 Nanjing massacre, and it aspires to assist partners with testimony in Bosnia, Darfur, and Guatemala. In all cases, its goal is to digitize, catalogue, and index these testimonies and integrate them into the Visual History Archive to enable users to search across all experiences in the archive—and to share its expertise with local groups engaged in creating new collections. Some concern has been expressed, says Stephen Smith, that including non-Holocaust testimonies somehow dilutes the archive's identity and power. He believes the opposite is true. "Each collection preserves its own identity, and the clarity and distinctness of its culture; each is independently searchable with our interface. But you can also find striking com-

monalities of experience. Human suffering must not be compared. But its causes and consequences must be if we are ever to really understand the nature of genocide in order to prevent it."

A related project called Preserving the Legacy seeks to expand the core collection of Holocaust-era testimonies. As custodians of the world's largest audiovisual archive of Holocaust survivor and witness testimonies, the institute is committed to becoming a digital repository for other audiovisual Holocaust testimonies. Organizations with such collections can benefit from the institute's infrastructure and expertise in cataloguing and indexing, digitization, preservation, digital storage, and access. Thus this project can potentially bring together collections into one shared space, while enabling them to live at their own institutions, museums, or websites.

An exciting prospect for the future, says Smith, is gathering or conducting testimony from people who experienced the Nazi era from perspectives not currently reflected in the archive—for example, Jews living in Arab lands during the Holocaust. "Because North African countries had varying relationships with the Nazis, there was a great variety of experiences. We want to do future educational programming in the Middle East, so we will need to have content in those languages and that cultural context."

> 66 I saw the kids from Rwanda who were here, and I spoke to the interns from Cambodia. They all are now realizing how important the Holocaust testimonies were. Now they are going to be doing it also. 99 —Renée Firestone

OPPOSITE: Guixiang Chen, a survivor of the Nanjing massacre of 1937, with Ana Lee, a USC doctoral student who assisted in the project.
ABOVE LEFT: Donna Casey, archivist, and Karen Jungblut working with Kigali Genocide Memorial Centre staff learning to index testimony.
ABOVE RIGHT: Ita Gordon, content specialist, works with Fatily Sa, staff member of the Documentation Center Cambodia (DC-Cam).

THE TESTIMONY OF **THEARY SENG**

Date of birth . . . . January 1971
Place of birth. . . . Phnom Penh, Cambodia
Date of interview . . . . January 13, 2011
Location of interview. . . . . . . Los Angeles,
California, USA
Experience. . . . . .Cambodian survivor
Language. . . . . English

THEARY SENG *describes the night her family was taken from the village and imprisoned. They believed that they would be executed that night. The family walked for hours (Theary believes the distance to be about twenty miles), finally coming to the prison, the first of several they were kept in. She was seven years old at the time.*

That day I was at home with my youngest brother and my mom, and my three oldest brothers were tending water buffaloes. That's what they did during the daytime with a few Khmer Rouge guards. That day in the late afternoon already there was tension in the house. My mom was crying; my aunts were crying; there was a lot of conversation and cacophony because we had been told the news that we would be arrested, and of course there was the understanding that we would be killed that night.

And then my brothers came back, that evening. And right away, even before they entered the house, my three older brothers saw the gathering and saw the Khmer Rouge soldiers. They understood that we were being taken to be executed. [My brother] Londhi right away jumped off his water buffalo and ran [to] hide and shrieked, "I don't want to die!" The other brothers knew, and they came and we were told that we would be taken and arrested. And so, after what seemed like several hours, they physically tied up my mom in this manner [Theary puts her hands behind her back] and they tied up my father's father and they led us from the home on the main road, village road, which was just basically a dirt road running through the village. And everyone saw us.

It was already dark. So there was this silhouette of two or three Khmer Rouge soldiers, two up front, one in the back, leading this family into nowhere, into the darkness. The whole time we were thinking that we were going to die, that we were being taken to be executed. What I remember that night, which is still fresh, is just being exhausted from walking . . . twenty miles for a seven-year-old on [an] uneven dirt path, in the middle of the night, with the heaviness of the events, so I just remembered being extremely tired and having my legs became jelly. And then we saw a structure. We were not taken to an open grave, [so] there was rejoicing, even though we were put in prison, and that was the first prison that we stayed in.

Later in her interview, Theary describes the night that her mother and all the other prisoners were killed. She and her brothers, who were children at the time, were kept alive and woke up to find the prison empty.

That night two or three prison guards came into the [cell]. I caught their eyes, they caught my eyes. And then they left right away. And that was really strange to me. It was so strange that I remember turning to my mom and I asked her, "Mom, why were those guards carrying wet robes and why are they coming back again?" I was thinking they had already shackled [our]

There was this silhouette of two or three Khmer Rouge soldiers, two up front, one in the back, leading this family into nowhere, into the darkness. And the whole time we were thinking that we were going to die, that we were being taken to be executed.

ankles, we were already preparing for bed. Why did they come back a second time? And so I asked her, "Mom, why were those men carrying wet robes?"

My mom knew, and she said, "My daughter, go back to sleep," and I did. And those were her last words to me. I woke up the next morning with just my youngest brother in this empty room, in this empty [cell]. We woke up and we cried and cried and cried. I knew right away that my mom was no longer on the earth, that she had been killed, even though I had awoken to an empty cell before. ∎

BELOW: Still photo taken during Theary's interview in 2011.

"THEY ARE ALL EDUCATORS NOW"

"I have seen young students who have watched these testimonies. It does change them. These survivors—who are now educators—they can change the world." —STEVEN SPIELBERG

As the first decade of the new millennium closed, the tools were all in place for the USC Shoah Foundation to become an eloquent voice in emerging conversations not only about Holocaust Education, but also about digital learning and twenty-first century literacy.

In February 2013, Universal Studios and Steven Spielberg were preparing to release the meticulously restored Blu-ray edition of *Schindler's List* on the occasion of the film's twentieth anniversary. The public's unflagging interest in the film made it the ideal time for a simultaneous announcement about the Shoah Foundation, then nearing its twentieth year as well. At a press conference, Spielberg invited high school and middle school students in the United States and Canada to take the IWitness Video Challenge: to act on the legacy of *Schindler's List* and do something positive in their community that exemplified the movie's message that one person can make a difference.

IWitness is the institute's educational website, the flagship in its fleet of educational offerings. Developed over three years using Web 2.0 technology and provided free of charge to educators and schools around the world, IWitness brings the human stories of its Visual History Archive to teachers and students via engaging multimedia learning activities, and makes almost thirteen hundred testimonies available in an interactive environment. For the Challenge, students viewed testimonies that guided them to themes such as highlighting racism or finding solutions to bullying, then used the website's simple video-editing tool to create one-to-four-minute video essays—thus linking their voices to those in the archive who inspired them to act.

"It was my goal when I established the Shoah Foundation that future generations would learn from the incredible life stories preserved in the Visual History Archive," said Spielberg in his announcement. "I've seen how students connect with survivors through watching their testimony, and the impact it has on them. They experience a kind of learning that is profound and personal. And they take that with them into their lives."

IWitness and the institute's other testimony-based educational offerings leverage the mobility and connectedness of the new student generation, while addressing educational standards. Today's students are deeply engaged with visual and digital media, socially, recreationally, and for education, and must be literate in those media to stay competitive. Furthermore, says Kori Street, who became the institute's director of education around the time IWitness was launched in early 2012, "It is not enough to teach them to search; students must know how to understand the value of what they find, whether in digital, visual, or textual form. And they need to understand the meaning of what they find in the context of their world, and then act on those understandings."

Designed to address those needs, IWitness is the institute's first classroom tool by which students can access, search, and interact with testimonies somewhat independently. Using IWitness, students engage with testimony using the same thesaurus of keywords that researchers use to search the VHA. They develop video projects and essays using the innovative built-in editing tool, and share them with other students and teachers. The site includes an array of contextual materials, from archives such as Yad

> **❝ Working with testimony effectively requires that we live at the intersection of critical literacies . . . including history, the Holocaust, and other genocides. It also requires that we occupy that space with integrity and great care.❞**
> —Kori Street, director of education

Opposite: Steven Spielberg with students at the IWitness Video Challenge launch, February 2013. Above: Stephen Smith interacts with students at the launch of IWitness at the United Nations, January 2012.

Vashem and the United States Holocaust Memorial Museum, to enhance students' learning experiences, as well as a media library to source material for their projects, and it offers guided, student-centered activities.

Learning activities in IWitness lean on a framework of teaching principles known as the "four Cs," found to make learning most effective: students are asked to *consider* new material; to actively *collect* research; to *construct*, or bring their own voice, to the subject; and to *communicate* their discoveries respectfully and ethically. "Building specific historical knowledge is part of a process," Street says, "in which students then go on to make cognitive links to the challenges and implications the events present. The importance of knowledge cannot be underestimated as one side of responsible citizenship. Developing critical thought, respectful attitudes, and thoughtful actions follows as an outcome of that acquired knowledge."

> ❝ There is nothing more real than hearing a person tell their story in their own words. IWitness allows students to meet survivors and experience history in a personal and life-changing way. ❞
>
> —Michelle Sadrena Clark, High Tech High School, San Marcos, California

IWitness was quickly recognized as a revolutionary educational resource. Accreditation from the International Society for Technology in Education (ISTE) aligns IWitness with National Education Technology Standards. The American Association of School Librarians named it as a top website for learning resources in 2012.

ETHICAL EDITING

IWitness doesn't stand in isolation; it's just the most currently visible of the USC Shoah Foundation Institute's exploratory forays into the new field of digital literacy. In one of many collaborations with scholars at USC, the institute embarked on a collaboration with the Institute for Multimedia Literacy in 2010, a research unit within USC's School of Cinematic Arts designed to study new forms of literacy in a digital culture. The goal was to develop best practices for teaching students how to work with testimony from the Visual History Archive. As high school students, undergraduates, and graduate students began to watch, edit, combine, and reconfigure clips from the testimonies, what did they need to know? From this emerged the IWitness "ethical editing" tool, which demonstrates for users how meaning can be changed through editing, With such tools, students learn to be good digital citizens.

A rigorous evaluation of the website's use by students produced noteworthy results. To cite just a few: Students expressed greater interest in studying the Holocaust after using IWitness, and felt it had more relevance to their individual lives. Nine out of ten students rated IWitness better than other websites used for school; 69 percent wanted to use IWitness outside the classroom for other school projects and/or personal research. Results from ongoing evaluation conducted by the institute showed that students' use of IWitness significantly increased two social-action measures—"speaking up" and "one person can make a difference." The long-term reward that Street and her colleagues hope for is a society that benefits from these engaged digital citizens, its future leaders.

GIVING OF THEMSELVES

To those who gave testimony I would say thank you from the bottom of my heart. Their willingness to bear witness about that horrific time in their lives—to revisit that time on a regular basis for the benefit of younger generations—must be anything but easy. But what an impact they have. They are opening our children's eyes and giving them knowledge that is critically important. I want to thank the survivors for their willingness and courage to give so much of themselves to our children." —*U.S. Secretary of Education Arne Duncan*

66 There is a thing that happens when a student watches testimony... it is almost like your DNA and the DNA of the story mix. You walk away from that experience, and it changes you. 99

—Corey Harbough, teacher, Gobles High School, Gobles, Michigan

TEACHERS AT HOME AND ABROAD

Steven Spielberg talks about how the institute fulfills what he calls the "five Ts": "teaching teachers to teach tolerance." Teachers remain the institute's indispensable partner in all its educational work using testimony-based resources, including IWitness. From its earliest outreach, the foundation explored with teachers how testimony can best be used in the classroom. By 2008 it had conducted two-hundred-twenty teacher trainings in fourteen countries, incorporating the use of visual history. Each was tailored for the teachers in the specific location and designed in partnership with local educators.

In-depth professional development workshops for highly motivated secondary-level educators prepare them to integrate testimony into existing curricula, and to become ambassadors for testimony-based education in their communities. By 2012, this cutting-edge teaching program had gone international. The first workshop abroad was held in July 2012 in Budapest, at Central European University, which provides public

OPPOSITE AND RIGHT: Students using IWitness.

THE TESTIMONY OF **PHILIP DRELL**

Date of birth . . . . March 7, 1919
Place of birth . . . . . . Chicago, Illinois, USA
Date of interview . . . . April 4, 1997
Location of interview . . . . .Skokie,
Illinois, USA
Language . . . . English
Experience . . . . .Liberation witness,
war photographer

PHILIP DRELL, *a photographer with the U.S. Army Signal Corps, served with the Special Motion Picture Coverage Unit (SPECOU) headed by film director George Stevens. This unit was responsible for documenting D-Day and other events of the war, including the liberation of Paris and of the Dachau concentration camp. In his testimony, Philip describes what he witnessed when his unit arrived at Dachau on August 29, 1945.*

The first thing that we saw was the train. It was along a siding. We opened up a door, and a body rolled out into a sitting position, right at the edge of the train. There were, I believe, about forty cars there, they claimed to have three thousand bodies in the train. Some of the cars had roofs, and others were just open. And we went along, and I made a whole series of photographs of the bodies in the train. There were some guards next to it who were shot immediately.

After, we went into the camp, and we wound up at the crematoria, this large building. They had run out of fuel for stoking the furnaces, so the bodies accumulated in a huge pile. Rooms inside were loaded with bodies. They couldn't process them anymore. So that's what we concentrated on: photographing that. And then these 120-some guards were rounded up and shot. When the guards saw what was happening, they tried to hide. They put on prisoners' striped uniforms, which was kind of silly.

A few days later we lined up everybody in the camp and checked out each person, to look for all the guards that tried to hide. Some of the guards were caught by some of the prisoners, the survivors, who beat them to death. And we photographed in the camp. George Stevens set up a sound camera and he interviewed people there. Probably one of the earliest interviewers of survivors there is. ■

ABOVE RIGHT: Philip with his camera during the war; the photos below are his. MIDDLE LEFT: Bodies stacked in a train car discovered in the liberation of Dachau. LOWER LEFT: German soldiers who surrendered on August 25, 1944, the day Paris was liberated.

access to the Visual History Archive. The Teaching with Testimony for the 21st Century program is currently offered in the United States, Hungary, France, Poland, Czech Republic, and Ukraine.

Some of the institute's staff in Europe have deep backgrounds with the organization and deep roots in their native communities. Two of these are senior international program consultant Martin Šmok and Andrea Szönyi, senior international training consultant (living in the Czech Republic and Hungary, respectively). In bringing programs such as Teaching with Testimony to these countries, they must account for factors such as the fluidity of central and eastern European borders, ancient layers of bias, pedagogical approaches quite different from those in the United States, and the fact that they are working on ground where the Holocaust took place. Moreover, since those countries emerged from Communist rule just decades ago, there can be "competing narratives of suffering," as Szönyi puts it. Šmok speaks of a "topic fatigue" from media over-

STUDENTS OF HISTORY

The twentieth century abounds in examples of hatred, bigotry, and acts of prejudice. The USC Shoah Foundation Institute's work is concerned with the possibility that the twenty-first century will be more of the same. Will we again turn out to be bad students of history? Will we again step onto that same rake? The beginning of this century shows that we might. — *Mikhail Goldenberg, a teacher from Russia who participated in the institute's first international workshop for educators on the use of visual history in the classroom*

ABOVE: Left to right, former institute teacher trainer Sheila Hansen, educator Sandy Rubenstein, and Shoah Foundation intern Deborah Herman at a Teaching with Testimony workshop, 2011.

exposure of Holocaust material that can make some teachers initially resistant to the institute's offerings.

The institute's hard-learned emphasis on working locally provides a strong counterforce. "Because we provide testimonies in people's native languages, and that address their own history, regional consultants can work productively with teachers to integrate them into local curricula," says Szönyi. For students, says Šmok, the effects of direct encounters with testimony—"seeing the faces, hearing the voices"—are similar to what happens everywhere, with the added impact of hearing stories that might have unfolded near their own homes.

Led by local educators who serve as regional consultants, various other teacher development programs address the needs of educators from Melbourne to Kigali to Chicago. In Ukraine, the education team developed a multimedia teacher's guide for using the institute's film *Spell Your Name* in that country's curriculum, including a program focused on human rights. Several programs designed in Italy, including *Piramide dell'odio (Pyramid of Hate)*, use testimony to

> **❝**The workshop allows us to take what the archive has to offer and bring it into the classroom. And we all have colleagues who teach other subjects. [The impact will] just keep blossoming.**❞**
>
> —History teacher Jeremy Howard, Francis Parker Middle School (San Diego), who took part in the inaugural Master Teacher Program workshop

LOCAL TESTIMONIES

Some educators are already embracing the idea of using local testimonies to explain the often complicated history of our region. Teachers at our workshops are unlocking the power of individual narrative to shatter years of prejudice and propaganda, and they are becoming aware of the stereotyping and labeling that pervade our daily lives. Only with this knowledge can they help their students to understand the mechanisms of intolerance.

—Martin Šmok, senior international training consultant

help educators teach students about the consequences of bigotry and intolerance.

Programs in Australia, the United States, Rwanda, and Italy have conducted pilots with educators who integrate IWitness into their existing programs—not only as compelling lessons but also as a way to address educational standards and expectations around digital and media literacy. And the institute has supported efforts such as the Rwandan Peace Education Program, which uses testimony from survivors of the Rwandan genocide for peace-building activities with young people across Rwanda and to raise awareness of the pressures that move people to genocidal violence.

While delivery models may change according to location, all of the institute's programs for teachers focus on the effective and appropriate use of testimony in education across curricula. They introduce teachers to testimony, or help them engage with it more deeply, in their own learning environments, and help them present topics as varied as economics, history, or languages in ways that are relevant and compelling to students. As teacher Jeremy Howard observes, "Watching and listening to testimonies helps students gain insight, develop a more complex worldview, and can encourage them to act, making the world a better place."

OPPOSITE: *Andrea Szőnyi leads a Teaching with Testimony professional development program for Polish educators in Hungary, 2012.*
ABOVE: *Teacher Jeremy Howard uses the Visual History Archive.*

ENCOUNTERING MEMORY

Encountering Memory is a kit designed to help teachers make educational use of *Nazvy svoie im'ia (Spell Your Name)*, the institute's documentary film about the Holocaust in Ukraine. Through the Encountering Memory training program, some 3,200 teachers have been trained to use the kit materi-

als at seminars conducted throughout Ukraine and the Autonomous Republic of Crimea.

ABOVE: *Ukrainian students at School 288 in Kyiv take part in the Encountering Memory program.*

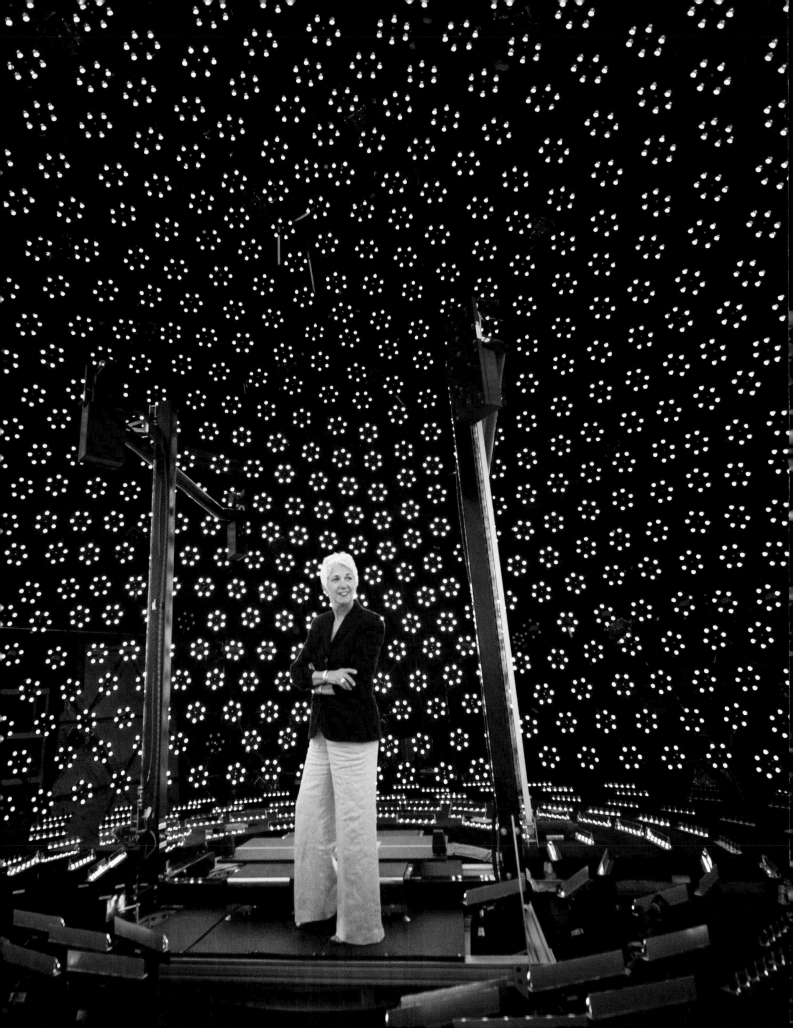

NEW HORIZONS IN USING TESTIMONY

The use of visual testimony has taken some startling new paths. Among the most intriguing have sprung from the institute's familial relationship with the USC Dornsife College of Arts and Letters, where some of the world's leading-edge research in human consciousness is conducted at the Brain and Creativity Institute (BCI), founded by Antonio Damasio and Hanna Damasio in 2006. For a major research project on "The Brain's Virtuous Cycle: An Investigation of Gratitude and Good Human Conduct," Glenn Fox, one of the project researchers and a doctoral candidate in neuroscience, used the Visual History Archive in his dissertation research on gratitude. Studying testimonies, Fox and his assistants searched for scenarios in which a survivor received some sort of gift or was the beneficiary of a good deed. Researchers took on the perspective of the survivor and read about his or her experiences while being monitored by a functional magnetic resonance imaging (fMRI) machine.

Other USC researchers are investigating the relationship of digital learning and the brain. In a talk moderated by the institute early in 2013, Mary Helen Immordino-Yang of the BCI discussed with world-renowned intellectual Howard Gardner how our expanding, data-packed digital world transforms today's students and their educational needs—a topic close to the institute's heart.

> ❝ It is amazing to think that young people will be able to hold the kind of conversation I have daily when I go out to speak. This is a truly good use for technology. ❞
>
> —Holocaust survivor Pinchas Gutter, speaking about New Dimensions in Testimony

Some innovators are looking at the VHA from a geographical perspective. Geography-based computing is literally in the institute's DNA: Sam Gustman applied his GIS mapping knowledge to creating the VHA's indexing system (see page 222). In 2012, researchers at USC's Integrated Media Systems Center pioneered a new concept called *geo-immersion*: capturing real-world spaces into a computer-generated replica that changes over time (the fourth dimension). Using geo-immersion, they aim to place the testimonies of Holocaust survivors within a "4-D space." Geo-immersive spaces not only create a different learning environment but also bring out information that might have been overlooked through conventional research methods.

OPPOSITE: *The institute's Daisy Miller on the 3-D capture stage of the New Dimensions in Testimony project.* ABOVE: *Glenn Fox, USC doctoral candidate in neuroscience, who has used the Visual History Archive in his research.*

THE TESTIMONY OF **ROMAN KENT**

Date of birth . . . . April 18, 1929
Place of birth . . . . Lodz, Poland
Date of interview . . . . April 29, 1996
Location of interview . . . . . New York City,
New York, USA
Language . . . . English
Experience . . . . Jewish survivor

ROMAN KENT *expresses his gratitude for all he has been able to accomplish since his arrival in the United States. He emphasizes the importance of getting involved in philanthropic projects that aid the less fortunate. He acknowledges the contribution of the "Righteous Gentiles" who put their own lives on the line in order to save Jews during the war.*

I came here with nothing, went to school, went to university, went into business. And some people may say, "You accomplished a lot." That may be so. But therefore I feel that, after what I went through, I should give something back to this society. And I feel that it is important for us. What I have instilled in my children, I hope, is not to be a

bystander. I think the atrocities happened because the world stood by and did nothing. But the world consists of individuals. And it is important that individuals get involved.

So, yes, I am involved in values projects. I am involved in the projects of keeping the memory of the Holocaust alive. So that maybe the new generation can learn something from it so that it will not be repeated again.

I am involved in helping the Righteous Gentiles, the few individuals that saved the Jewish life during the war. Because I think they are the perfect example that even among the most horrible circumstances, people who are moral and ethical can do something. And particularly important [was that] to help a Jew meant that if the Gentiles are caught, they lose their life, their family loses their life. So I want to bring up that even in the midst of

the atrocities, there is some goodness. And it is always easier to teach the new generation, if you show them not only the evil, but [that] you have the right to be good, you should be good. So the memory and the acts of the Righteous Gentiles serve a dual purpose, of teaching what happened, but also of teaching what can be done, if people care. ∎

The memory and the acts of the Righteous Gentiles serve a dual purpose, of teaching what happened, but also of teaching what can be done, if people care.

LEFT: *Roman, far right, with fellow members of a band called Happy Boys, in Cham, Germany, shortly after the war.* ABOVE: *Roman took part in a documentary film called* Children in the Holocaust; *he is pictured here with narrator Liv Ullmann.*

New Dimensions in Testimony is a future-facing research project conceived by Conscience Display, an exhibition design company, and developed in concert with USC Institute for Creative Technologies. "We wanted to capture the interaction between students and survivors for the benefit of future generations" says concept designer Heather Maio. The project captures new, three-dimensional interviews with a number of survivors so that in the future people can engage with them conversationally in real time, asking their own questions.

The effort hinges on cutting-edge technologies in language and visual reproduction. New Dimensions will gather survivors' answers to hundreds of questions—some that they are asked on a daily basis, and some that they may never have been asked before—on topics such as family, tradition, memory, belief, identity, and ethics. Their answers will be placed in a database, which then will be used to sustain the dialogue between students and the survivor. A technology called Natural Language Understanding enables the computer to find the most appropriate answer from the many available. And the most advanced 3-D techniques will record these new interviews, so that future 3-D display technology will allow students and others to interact personally with testimony through true holographic display.

Top: Stephen Smith with survivor Pinchas Gutter during filming for the New Dimensions in Testimony project, 2012. Above: Visitors view testimony from the Visual History Archive at the exhibit "Some Were Neighbors" at the U.S. Holocaust Memorial Museum.

THE FUTURE OF THE PAST

In a conversation about how the USC Shoah Foundation has evolved over the years, Netherlands regional consultant Denise Citroen observed that no matter how much had changed, the core of its work remains the same: the survivor who "takes you by the hand, takes you in [to her life], and takes you back out again." It's a comment that speaks to how personal the connection with survivors became for foundation staff, and also to a fundamental dynamic of the work itself: you are invited into relationship with another human being with something vital to impart, and then commissioned to take that message back out into the world.

Bonnie Samotin is a former manager at the foundation (1994 to 2003). In a 2009 article for *Jewish Journal,* she reminisces about the enduring friendships she and fellow staffers formed with survivors who volunteered or in other ways stayed involved with the foundation for many years—focusing especially on the life and death of Silvia Grohs-Martin, "a feisty, spirited woman whose fair complexion was offset by fiery orange curly hair, ruby lipstick and vibrant outfits. . . . Silvia would make her arrival known with her singsong greeting, uniquely punctuated with her thick Austrian accent." An actress in her youth, Grohs-Martin toured Europe before the Nazi occupation; much later, her testimony would be featured in the foundation's first CD-ROM (see page 250).

Samotin affectingly describes her final reunion with Silvia, who, she says, had

a "special spark that drew people to her." She characterizes her work at the foundation as "at once a privilege and a burden, an honor and a challenge, a workplace and a family, an education and a responsibility." Samotin recalls that while they "were doing purposeful work together, documenting personal and historic tragedy of monumental proportions . . . when we gathered socially, it was often funny, lighter moments we shared, interspersed

TOP: *Survivor Sidonia Lax with teenagers visiting the institute, c. 2003.* ABOVE: *Silvia Grohs-Martin with students at the New York City launch of* Survivors: Testimonies of the Holocaust, *the foundation's first CD-ROM, 1999.* OPPOSITE: *Paula Lebovics with students at Canoga Park High School in Los Angeles, 2003.*

with poignant remembrances of a life long ago. . . . Sometimes it was sharing deep wisdom about personal accountability, taking a stand and how an act of kindness can make a world of difference."

And, even while mourning the mounting losses of these remarkable friends, Samotin finds comfort and inspiration in the mission to keep their memories alive. "I am blessed," she writes, "to have had personal relationships with many survivors and to know that I played a part in ensuring their voices will be heard, as their legacy to the future. . . . With the help of educators, technology, and all of us, the testimonies of Holocaust survivors will live on for generations."

If organizations have their own characters, it's tempting to say that the USC Shoah Foundation shares something of the natures of both an extended family and a faith. Staff members go at their work with a striking dedication, and they speak of

MESSAGES FOR THE FUTURE

Research into the archive provides insights into testimony from many angles. One student research project examined more than three hundred hours of testimony from more than one thousand Jewish survivors who left messages for the future, and revealed some clear patterns. The average testimony contained more than sixteen minutes of a survivor speaking about a future mes-

sage. More than 25 percent of them used the exact words "never again" in their message. Some 44 percent men-

tioned Holocaust remembrance and prevention of future genocides together linking memory to action

319

caring for the survivors and their testimonies as if they were much-loved relations. Regarding the testimonies in the Visual History Archive, Stephen Smith speaks of a "duty of care"—a term that covers multitudinous ways of caring: preserving the testimonies in perpetuity and protecting them from

A FIRST-PERSON IMPRINT

The survivors are leaving us an indelible imprint of man's inhumanity to man, as well as a wealth of material about Jewish culture before the war. This is a first-person imprint, not a hand-me-down. This is the person the students are learning from—the direct link to that event, to the witness and teacher who impresses upon them that they must respect and value life. —*Steven Spielberg*

possible misuse, as well as the responsibility he and his colleagues feel toward the survivors still living, and to the dead. "The wishes of those who gave testimony have to be at the heart of our mission," states Smith. "Without them there would be no archive, and only with them can the institute achieve its aims. That is what I mean by the 'duty of care.'"

Existing in creative tension with that urge to protect the survivors' memories is the mandate to use and share the testimonies, which these days means coming to grips with all the promise and perils of new technologies. Digital technology is four hundred times faster, some experts say, than it was when the foundation began collecting testimony. That same twenty-year period, Smith notes, "has

ABOVE: *High school student Maritssa Turcios shares her IWitness project with survivor and educator Renée Firestone, 2013.*

brought dramatic changes to the education landscape as well, and it has fundamentally changed the way testimony is used for learning."

But, he adds, "Technology is not an end in itself. What's really interesting is how the content of the testimonies is being optimized, through emerging technologies and new media, to become the worldwide educational resource it was always intended to be." Nor, most agree, is informal participation in the digital milieu enough to give students the skills they need to thrive. "That's why we are committed to designing resources that use testimony for digital literacy as well as character development."

Asked about their visions for the future of the USC Shoah Foundation, its leaders speak mainly of further developing the paths they are already embarked on:

- Expanding the Visual History Archive by various means, thereby helping to save other collections that may be in peril; and giving other organizations access to the tools and systems to process their own content, as the institute has done with Rwandan groups.

- Continuing to build digital literacy in schools through teaching with testimony.

- Leveraging technology to engage users of testimony most effectively in meaningful interactions that promote ethics development and action in the real world.

- Making sure that researchers in as many places as possible can get the complete archive in large volume and at high quality.

- Rendering the preservation effort even more secure, by making sure the digitized archive (including all the collections) is geo-diversified and globally distributed.

FUTURE LEARNING

"IWitness is just the beginning," believes Kori Street, "because we are in a sea change in teaching and learning and technology, and we can leverage technology to serve our ends." Sam Gustman notes: "The tech landscape is constantly changing. We look ahead to a time when you're not tied to a desk for learning but rather using tools like mobile devices and Google Glass." Already IWitness is available for iPad and tablets, and mobile solutions are being developed to meet the demand for video content on handheld devices. This is how the Visual History Archive will be accessed by more and more users in the future.

But in the end it all comes back to keeping faith with the givers of testimony, who hoped above all that telling their stories to the institute would help make a world a better place. "Genocide never happens by chance, and we know from research that it happens in cycles," says Stephen Smith. "Testimony can help us to break the cycle of hate. That's why we work with testimony in Rwanda." Recent foci of research and discussion center around how the signs of impending genocide can be recognized so that it can be forestalled. Testimonies are being re-scrutinized for clues to factors that facilitate individual resistance to persecution.

No one knows better than the survivors how hard this task will be, how imperative it is nonetheless, and how much

individual learning and growth will be required to transform society. One of the *Schindlerjuden*, Poldek Pfefferberg, says in his testimony, "The thing to remember is that the tragedy that happened was on account of hatred and prejudice, and this is the worst killer. This is what you have to remember: Love everybody around you. Love is building and hatred is killing."

The interviewer who took Poldek's testimony was *Schindler's List* co-producer Branko Lustig, who says, "As a survivor of the Holocaust, I want the Shoah Foundation to push the boundaries of technology not for the sake of it, but to make sure that we fulfill the promise we made to the survivors in the Visual History Archive. We always said that the testimonies would be kept in perpetuity, which requires a huge technological effort. We also said that we would teach from them for generations to come, which in a world wired for the Internet, means bringing the Visual History Archive directly to their screens."

HOW WE TELL THE STORY

As a filmmaker, I am interested in how we communicate the story of the Shoah. The next generation will tell their own story in their own words with whatever means they have at their disposal. Our job is not to dissuade them from using their voice and the technology at their fingertips but rather to encourage them to do it with care, with dignity, and humanity."

—*Branko Lustig*

His "message for the future" is much like Pfefferberg's: "I hope that one day people will love each other and that this will never happen again; that's why I was so involved with this Shoah project. Because I think that these tapes—what we've made—they will help the people to love each other and to forgive . . . and to live, somehow, in a new world.." ∎

ABOVE: *Branko Lustig.* OPPOSITE: *A student learns about the "Pyramid of Hate," in an exercise developed jointly by the Anti-Defamation League and the USC Shoah Foundation.*

BESHERT

"It has been said that it is far better to light a candle than curse the darkness.
The testimonies videotaped and maintained by the Shoah Foundation have
brightened our often dark and troubled civilization with the living presence
of survivors whose permanent record of perseverance in the face of evil
offers us, and our progeny, inspiration to work toward the highest human
good—*tikkun olam*, the repair of our broken but perfectible world."
—*The Honorable Bruce J. Einhorn, U.S. Federal Court judge, retired*

Behind the opening titles of *Schindler's List,* a single wavering candle flame
pierces the darkness—the only frames filmed in color until the very last
scene. As *Schindler's List* and the Shoah Foundation mark their twentieth anniversaries in the world, it seems fitting that a jurist and humanitarian renowned for civil rights activism (especially on the issue of immigration reform)
draws attention to the joint role of the film and the foundation in illuminating the
shadows of prejudice that still darken our lives.

The Yiddish word *beshert* often refers to a fortuitous relationship that seems
to have been miraculously preordained—such as the confluence of people, places,
and circumstances that led to the establishment of the Shoah Foundation in 1994.
In 2010, Steven Spielberg, who made *Schindler's List* and has been the driving force
behind the foundation and the institute, sat down for a conversation with Executive
Director Stephen Smith and Renée Firestone, a Holocaust survivor, interviewee,

OPPOSITE: "Whoever saves one life . . ." Steven Spielberg and Liam Neeson, as Oskar Schindler, on the set of Schindler's List.

interviewer, trainer, and educator who has represented the organization in countless classrooms and appearances. The film director and the survivor are two of the many thousands of individuals whose lives converged in the realization of a dream: to preserve Holocaust-witness testimony as a legacy for all generations.

The three-way conversation ranged widely: reflecting on the past, taking inventory of the present, and considering the future of testimony-based education. Spielberg summons up the memory of his long-ago encounter on the *Schindler's List* set with Niusia Horowitz—an encounter (described in the prologue of this book) that set everything in motion. Renée recalls viewing the testimony of a one-time partisan in Slovakia who tells an enthralling story of how a young man created false papers that helped some Jews escape the Nazis. She discovered at the end that the young man was her own brother—another striking case of *beshert* from an archive rich in potential discoveries of all kinds.

As the conversation moves to the institute's later initiatives and the twenty-first-century technologies they depend on, Spielberg reflects on the timely emergence of Internet-based communication in shaping that work. "It's *beshert* that we're here at the same time, doing this now, as opposed to fifteen years ago when none of this ever existed." When Renée mentions, "We just did a Skype with two schools at the same time," he elaborates: "You can see how you can quickly organize an event in a school, and Renée can be there to be the moderator; but then, she's also surrounded by fifty-two thousand survivor testimonies, all digitized and standing by to express themselves about what happened in the twentieth century."

> "I saw that the final act of this endeavor would be to change educational systems across the globe to include tolerance education, genocide education, and Holocaust education as a basic precept in social science curricula." —Steven Spielberg

Spielberg's comment on the scale of the Visual History Archive and its accessibility to millions makes it clear that much more than fate and good fortune went into making the foundation the force and resource it is today. Its power to light many candles has been fueled by the work of thousands of staff and volunteers and supporters and donors over the decades. Most of that work was highly intentional, and meticulously planned and executed: the production of interviews, their cataloguing and indexing, and then their carefully phased journey out into the world.

Stephen Smith, who is charged with directing the mission to carry the survivors' legacy forward, emphasizes the intentionality but also recognizes the remarkable confluence of timing and events that formed the organization. "The

timing was so critical," he says. "If we had started any later, we wouldn't have the archive that exists today." He also points to Spielberg's insatiable drive to gather as many stories as possible. "He was modeling the character of Oskar Schindler in this, I think: always saying 'Just one more!'"

In this and many things, Smith believes, Spielberg's leadership and "the breadth of his global vision" were fundamental. "He has a profound understanding that the archive is so much greater than the sum of its parts," Smith says. "Each individual piece is remarkable in its granularity and detail, but put them together and you get an undeniable, indelible voice speaking to the conscience of the world. Those 105,000 hours of testimony become the voice of humanity.

"None of us knows where conscience resides within us, but we can hear it and respond. And maybe, if enough people are exposed to that voice in effective ways, there may come a time when someone hears about a government policy, or a private hate group, that targets and endangers another group of humans—maybe they will recognize the wrong and take action."

Just as Oskar Schindler did. Twenty years on, *Schindler's List* remains a formidable teaching tool in support of the institute's mission. Both the film and the testimonies in the Visual History Archive embody the power of storytelling, in different forms. The origin story of the Shoah Foundation has always begun with *Schindler's List,* but these days it's possible to imagine new generations coming to the movie from the other direction: perhaps because they've encountered testimony in school. And so they settle in to watch those opening titles with the evocative, beckoning candle flame. They go along on the film's journey into darkness and back out into the light. ■

ABOVE: *Stephen Smith, Renée Firestone, and Steven Spielberg discuss the past and future of the USC Shoah Foundation.*

TIMELINE OF THE USC SHOAH FOUNDATION: HIGHLIGHTS OF THE FIRST TWENTY YEARS

"I didn't know it then, but my experience on Schindler's List *was preparing me for the most important work of my professional life: Survivors of the Shoah Visual History Foundation."* —STEVEN SPIELBERG

1993

Steven Spielberg begins and completes principal photography on *Schindler's List* in Krakow, Poland. Opens December 15th.

1994

Survivors of the Shoah Visual History Foundation is established in Los Angeles. Its mission is to videotape, before it is too late, the first-person accounts of 50,000 Holocaust survivors and other witnesses.

Interviewer training begins.

Regional offices open in New York and Toronto.

The first Holocaust survivor testimony is videotaped.

1995

Regional offices open worldwide.

Digital video preservation and indexing software development begin.

An international network of coordinators, interviewers, videographers, and volunteers is trained to schedule and conduct interviews around the world.

The first multinational interviewer training session is held in Amsterdam.

1996

The 10,000th testimony is recorded.

Prototype digital preservation and indexing systems are tested.

The *Survivors of the Holocaust* documentary airs on TBS and subsequently earns multiple awards, including two Emmys, a Peabody, and a CableACE.

1997

The 25,000th testimony is recorded.

Pioneering database storage and networking techniques are tested.

The Lost Children of Berlin documentary premieres on A&E and is honored with the Edward R. Murrow Award.

1998

The 40,000th testimony is recorded.

The 1,500th testimony is indexed.

The Last Days feature documentary premieres in New York and Los Angeles and subsequently earns the Academy Award for Best Documentary in 1999.

The Shoah Foundation releases its first English-language educational product based on testimonies: a CD-ROM entitled *Survivors: Testimonies of the Holocaust.*

1999

The goal of collecting 50,000 testimonies for the Visual History Archive is reached.

The Shoah Foundation installs its first digital access system, a one-terabyte cache, at the Simon Wiesenthal Center.

The Shoah Foundation unveils its first foreign-language educational product, the German-language CD-ROM *Erinnern für Gegenwart und Zukunft (Remembering for the Present and the Future).*

2000

The Pilot Education Initiative launches; over three years it examines the use of testimony-based educational products in five public school districts in California, Virginia, Florida, Illinois, and Oregon.

The Tapper Research and Testing Center is dedicated as the first public space in which researchers, students, and educators can conduct independent research in the Visual History Archive.

Broken Silence, a series of five documentaries representing the Holocaust as experienced by survivors from Argentina and Uruguay, the Czech Republic, Hungary, Poland, and Russia, is completed for broadcast to global audiences.

2001

The Shoah Foundation adopts a new mission: *To overcome prejudice intolerance, and bigotry—and the suffering they cause—through the educational use of its Visual History Archive.*

The first teacher-training workshop on the use of visual history in the classroom is hosted in Los Angeles with educators from diverse areas throughout the United States.

The first national collection of testimonies is established at the Joods Historisch Museum in Amsterdam with more than 1,000 testimonies from the Visual History Archive related to the Dutch experience.

2002

A subscription service for universities and institutions is established to make the entire Visual History Archive available over Internet2, with the first connections made at Rice University, Yale University, and the University of Southern California.

The first regional collection is established at the Charleston County Public Library in South Carolina, with 28 testimonies of state residents.

A collection of Sinti and Roma Holocaust survivor testimonies opens at the Dokumentations und Kulturzentrum Deutscher Sinti und Roma (Documentation and Culture Center for German Sinti and Roma) in Heidelberg, Germany.

2003

The 25,000th testimony is indexed.

"Racism-Antiracism," the first university course based on the Visual History Archive, is offered to students at Bárczi Gusztáv College in Hungary.

The Shoah Foundation releases *One Human Spirit*, its first classroom video with accompanying study guide.

2004

The Shoah Foundation commemorates its tenth anniversary with the release of a new documentary, *Voices from the List*, and a new classroom video, *Giving Voice*, concurrently with the release of *Schindler's List* on DVD.

The Shoah Foundation's *Visual History in the Classroom* initiative brings six educational products to 54,000 schools, reaching 1.6 million students in 11 countries.

A regional collection of more than 1,000 testimonies is established at the Jewish Museum Berlin.

2005

The 49,000th testimony is indexed, making 95 percent of the collected testimonies digitally searchable.

Echoes and Reflections, a multimedia curriculum on the Holocaust for secondary school teachers in the United States, is launched in partnership with the Anti-Defamation League and Yad Vashem.

A total of 25 university courses incorporate testimony at Visual History Archive sites.

2006

The Shoah Foundation becomes part of the Dana and David Dornsife College of Letters, Arts and Sciences at University of Southern California and is renamed USC Shoah Foundation—The Institute for Visual History and Education.

The documentaries *Spell Your Name* and *I Only Wanted to Live* premiere in Ukraine and Italy, respectively.

Creating Character, a free online educational resource, incorporates streaming video testimony in easy-to-use, downloadable character education lessons.

The Visual History Archive digital preservation system migrates to a state-of-the-art 200-terabyte digital disc array.

2007

Local organizations in Rwanda invite the institute to partner in collecting video testimonies of the Rwandan Tutsi Genocide.

The Corrie ten Boom scholars program begins, enabling postdoctoral scholars and dissertation candidates to conduct research at the institute for periods of one to six months.

Segments for the Classroom launches on the institute's website, providing educators with testimony-clip reels that highlight a theme or historical event for use in curricula.

2008

Nearly 4,000 university students have enrolled in 137 university courses worldwide that have incorporated testimonies from the institute's archive.

The institute partners with Documentation Center of Cambodia to support its testimony recording efforts and conduct pilot interviews with Cambodian survivors for the Visual History Archive.

The Faculty Advisory Council convenes 16 scholars to promote linkages with the institute at USC.

Access to the full Visual History Archive is available at 21 institutions, with 102 regional collections in 23 countries.

2009

An *IWitness* prototype website is developed to provide compelling, testimony-based learning experiences for secondary education.

The institute launches its YouTube channel.

The institute's Teacher Innovation Network and Master Teachers programs launch.

Three pilot interviews are conducted with Rwandan Tutsi genocide survivors in partnership with the Kigali Genocide Memorial.

The institute convenes an international workshop in Budapest with ten countries represented, to advance best practices on the use of video testimony in education.

2010

The Armenian Film Foundation and Dr. J. Michael Hagopian sign a historic agreement with the institute to digitize, preserve, and disseminate filmed interviews with survivors and witnesses of the Armenian genocide.

The first International Digital Access, Outreach, and Research Conference convenes scholars from 25 institutions to discuss their use of the Visual History Archive.

Access to the full Visual History Archive is available at 26 institutions, with regional collections at 140 institutions in 29 countries.

A total of 200 university courses have incorporated testimony from the Visual History Archive.

2011

The entire Visual History Archive is digitally replicated and saved at a location outside the earthquake zone of Southern California.

The institute launches fellowship programs for senior scholars and doctoral fellows.

The institute publishes *Visual History Archive in Practice.*

The institute's Student Voices Film Contest launches at USC; it encourages undergraduates to make short films based on testimony that address the themes of genocide and human rights.

2012

VHA Online launches, enabling the public to search the Visual History Archive metadata and view of a selection of 1,000 English-language testimonies.

IWitness receives the International Society for Technology in Education Seal of Alignment for Proficiency.

USC Shoah Foundation launches its two-year professional development program, *Teaching with Testimony in the 21st Century,* with more than 100 participants from the United States, Ukraine, Czech Republic, Hungary, and Poland.

Days of Remembrance video-on-demand series on Comcast offers ten of the Institute's award-winning documentary films to global viewers.

The institute welcomes its first Yom HaShoah Scholar-in-Residence, Yehuda Bauer, of Hebrew University of Jerusalem.

2013

The first 65 testimonies of survivors of the 1994 Rwandan Tutsi genocide are integrated into the Visual History Archive.

USC Shoah Foundation commemorates the 20th anniversary of the filming of *Schindler's List* by launching the IWitness Video Challenge with founder Steven Spielberg.

The Visual History Archive integrates Google Maps to enhance testimony search by geographic location.

Access to the full Visual History Archive is available at 44 institutions, with regional collections at 195 institutions in 31 countries.

A total of 370 university courses have incorporated testimony from the Visual History Archive.

AWARDS, HONORS, AND PATENTS

SCHINDLER'S LIST

Schindler's List received the equivalent of the "Best Picture" award from all of the following organizations in the period immediately following its release:

Academy Awards	Best Picture
Amanda Awards, Norway	Best Foreign Feature Film
American Cinema Editors	Best Edited Feature Film
Australian Film Institute	Best Foreign Film
Awards of the Japanese Academy	Award of the Japanese Academy
BAFTA Awards	Best Film
Boston Society of Film Critics Awards	Best Film
Chicago Film Critics Association Awards	Best Picture
Cinema Writers Circle Awards, Spain	Best Foreign Film
César Awards, France	Best Foreign Film
David di Donatello Awards, Italy	Best Foreign Film
Golden Globes	Best Motion Picture—Drama
Hochi Film Awards, Japan	Best Foreign Language Film
Humanitas Prize	Feature Film Category
Kansas City Film Critics Circle Awards	Best Film
Los Angeles Film Critics Association Awards	Best Picture
MTV Movie Awards	Best Movie
National Board of Review	NBR Award Best Film
National Society of Film Critics Awards	Best Film
New York Film Critics Circle Awards	Best Film
Southeastern Film Critics Association Awards	Best Picture

In addition, the film won scores of additional awards for film production, direction, screenwriting, cinematography, production design, costumes and makeup, sound, and acting. A full list can be found at www.imdb.com/title/tt0108052/awards

USC SHOAH FOUNDATION

Here are listed awards, honors, and patents the institute has received for its programs, documentary films, website and other media, exhibits, and achievements in information technology.

2013 Peace Over Violence Humanitarian Awards: Media Award

2012 LA Weekly's Best of LA: Best Video Art Exhibit (Los Angeles Museum of the Holocaust's "Tree of Testimony" featuring the institute's 51,696 testimonies)

The Source for Learning: Featured Site, TeachersFirst.com (*IWitness*)

International Society for Technology in Education: Seal of Alignment for Proficiency (*IWitness*)

Arpa Foundation Award (Arpa International Film Festival)

American Association of School Librarians: Top Website for Teaching and Learning (*IWitness*)

2010 Walter Cronkite Civic Engagement Leadership Award (What's Your Issue)

2007 National Multicultural Media Award (National Association for Multicultural Education) (*Echoes and Reflections*)

Lerici Città di Pace e di Poesia (*Volevo solo vivere*)

Jerusalem Film Festival: Special Mention, Yad Vashem Chairman's Award for Artistic Achievement in Holocaust Theme (*Spell Your Name*)

International Film Festival Jewish Motifs, Warsaw: Gold Warsaw Phoenix (Grand Prize) (*Volevo solo vivere*)

BAFTA Award (*Recollections: Eyewitnesses Remember the Holocaust*)

2006 Donatello Nomination, Italy: Best Documentary *(Volevo solo vivere)*

2005 Philip M. Hamer and Elizabeth Hamer Kegan Award (Society of American Archivists)

2003 AT&T Spirit of Communication Award

2002 Gardel Nomination, Argentina: Best Classical Music Album *(Algunos Que Vivieron)*

2001 Giga Mouse: *Eltern für Familie (Parents for Family)* magazine *(Erinnern für Gegenwart und Zukunft—Remembering for the Present and the Future)*

2000 Districts' Choice Top 100 Products—Curriculum Administrator Magazine *(Survivors: Testimonies of the Holocaust)*
Friends of the United Nations Global Tolerance Award for Education

1999 Gold Apple Award (National Educational Media Network) *(Survivors: Testimonies of the Holocaust)*
Codie Award Nominee: Best Software Product *(Survivors: Testimonies of the Holocaust)*
Academy Award: Best Feature Documentary *(The Last Days)*

1998 Edward R. Murrow Award: News Documentary *(The Lost Children of Berlin)*
Commitment to Justice Award (Bet Tzedek–The House of Justice)
Finalist, Computerworld Smithsonian Award in Education & Academia category

1997 Amicus Award (International Documentary Association)

1996 Peabody Award: Significant and Meritorious Achievement in Broadcasting and Cable *(Survivors of the Holocaust)*
Excellence in Media Award (International Television Association)
Emmy Nomination: the President's Award *(Survivors of the Holocaust)*
Emmy Award: Outstanding Informational Special *(Survivors of the Holocaust)*
Emmy Award: Outstanding Individual Achievement in Editing (Informational Special) *(Survivors of the Holocaust)*
CableACE Award: Documentary Special *(Survivors of the Holocaust)*
Award for the Advancement of Learning through Broadcasting (National Education Association)

PATENTS

The following patents cover USC Shoah Foundation's technology for the storage, retrieval, cataloguing and indexing of nearly 52,000 video testimonies of Holocaust survivors and witnesses.

Method and Apparatus for Management of Multimedia Assets (Number: 5,813,014)

Method and Apparatus for Cataloguing Multimedia (Number: 5,832,495)

Digital Library System (Number: 5,832,499)

Digital Library System (Number: 6,092,080)

Method and Apparatus for Management of Multimedia Assets (Number: 6,199,060)

Method and Apparatus for Cataloguing Multimedia (Number: 6,212,527)

Digital Library System (Number: 6,353,831)

Method and Apparatus for Management of Multimedia Assets (Number: 6,477,537)

Method and Apparatus for Cataloguing Multimedia Data (Number: 6,549,911)

Method and Apparatus for Cataloguing Multimedia Data Using Surveying Data (Number: 6,574,638)

Surveying System and Method (Number: 6,581,071)

FILM CREDITS

CAST

Oskar Schindler	LIAM NEESON
Itzhak Stern	BEN KINGSLEY
Amon Goeth	RALPH FIENNES
Emilie Schindler	CAROLINE GOODALL
Poldek Pfefferberg	JONATHAN SAGALLE
Helen Hirsch	EMBETH DAVIDTZ
Wiktoria Klonowska	MALGOSCHA GEBEL
Wilek Chilowicz	SHMULIK LEVY
Marcel Goldberg	MARK IVANIR
Ingrid	BEATRICE MACOLA
Julian Scherner	ANDRZEJ SEWERYN
Rolf Czurda	FRIEDRICH VON THUN
Herman Toffel	KRZYSZTOF LUFT
Leo John	HARRY NEHRING
Albert Hujar	NORBERT WEISSER
Mila Pfefferberg	ADI NITZAN
Juda Dresner	MICHAEL SCHNEIDER
Chaja Dresner	MIRI FABIAN
Danka Dresner	ANNA MUCHA
Mordecai Wulkan	ALBERT MISAK
Mr. Nussbaum	MICHAEL GORDON
Mrs. Nussbaum	ALDONA GROCHAL
Henry Rosner	JACEK WOJCICKI
Manci Rosner	BEATA PALUCH
Leo Rosner	PIOTR POLK
Rabbi Menasha Levartov	EZRA DAGAN
Rebecca Tannenbaum	BEATA NOWAK
Josef Bau	RAMI HEUBERGER
Investor	LEOPOLD KOZLOWSKI
Investor	JERZY NOWAK
Chaim Nowak	URI AVRAHAMI
O.D. / Chicken Boy	ADAM SIEMION
Niusia Horowitz	MAGDALENA DANDOURIAN
Dolek Horowitz	PAWEL DELAG
Garage Mechanic	SHABTAI KONORTI
Red Genia	OLIWIA DABROWSKA
Mr. Löwenstein	HENRYK BISTA
DEF Foreman	TADEUSZ BRADECKI
Lisiek	WOJCIECH KLATA
Diana Reiter	ELINA LÖWENSOHN
Irrational Woman	EWA KOLASINSKA
Regina Perlman	BETTINA KUPFER
Mietek Pemper	GRZEGORZ KWAS
Investigator	VILI MATULA
Doorman	STANISLAW KOCZANOWICZ
Julius Madritsch	HANS JORG ASSMANN
Majola	GENO LECHNER
Dieter Reeder	AUGUST SCHMOLZER
Josef Liepold	LUDGER PISTO
Club Singer	BEATA RYBOTYCKA
Nightclub Maitre d'	BRANKO LUSTIG
Treblinka Commandant	ARTUS MARIA MATTHIESSEN
Rudolph Hoss	HANS MICHAEL REHBERG
Waiter	EUGENIUSZ PRIWIEZENCEW
Montelupich Colonel	MICHAEL Z. HOFFMANN
SS Waffen Officer	ERWIN LEDER
Wilhelm Kunde	JOCHEN NICKEL
Dr. Blancke	ANDRZEJ WELMINSKI
Dr. Josef Mengele	DANIEL DEL PONTE
DEF SS Officer	MARIAN GLINKA
SS Sgt. Kunder	GRZEGORZ DAMIECKI
DEF Guard	STANISLAW BREJDYGANT
Auschwitz Guard	OLAF LINDE LUBASZENKO
Auschwitz Guard	HAYMON MARIA BUTTINGER
Auschwitz Guard	PETER APPIANO
Brunnlitz Guard	JACEK PULANECKI
SS Waffen Man	MARTIN SEMMELROGGE
Gestapo Agent	TOMASZ DEDEK
	SLAWOMIR HOLLAND
Gestapo Brunnlitz	TADEUSZ HUK
SS Bureaucrat	GERALD ALEXANDER HELD
Ukrainian Guard	PIOTR CYRWUS
Gestapo Clerk Klaus Tauber	JOACHIM PAUL ASSBOCK
Border Guard	OSMAN RAGHEB
German Clerk	MACIEJ ORLOS
Toffel's Secretary	MAREK WRONA
Scherner's Secretary	ZBIGNIEW KOZLOWSKI
Czurda's Secretary	MARCIN GRYZMOWICZ
Bosch	DIETER WITTING
Goeth's Girl	MAGDALENA KOMORNICKA
Czurda's Girl	AGNIESZKA KRUK
Polish Girl	ANEMONA KNUT
Brunnlitz Man	JEREMY FLYNN
Brunnlitz Girl	AGNIESZKA WAGNER
Russian Officer	JAN JUREWICZ
Plaszow Depot SS Guard	WIESLAW KOMASA
SS Guard Zablocie	MACIEJ KOZLOWSKI
SS NCO Zablocie	MARTIN BERGMANN
SS NCO Ghetto	WILHELM MANSKE
SS NCO Ghetto	PETER FLECHTNER
SS NCO Ghetto	SIGURD BEMME
Ghetto Woman	ETHEL SZYC
Ghetto Woman	LUCYNA ZABAWA
Ghetto Old Man	JERZY SAGAN
Old Jewish Woman	RUTH FARHI
Clerk at Depot	DIRK BENDER
Prisoner at Depot	DARIUSZ SZYMANIAK
Ghetto Doctor	HANNA KOSSOWSKA
Black Marketeer	MACIEJ WINKLER
Black Marketeer	RADOSLAW KRZYZOWSKI
Black Marketeer	JACEK LENCZOWSKI
Frantic Woman	MAJA OSTASZEWSKA
Stable Boy	SEBASTIAN SKALSKI
Pankiewicz	RYSZARD RADWANSKI
Man in Pharmacy	PIOTR KADLCIK
NCO Plaszow	BARTEK NIEBIELSKI
Grun	THOMAS MORRIS
Engineer Man	SEBASTIAN KONRAD

Clara Sternberg	LIDIA WYROBIEC-BANK
Maria Mischel	RAVIT FERERA
Ghetto Girl	AGNIESZKA KORZENIOWSKA
Ghetto Girl	DOMINIKA BEDNARCZYK
Ghetto Girl	ALICJA KUBASZEWSKA
Ghetto Men	DANNY MARCU
Ghetto Men	HANS ROSNER
Montelupich Prisoner	ALEXANDER STROBELE
Brunnlitz Priest	EDWARD LINDE LUBASZENKO
Depot Master	GOERGES KERN
Plaszow SS Guard	ALEXANDER BUCZOLICH
Plaszow SS Guard	MICHAEL SCHILLER
Plaszow SS Guard	GOETZ OTTO
Plaszow SS Guard	WOLFGANG SEIDENBERG
Plaszow SS Guard	HUBERT KRAMER
Plaszow Jewish Girl	RAZIA ISRAELI
Plaszow Jewish Girl	DORIT ADY SEADIA
Plaszow Jewish Girl	ESTI YERUSHALMI

THE CREDITS

Directed / Produced by	STEVEN SPIELBERG
Screenplay by	STEVEN ZAILLIAN
Based on the novel by	THOMAS KENEALLY
Produced by	STEVEN SPIELBERG
Producer	GERALD R. MOLEN
Producer	BRANKO LUSTIG
Executive Producer	KATHLEEN KENNEDY
Director of Photography	JANUSZ KAMINSKI
Film Edited by	MICHAEL KAHN, A.C.E.
Production Designer	ALLAN STARSKI
Music by	JOHN WILLIAMS
Co-Producer	LEW RYWIN
Violin Solos by	ITZHAK PERLMAN
Costume Designer	ANNA BIEDRZYCKA-SHEPPARD
Casting by	LUCKY ENGLANDER and FRITZ FLEISCHHACKER
	MAGDALENA SZWARCBART
	TOVA CYPIN and LIAT MEIRON
	JULIET TAYLOR
Unit Production Manager	BRANKO LUSTIG
First Assistant Director	SERGIO MIMICA-GEZZAN
Second Assistant Director	MICHAEL HELFAND
Production Associates	BONNIE CURTIS
	KAREN BITTENSON KUSHELL
Consultant	LEOPOLD PAGE
Associate Producers	IRVING GLOVIN, ROBERT RAYMOND
Camera Operator	RAYMOND STELLA, A.S.C.
1st Assistant Camera	STEVE TATE, STEVE MEIZLER
2nd Assistant Camera	MOLLIE S. MALLINGER
Production Sound Mixers	RONALD JUDKINS, C.A.S.
	ROBERT JACKSON
Make-up Supervisor	CHRISTINA SMITH
Hair Supervisor	JUDITH CORY
Unit Publicist	ANNE MARIE STEIN
Still Photographer	DAVID JAMES

Assistant Editors	ALAN CODY, PATRICK CRANE
	MICHAEL FALLAVOLLITA, PETER FANDETTI
Gaffer	MAURO FIORE
Electrical Best Boy	JAREK GORCZCKI
Rigging Best Boy	MAREK BOJSZA
Key Grip	ANDRE SOBCZAK
Dolly Grip	JIM KWIATKOWSKI
Rigging Grip	SCOTT BUCKLER
Special Effects Coordinator	BRUCE MINKUS
Prop Masters	BATIA GRAFKA, CESAR DIEZ ALAVA
Production Coordinators	MICHAEL THEURER, JIM WIGGINS
Production Controller	JANE GOE
Production Accountant	KAREN GORDON
Assistant Accountants	SHELIA CLARK, ARMEN TATOIAN
Additional Make-up	MATTHEW MUNGLE
Assistant to Mr. Spielberg	KATHLEEN MIRANDA
Assistants to Mr. Molen	DIANA TINKLEY, LORI HELFAND
Production Assistants	STEVEN W. BAUERFEIND
	KRISTEN O'NEILL
	JOSEPH J.M. KENNY
Interns	JESSICA CAPSHAW, AMANDA CODDING
	ALISON MACE, JENIFER MALLORY
Projectionist	RENE GONZALEZ
Post Production Supervisor	MARTIN COHEN
Post Production Coordinator	MICHELLE FANDETTI
Supervising Sound Editors	CHARLES L. CAMPBELL
	LOUIS L. EDEMANN
ADR Supervisor	LARRY SINGER
Re-Recording Mixers	ANDY NELSON, STEVE PEDERSON
	SCOTT MILLAN
Re-Recordists	ANDREA LAKIN, SAMUEL F. KAUFMAN
Sound Editors	DONALD J. MALOUF
	PAUL TIMOTHY CARDEN
	JEFF CLARK
	LENNY GESCHKE, M.P.S.E.
	DOUG JACKSON
	NILS C. JENSEN
	GARY KRIVACEK
	GARY MUNDHEIM
	CHUCK NEELY
	KERRY DEAN WILLIAMS
	BERNARD WEISER
ADR Editors	ANDREA HORTZ, ALLEN HARTZ
Assistant Sound Editors	ANGIE LUCKEY
	ROB MORRISEY
	JERRY EDEMANN
ADR Assistants	ROD ROGERS
	STEPHANIE D. KRIVACEK
Processed Sound Effect	MEL NEIMAN
Foley Artists	JOHN ROESCH
	KEVIN BARTNOF
	ALICIA STEVENSON
	ELLEN HEUER
Foley Mixers	MARY JO LANG, ERIC GOTTHELF
Foley Recordists	CAROLYN TAPP, RON GRAFTON

ACKNOWLEDGMENTS

Esther Margolis, on behalf of Newmarket Press for It Books/HarperCollins; and Diana Landau, book producer at Parlandau Communications and project editor and co-writer, thank the following for their invaluable contributions to the making of this book:

First and foremost, Steven Spielberg, for the vision, conscience, compassion, craft, and collaborative spirit that enabled him to make *Schindler's List*, to recognize and articulate the urgent need to record survivor testimony, and to establish the Shoah Foundation; and for his eloquent essay that introduces this book.

Branko Lustig, co-producer of *Schindler's List* and the fifty-thousandth witness to be interviewed for the Visual History Archive, for his inspiring example and words, and for contributing so much to the book by granting us a new interview.

Gerald Molen, co-producer of *Schindler's List*, for his careful reading of the manuscript and invaluable memories of the production.

Stephen D. Smith, executive director of the USC Shoah Foundation, for his preface, which helps us understand the significance of testimony for the past, present, and future; and for the keen interest, unflagging attentiveness, and great good will with which he help steer this book project to completion.

June Beallor and James Moll, founding executive directors of the Shoah Foundation: June championed this book from the start as an essential component of the twentieth anniversary commemoration, and followed through from concept through contracts to completion with her usual foresight, energy, and persistence. She and James both contributed crucial background on the organization's early history and insightful comments on the text; James also gave us access to priceless early documents and photos long dormant on his hard drive and awaiting this moment. Sandy Gervay at June Beallor Productions and Madison McCabe at Allentown Productions provided key support.

At Universal Studios: Bette Einbinder, vice president, Stills Department; Chante Hardesty, manager, Stills Department at Universal Pictures; Deidre Thieman, manager, NBC Universal Archives; and Jessica Taylor, archivist, NBC Universal. At West Coast Photos: Pam Lord, general manager.

At DreamWorks Studios: Marvin Levy, Kristie Macosko Krieger, Samantha Becker; Kristin Stark, Mary Hulett, Tommy Sobel, Samantha Stogel, Nelson Oliver, and Michelle Fandetti.

David James, whose glorious black-and-white still photographs of the *Schindler's List* production so superbly evoke the film.

At the USC Shoah Foundation, there are so many people without whom this book could not have been done. In addition to Stephen Smith, acknowledged above, other leaders and staff of the institute gave interviews, provided source material, reviewed manuscript and layouts, and made themselves available for consultation; they include Managing Director Kim Simon, Chief Technology Officer Sam Gustman, Director of Research and Documentation Karen Jungblut, Director of Education Kori Street, Content Specialist Ita Gordon; Senior International Program Consultant Martin Šmok, and Senior International Training Consultant Andrea Szönyi. ITS Director of Technology Anita Pace initiated us into the mysteries of the data center. Senior Program Writer Aaron Zarrow consulted and lent his editorial expertise. Director of Communications Anne Marie Stein was the project's fulcrum: as the original unit publicist on *Schindler's List* she brought a unique perspective to the filmmaking story and the origins of the Shoah Foundation. Thanks also to Lukas Binder, Crispin Brooks, Danielle Gomez, Kathy Guyton, Judy Huang, Deanna Pitre, Linda Sturm, and Lauren Thomas.

Director of Administration Ari Zev, as the longest-serving employee of the institute, was a key source of facts, figures, and information about the organization.

Very special thanks go to Sherry Bard, former project director, educational programs, and to Krystal Szabo, coordinator, external relations, whose dedicated liaison work and assistance over many months were indispensable in getting the project launched and seeing it through. Among countless contributions, they set up interviews, provided source materials (sometimes from very deep storage), worked on the excerpted testimonies, transmitted text and proofs, tracked down and organized photos, and arranged for the use of copyrighted material.

Douglas Greenberg, president and CEO of the foundation from 2000 to 2006, read the text of Part Two with great care and offered essential feedback. Professor Jeffrey Shandler of Rutgers University also served as a reader as well as contributing his insightful essay "Survivors and *Schindler's List*."

Judith Cohen and Caroline Waddell, photo archivists, at the United States Holocaust Memorial Museum; Naama Shilo at Yad Vashem Photo Archive; Glen Powell, former studio manager at the Holocaust Centre and Aegis Trust; Lawreen Loeser, Rights and Clearances,

and Faye Thompson, photograph archive coordinator at the Academy of Motion Picture Arts and Sciences Margaret Herrick Library; and Susan Carlson and Maya Benton at the International Center of Photography.

Our book team: Co-writer Linda Sunshine, who researched, organized, and movingly told the story of the making of *Schindler's List*, along with editing the photos for Part One; Timothy Shaner of Night & Day Design, for his typically brilliant work in melding disparate text elements and illustrations into visually coherent pages; Christopher Measom at Night & Day Design for editorial and layout assistance; copyeditor Karen Wise and proofreader Kathy Shorr for helping to ensure a professional result on challenging schedules; and the publishing, editorial, production, legal, sales, publicity, and marketing staff at HarperCollins, whose expertise and patience helped marshal the book to the finish line.

To all the survivors and witnesses—especially those quoted or profiled in the book—and to our patient families, our deepest gratitude.

■

The USC Shoah Foundation wishes to acknowledge the contributions of all those who have served the organization and its mission over the two decades since its founding:

Staff: More than 350 staff members; *Interviewers*: More than 2,600 interviewers; *Videographers*: More than 1,100 videographers; *Regional Coordinators*: More than 100 regional and assistant regional coordinators; *Volunteers*: More than 1,000 volunteers

BOOK CREDITS

Permission is gratefully acknowledged to reprint passages from *Schindler's List* by Thomas Keneally, copyright © 1982 by Serpentine Publishing Co. Pty. Ltd. By permission of Simon & Schuster Publishing Group. All rights reserved.

Unless otherwise identified below, all photographs in Part One are by David James, courtesy of Universal Studios Licensing LLC. All other photographs are credited below, are from the USC Shoah Foundation archives, or are provided courtesy of past and current foundation staff. USC Shoah Foundation and the publisher have made every effort to contact copyright holders and sources of photographs; any errors or omissions are inadvertent and will be corrected upon notice in future printings.

Allison Rodriguez, courtesy of the Holocaust Memorial Museum of the Jewish Federation of San Antonio, page 261; Abraham Zuckerman, courtesy of Steve Katz and Wayne Zuckerman, pages 134, 199 (top); Academy of Motion Picture Arts and Sciences, page 147; AMP Studios, page 243; Aubrey Graham, page 296 (opposite); Bernice Krantz, pages 200, 203, 206; Bill Harder, page 210; Celina Biniaz, page 152; Chris Polk, courtesy of FilmMagic, page 277; David Strick Photography, page viii-ix; Derek Bauer Photography, courtesy of the Los Angeles Museum of the Holocaust, page 236; Edward Serotta, pages 226-227; Eric Weber, page 209; Fred Marcus Photography, page 199 (bottom); Freie Universität Berlin, page xiv-xv; Geoffrey Clifford, page 240-241; Gerald R. Ford Presidential Library, page 253; Holocaust Centre, page 148 (left), 149 (left); Italian Central State Archives, page 259; Jemal Young, page 282 (bottom), page 301; Jerry Fowler, United States Holocaust Memorial Museum, Committee on Conscience, page 298; Jewish Historical Museum Amsterdam, page 255 (bottom), 260; Joel Carnes, page 291 (top); John Livzey, page 265; Kim Fox Photography, pages xi, xii, xvi, 169, 216, 217, 234, 267, 276 (top two), 278-279, 282 (top); 285, 290, 291 (bottom), 294, 299 (right), 303 (right), 304, 305, 306, 308, 309, 311, 313 (top), 314, 322; Krystal Szabo, page 204 (bottom); Larry Busacca, courtesy of Getty Images, page 276 (bottom right); Lee Salem Photography, page 175; Leo Hsu, page 295; Mara Vishniac Kohn, courtesy of International Center of Photography, photographs by Roman Vishniac on page 63: Students discussing the Chumash in *cheder* (Jewish elementary school), Brod, ca. 1938 (top); Interior of the Anhalter Bahnhof railway terminus near Potsdamer Platz, Berlin, late 1920s–early 1930s (bottom); Mark Berndt, pages 194, 214, 281, 284; Mathieu Asselin, page 307; Melanie Einzig, courtesy of the Museum of Jewish Heritage, page 237; Melanie Kotsopoulos, page 297 (above); Michael Priest, courtesy of United States Holocaust Memorial Museum, page 317 (above); Michelle Kleinert Bader, page 163; Michelle Zousmer, page 317 (top); Peter Olson, page 174; Ryan Fenton-Strauss, page 300 (top and bottom); Sala and Aron Samueli Holocaust Memorial Library at Chapman University, page 195; Stephen Smith, page 297 (top); Todd Williamson, page 276 (bottom left); Two Point Pictures, pages 315, 320; United States National Archives and Records Administration, page 252; United States Holocaust Memorial Museum, pages 13, 24, 26, 27, 37, 96, 148 (right), 149 (two on right), 154, 155, 264, 271; Universal Studios Licensing LLC, page 158. Unknown, page 299 (left); Yad Vashem The Holocaust Martyrs' and Heroes' Remembrance Authority, pages 135, 146, 184; Zachary Goode, page 286.